The Eleusinian Method and The Philosopher's Way

by

Ralf Smith

From the beginning, I would like to state that this book is entirely fiction and is for entertainment purposes only. All parties and locations mentioned are complete fiction and any similarities between the characters portrayed in this book to those you may know are coincidences.

The author does not support or endorse using psychedelics for therapy or otherwise, especially where it is illegal. Due to rapidly increasing changes in the law globally where psychedelics are no longer seen as a racial profiling tool and with the recognition of their medical benefits, they are now gathering positive awareness, legal acceptance and reducing overall financial costs covering potentially reduced therapy time and reduction of medication consumption.

Should the reader consider taking such substances by going through such therapy, the author does recommend that the reader takes advice from an expert first. Although the outcome can be astounding, the journey can be fraught reliving those past events under the powerful influence of such substances.

Dedication

This dedication goes to mum and dad for the unconditional love you gave me and whom I miss since you are both no longer here.

A special thanks to The Instructor for showing me the way and a heartfelt thanks to Steve and Marie for being there in my moments of doubt, for listening when I didn't know what to do and for providing a shoulder to lean on when my new life gave me a challenge I didn't know how to tackle.

A big thanks to Dave and his girlfriend, Andrea, for introducing me to The Instructor to deal with my past. And thank you for the many wonderful evenings we have shared since undergoing this part of my Journey.

Forward

To begin with, I would like to highlight that it took me a long time of contemplation before I decided to release this book because I was concerned about the reaction that it would cause. However, upon reflection, there are many products on the market that have the potential to cause mental as well as physical damage. Even something as simple as drinking water can risk our health if we don't pay it the necessary attention. If something as simple as drinking water kills several people per year internationally, what are the numbers of people who die from medication per year and how many didn't research its risks before taking a mix of unknown concoctions? Even considering two simple legal drugs, smoking and alcohol, the death rate is around eleven million people worldwide. Add the deaths related to medicated drugs and the number increases significantly higher. Deaths through the use of illegal psychedelics (all types) are around 0.1% in comparison to alcohol and tobacco alone. That is around 11,000 per year.

In being able to write this book, I am grateful for the participants' support and guidance. I am also grateful for The Instructor's help in publishing this book to avoid revealing identities, locations, personal details and for help in recording my experiences and what to be aware of. Along with The Instructors guidance, we have agreed on what could and couldn't be written about the sessions themselves and we hope this explains why certain parts of the sessions and exercises are missing. The Instructor's opinion is to ensure the reader does not try to deal with their inner burden with psychedelics alone.

It is also worth pointing out that after these sessions, myself included, some of the participants needed to unlearn, relearn and re-adapt their way of thinking to help them rebuild their new lives once the sessions were over. These steps took from several days to a couple of years of active reflection, experimentation and new life adaptation. This doesn't mean to say their experiences or relearning are over, as we all are relearning many things about life all the time.

Until one goes through such a life-changing experience, it is impossible to know how our language fails to bring such profound information across without the risk of sounding a little crazy, lost or disorientated concerning the inexperienced listener's world. Such psychedelic participants tend to start seeing the world and its varying systems differently than before. This could be a fearful experience without being willing to change one's mental perspective of one's life. Yet, it can be incredibly liberating once those limiting pre-programmed perspectives have been obliterated. This could be true for those with restrictive beliefs by potentially providing a clearer view of one's life on this beautiful planet. I have read and heard several times that once you have gone down the rabbit hole, life will never be the same again when you reappear on the other side. I can vouch for that.

And that leads me to another point I would like to address. In this story, I describe two intense hallucinogenic sessions that I went through. Those who have experienced the effects of psychedelics before may be aware that how I have written them doesn't truly represent what happened in the sessions. Not only that, no two sessions are the same and each person's experience is unique. It took me ages to work out how best to write them down to try to bring across what was happening for a non-experienced psychonaut to get a glimpse of the effects it had on me, yet trying not to be too abstract at the same time. Some things I experienced happened so quickly I can't remember what happened and some were in some convoluted order that made sense within the trip (or later) but not on paper and thus, I have chosen to leave them out. Although they were helpful within the session, I felt they would detract from the story. If they can be documented in a certain way, I will admit I don't know how. That's all I can offer you, I'm afraid and I hope you will understand what I am trying to convey.

Those who recognise these Mystery sessions from personal experience with The Instructor will understand why certain parts are missing. This is done to ensure some reader protection who doesn't realise how intense these sessions can be and could be freaked out in some way if they can't get out of a highly emotional experience. Nor am I willing to take The Instructor's therapy sessions away from them. I needed this person's help and believe that others should, too, if they consider this a rapid but challenging avenue. I you are going to do it, then better do it with an expert than on one's own. I would never have been able to have managed this if I hadn't had that excellent support around me.

Carrying out a session with something as powerful as psychedelics breaks the law in some countries. I know I broke the law in my country by doing this, however, in the end, it was my ultimate decision to participate and I was well aware of the risks. Being naturally a fearful person, it was a terrifying decision for me. Yet, it was my desperation that overweighed what could have happened if I had been caught. I believe I made the right decisions for myself. Would I do it again? Definitely! The quality of my life today far exceeds the life I had before I started this incredible journey. I have been released from the internal prison that debilitated me in every aspect of my life for many years. This mental freedom is something nobody can take away from me again. Even if I should be incarcerated for setting myself free through illegal activities I carried out as written in this book, mentally, I am still free.

Ultimately, once our life game is over and we return to our spiritual home, I believe it will be the human persecutor in this life will have that balanced opportunity to live the role of a persecuted person in their next karmic life, just as myself and many are doing in this current life. The problem is, that we don't know what karma we could receive in the next life based on what we are doing in this one. Maybe we conned someone out of something, hurt or killed an innocent person, were simply rude to someone, denied someone from something or hurt another living creature in some way. Whatever it was, it doesn't matter as we get a chance to understand both sides of that event. And if I am wrong? Who cares? It doesn't matter. We will all find out what comes next in our own good time.

I am aware that I think differently from the majority of society, which still keeps me as an outsider. I have been such a person all my life and feel comfortable here. There is inner peace and inner trust with those close to me. I have lived my life with what is important to me and not what is important to others which

I think is important. However, by going down the rabbit hole, I am lucky to have found other like-minded individuals I can relate to and talk to when I am unsure of something. I am grateful they are in my life for their friendship and support.

What you think and feel about my approach to life and in dealing with it is your opinion and is your free choice. I am not here to convince you. I am here to show you what worked for me. Still, if you disagree, please respect my opinions and of others who may think differently because these options are a part of what makes life interesting. Their game and the systems they are using may be different to yours and that's fine. If you are unaware of them, don't become the persecutor and judge them on something you know nothing about. Just respect their choices and decisions within their life journey is different to yours.

I think it is important to say that what I have experienced in dealing with my past is one possible opportunity available to us. It is an approach we have successfully done as a species for thousands of years before established religions and man-made gods reared their fictional heads. It doesn't matter whether we use magic mushrooms, Ayahuasca, mescaline or another potent plant. It doesn't matter what we use or whom we speak to in these sessions as long as we set ourselves free from imagined fear and unseen bounds. For some of us, mind-numbing medication may be what we need until we are ready to deal with it head-on or whether we want to suffer under it in some way for the rest of our lives. Maybe that is what you want or maybe it is a part of our chosen karma.

Please respect my choice because the results clearly show that it worked exceptionally well on me and many other participants. It has worked far better than I could have ever dreamed of. Even several participants who needed further work (I needed some extra guidance I haven't included in this book) say that a burden has been lifted enough to help them get on with lives easier and to have less dependency on those external crutches they were clinging onto beforehand. Isn't that what we want? Or is it better to complain and rely on external crutches we want to hide behind?

If do find you are judging yourself, me or other participants based on your education, experience, etc, please remember those thoughts are not universal. They belong to you and you only. Even if someone else shares your views, no two views are alike. I ask that you observe and reflect on the whole picture and not remain on one judgemental side. Even when we have had the chance to eliminate those limiting beliefs and think we live a belief-free life, I don't think it is. Our free choice is still based on our past and what we have learnt from it, isn't our life direction choices biased decisions based on beliefs we have realised through release, too? After all, isn't freedom when we have no issues, so the freedom we think we have chosen is a part of our journey to support the things that aid us?

You decide.

How It All Began...

Do you know what it is like to fall into an increasing role of ever-increasing procrastination? Even when you think it can't get any worse, it does. You get up late and plan to do nothing for the remainder of the day while brewing a cup of tea. It makes this type of day the same as all the others by staring at a screen until it is time to go back to bed before repeating it. It's tedious, I know. Nevertheless, it has become a non-provocative routine to live by that causes little risk of extra-worthlessness. The problem is, even if I wanted to do something different with my life, I don't know how to change whatever I need to change to do whatever I would want to do differently, even if I know what I wanted to do that was different to what I am currently doing. I am someone nobody knows or recognises, even when I occasionally leave my bedsit. I'm anonymous in every way. But even I have to admit, it's not what I want to carry on being for the rest of my life and I don't know what to do about it.

Today, on the internet, for example, I'm flicking through some trashy personal stories, hoping to find someone who is just a little bit worse off than I am. Yeah, I know all I have to do is go into the town centre to look at the homeless to consider what a hard life they have experienced. I don't do that because it reminds me how close I am to being one step away from joining them. So, instead, I sit in front of another irrelevant website or two and while the time away. This lasts the whole day until the early hours before I give up, feeling even more depressed than ever and head to bed. Then that day has gone with nothing left of value, forever gone. Never be recovered. Ever.

Just like me.

How long has this been going on? You would think if you were curious. I guess you aren't. Who would? As far back as I can remember, there hasn't been any sign that this emptiness will be easing up anytime soon either.... Since I left the family home, I thought I would have found my drive and motivation to move on with my life by now, but I guess that deserted me too.

My parents often told me I'm lazy and a waste of space. They've reminded me numerous times that I should be constantly reminded of what kind of impact I have had on their lives. I can't argue with that as it seems to be true when I think about it. They have often told me how supportive they were by constantly pointing out my mistakes. It's not that I couldn't disagree with them. That is precisely what I am – a waste of space.

Reflecting on their comments, you may be thinking, what kind of issues am I wading through that's holding me back? I have to say. I don't know. I don't really have some shit that is bothering me, exactly. A person like me doesn't have such problematic shit when I compare myself to successful and creative people who have proper shit to deal with. Maybe it's just some lethargic shit I have bothering me and that's why I can't visualise a future for myself. If you ask me to imagine a cat, a dog, or some other object, I can, and in detail. But when I try to focus on what is distracting me in my life, there's nothing of value that I can clearly define. Maybe that's what defines me as not being good enough when I think about the other things I've failed in my life, which is pretty much everything.

My psychologist asked me what my friends thought of my behaviour (I have to attend, it's not my choice). I had to reply that I didn't know. I don't have any friends. Never have and I guess I never will. Then my psychologist asked me what my parents thought about that. I replied that they have often told me I am a good-for-nothing and that I didn't take after my parents in any way, shape or form and that's why I don't have any friends or family. Not only that, but because of me, they lost theirs too.

My parents accused me of being their bad luck charm. The way they dealt with it was to lock me in my room day and night so I couldn't bother them. The beatings started when I was a little older, which I remember as a normal part of my life that gradually became their only source of attention towards me. I quickly learnt to keep my opinions to myself because, as they say, I am always wrong whatever I think and do. I don't want to mislead you about my family. I am at fault here. I let them down. I know it was wrong of me to do that. Let's leave that discussion here; otherwise, you may not want to read this book further.

Today is another one of those regular nondescript days. I slump on the shabby couch in my dingy little bedsit in front of the computer and flick from one website to the other. Bored to the bone, I notice the damp patch on the wall and type 'mushroom' in the search box and hit return.

I stumble across a small film about magic mushrooms that are known to be psychedelic. It says they can help people like me who suffer from lethargy and lack of self-worth. They can help sufferers to find their feet and get back on track with their life. I've never done psychedelics before. It's not because I don't want to. I know nothing about them. Not only that, but I haven't the foggiest where I would find them either. I know toadstools are poisonous, and I wouldn't want to risk picking the wrong ones in some field around here. And where would I find them even if I knew what to look for? Anyway, such life-changing things happen to other people, not me. I suppose I can dream of having a life like that. There's nothing wrong with daydreaming, is there?

That evening, my dreams don't let me forget about those magical mushrooms. Have you ever had those lucid moments when you can remember it in such detail that it was as though it had happened?

Even a few nights later, those dreams are still re-occurring. I remember being approached by someone with dark hair dressed in hippy clothes, but I couldn't see them too well. Their friendly eyes were staring into me, beckoning me to join them.

Behind this person was a flow of colours and shapes. Then in a wisp, the person was gone, leaving a colourful aura in an empty barn. I ask myself what this means. I don't know how to work through such an issue like this. Today is my psychologist's appointment. I'll ask her at the end of the session.

"Ah, good to see you again," my psychologist says with a hint of sarcasm. I missed the last appointment as I didn't think attending was worth my while. I've been coming here for more than a year and feel we're going in circles. I feel obliged to give her an answer to her confusing questions in each session. Yet, I know the unrelated answers I am offering are to appease her because I don't know what the real replies should be. I want the session to be finished before I leave my apartment to attend the appointment.

The other problem with playing this game with the psychologist is that I know I am avoiding the issue, whatever it is. Yet, I don't know how to recognise the honest answer she needs to hear. It's like there's some force field around whatever it is and it won't let me break through to find out what I need to find. Not that I try. I mean, what would it do for me even if I did? I suppose it would just confer that I'm more worthless than I currently think I am. I guess even I'm not willing to risk that level of humiliation.

Around ten minutes before the end, she asks whether I have any questions I would like to ask. I've been asked this question every time since I started coming here. Every time, I reply that I don't. Usually, I get up and grab my shoulder bag as she gives me a new appointment, to which I agree and leave. I mean, it's not as though I have my life thoroughly planned and need to get to the next irrelevant appointment on time.

"Yes," I reply, "I do," I say, and remain in the unforgiving chair.

The psychologist ignores me and gives me my next appointment date. I remember it and remain seated.

"Hmm?" the psychologist replies, looking up.

"Yes, I do."

"You do, what?" she asks.

"I have a question."

"Oh," the psychologist replies, glancing at the analogue wall clock as those valuable seconds of potentially undisturbed relaxation gradually tick away. I quickly see a frustrated look flash across her face. I feel guilty and almost cave in. I want to say, 'it doesn't matter,' and leave, but something inside me tells me to remain seated.

"Well?" the psychologist asks with a hint of irritation, "What is it?" She gives me that stare that tells me to hurry up.

"Could psychedelics help me?" I admit I hadn't thought about how I should ask this question. I wish I had as I see increased irritation furrow across her forehead, highlighting her greying roots a little more.

"Oh, I don't think this is the right place, nor do I think there's enough time for such a question," she replies as she clasps her hands together and rests them on her desk. I think she is expecting me to leave.

"I have time," I reply. "You owe me a fair amount of time due to previous sessions that have finished early." The psychologist must have seen the shock on my face once I realised what I had blurted out. Where that came from, I don't know. I learnt from an early age to be quiet and not answer back and I've just broken this family ingrained rule. It feels liberating, although I am shaking like a leaf inside. I remember as a child that when I spoke my mind, it would cause me immense physical pain from the insolence beatings, as my father called them. My parents always gave me the unwanted choice of either a hand, belt or anything else useful lying nearby when I asked a question that wasn't meant for them. Sadly, any question I had wasn't meant for them.

"Er… I don't know about that," the psychologist replies and glances at the clock again. "How about we address this in our next session?"

We still have time," I reply and remain in the chair more to try and calm my nerves than to wait for her answer. I watch the psychologist shift uncomfortably.

"What do you want to know about psychedelics?" the psychologist says with reluctance. A slight nod of the head indicates as if to say, 'C'mon, get one with it. I don't have all day.'

So, I ask her, "I've seen several films where people have taken psychedelics for their problems and due to their effects, these people have been released from their issues within one or two sessions. We've been meeting for more than a year and I don't feel any different from the first day I saw you."

"Oh, I don't know," she replies with a hint of fear flashing across her face. "I've seen a lot of changes in you since we started our sessions." She looks a little more under control again. "Maybe it's a good idea to continue with what we have been doing until you understand what is bothering you. Then maybe we could consider answering that question." The psychologist closes my file with a slap. "Yes!"

That sounded more like a command than a question.

"What's taking so long for you to help me?" I ask.

"Don't touch them!" the psychologist snaps at me. "All they will do is mess you up and end up in a mental institution. Or worse. Dead! And I don't want you to have that, now, do we?"

"But what about the others? Why has it worked-." I ask before she cuts me off. The clock shows I have another five minutes. Her next client session starts at five past the hour.

"That's it for today. I think it best we don't bring this subject up again," the psychologist replies. With a swift move, she dashes to the office door and opens it for me to leave.

I sit there a bit perplexed. In the film, I saw interviewed various psychologists on the benefits of psychedelics and spoke of them openly. Yet, mine is offended in some way.

"Thank you for coming and I'll see you at your next session," the psychologist replies curtly.

I glance at my watch and turn it to show the watch face that I still have a few minutes left. All I see is her beady eyes disappearing into her beetroot-red face. I'm sure I would see steam pumping out of her ears if it were a real possibility.

Disappointed, I realise this discussion is at an end and throw my bag over my shoulder as I leave without saying a word. A few yards down the street, I hear her shouting that I forgot to confirm my next session and to ring her.

After that, I must admit I don't want another session with her. There is something she is hiding at my expense.

That evening, after a good amount of searching on the internet, I am starting to understand that psychedelics can be used to deal with many mental issues. All I need is to have a therapeutic psychedelic trip with a prepared key question for my consciousness to use. The hallucinogens can assess those restricted mental problem areas, gather critical information from the darkest corners of the mind and break it down into elements to evaluate and understand it. This understanding should then release inner pain and restrictions from one's mind. Theoretically, that sounds reasonably straightforward. Easy, when you know how.

I feel an overwhelming emotional wave of hope flow over me that I haven't had since I left my parent's house. I think I am on the cusp of something new as I start to search on the internet for a psychologist with a psychedelic background that could help me.

And here my challenge begins. I can't find one person who offers this service. After a little more reading, I discovered that psychedelics are illegal here. According to the government, they are more dangerous than heroin, meth, cocaine, tobacco and alcohol. Why couldn't my psychologist just have said that to me if this is the case? What had scared her so much about my question?

I'm curious, so I dig a little deeper to discover why our government thinks they are dangerous. After some searching on the internet, I discover that this was used as propaganda material, first with cannabis starting as a racist tool against blacks and Hispanics in the USA. This happened when there was no medical justification that cannabis was riskier than prescribed pharma drugs. In some cases, it looks like cannabis has several benefits without the typical and sometimes life-threatening pharma side effects. Are we so gullible? I read on....

According to this article that several years ago, the UK government requested the help of a UK drugs expert, Dr David Nutt, to explain the dangers of illegal drugs like cannabis, LSD, Acid, and so on when compared to the 'not-so-dangerous' drugs like alcohol, cigarettes and medication. David Nutt informed the government that psychedelics are significantly safer than alcohol and tobacco. And that in comparison, psychedelics are even safer for one's health than a simple but expensive hobby like horse riding.

The UK government threw him out as an advisor. Instead, the article says they brought in some "yes, man" as an advisor to tow the political policy against such drugs. Who they were, it doesn't say. The article says that one of the reasons was probably that the government officials, or more likely, their sponsors, didn't know how to make money from non-conventional options that we could cultivate at home. But my question is, why does the government want their society to be mentally unstable and financially broke as a consequence? Does it just boil down to company profit and unethical power over us minions? I ask myself.

Using the provided data, I compare psychedelics' deaths against pharma medication, alcohol and tobacco, which shows that psychedelics have a risk of 0.1 per cent of death. I then reread the data to verify that I understood the results correctly. It looks like the scientists were surprised at how powerfully healing psychedelics are and the legal drugs that d be severely restricted or even banned for consumption. Not the other way around.

Since psychedelics are illegal, how can I go about this? My next step is to consider buying some on the black market and do this myself because I've read many people have done this with excellent results. One of the films I saw discussed using LSD for micro-dosing and therapy work. So, I search for where I could buy it. I find an alternative, but it isn't LSD exactly. It's called 1P-LSD and is legal. I don't understand the difference, so I decide not to buy it.

The other bit I read is that magic mushrooms can be used for micro-dosing and therapy depending on the dose. I also learn that buying them is legal in some European countries and illegal in others. In my country, they are illegal. The more I consider buying them, the more paranoid I am at the thought of being arrested and thrown in prison for the purchase of a plant in wanting to try to help rid me of my inner demons. Even I know I don't deserve to be thrown into prison for trying to help release something from within me. Is the risk worth it?

I fell asleep quite quickly that night and started dreaming. I see a man on a bike as he pedals through a rich, intensive blue sky. He struggles to keep the bicycle under control as he avoids various floating objects. Slowly, the man on the bicycle returns to earth and stops in front of someone. They speak. They laugh. The man on the bicycle pedals and flies away, bouncing from one red-capped mushroom to another and into the air. I stare at the other person the man on the bike spoke to. I know him from somewhere. Where?

Early that morning, I wake up with a start and cry out loud in recognition, 'I know him!' Remember that dream that involved the cycle and the cyclist spoke to someone? The person I saw was an old college student I knew before I dropped out. If I remember rightly, he was into the drugs and party scene. He once offered me some Ecstasy and told me it would do me good. I refused. Wish I hadn't. At least I now know where I can get my psychedelics! I jump out of bed, throw on my clothes, and dash out.

It's still dark outside and when I look at my watch, it is just past five in the morning. A little disappointed and wide awake, I head for the couch to read more on psychedelics.

It's near lunchtime when I take a break from my computer. I have just read about determining the question I need to ask myself for an improved chance of a successful psychedelic outcome. However, it says here that a specific outcome isn't guaranteed because it is impossible to know or influence what one will learn and what the resuming effects could be. My other problem is that I need to know what my problem is to help me formulate my question. This is proving to be extremely challenging.

It's early evening and I'm standing in front of the college student's house door. Not that he is a student anymore and am not sure what to call him since we were never friends. I can't bring myself to knock on the door. It's hard to believe how motivated I was at five in the morning compared to how I am now. Yet, something inside me tells me I need to go through with this and risk ridicule if there really is a way out of this mess.

After seemingly thirty minutes of standing there doing nothing, the door opens. A young woman's head pops out from the other side. Long curly hair falls to the side of her distrusting face.

"What do you want?" she asks, albeit none-too-friendly.

"I… er… I…" I stammer.

"Well, I haven't got all day."

"Who is it?" I recognise the voice coming from somewhere in the depths of the house.

"Dave!" I say aloud as though a vocal blockage has suddenly been removed.

"He wants to speak to you," she says, still watching me like a hawk.

"Who is it?" Dave asks from somewhere inside the house.

"Dunno," she replies, still checking me out.

Dave comes to the door. I recognise him instantly. His girlfriend disappears back into the house.

"Hi," I say with an uncomfortable grimace. Dave has lost some weight and hair since I last avoided him. "Do you remember me...? Er... From college? My name is-."

"Ah, I know you, he says. You're... you're... Ralf. What can I do for you?" He grabs the edge of the doorframe, half leaning out as he waits for my reply to come his way.

I stand there, staring at him as my paralysed mouth refuses to work. I'm beginning to believe my question is so ridiculous that he will tell me where to go and never bother him again.

"Come in," he says in a calm and friendly voice. I think he saw my uncomfortable expression matching my pained and twisted body. I notice some cramp building up along my tightened jaw as he closes the door behind me. He guides me into their kitchen. Except for the essential kettle on the worktop next to a coffee jar and a couple of mugs, there is a small table and two chairs pushed against the wall and that's about it. "Sit down", he says, "and tell me what's on your mind."

I guess I am that readable.

"Oh, yeah..." I say, fiddling with my fingers under the table. "I... er... wanted to ask you about something,"

"Yeah?" He sits down opposite me.

"It's private. Could we keep it that way?" I ask.

"Sure. What is it?" he replies, unperturbed.

"Well, remember when we were at college, and..." I say and fizzle out at the critical point of information.

"Did I offend you?" he asks and raises his hand. "If I did, I apologise. Not intended."

"No! No, you didn't... Oh, sorry. Maybe I should go."

"Look, whatever you have to say, stays here," Dave says.

"Promise?"

"Promise," he replies with a slight nod.

"Okay. Er…. Remember when you used to go clubbing, you used to… used to take drugs."

"What of them?" he asks, shifting in his kitchen chair.

"Well, I've discovered that psychedelics might help me…. I don't know where else to go."

"Oh, is that all," he says, breathing a sigh of relief. "What do you need?"

"Eh! Oh, er… I don't know," I reply. I am shocked at how easy this went. "That's my problem."

"Ah. Would you like a cuppa?" Dave asks, standing up. "This might take some time."

Now that was an informative evening. It's just gone three in the morning and I have just arrived home. I'm lying on the couch buzzing. I found it surprising that Dave was so easy to talk to. He's easier to have a conversation with than my psychologist. Shouldn't it be the other way around? Firstly, he asked whether the psychedelics were for pleasure or therapy. Naturally, I asked him what the difference was, just to make sure. I need the therapy version. That became even clearer after I told him about my thoughts, especially how he summed me up as an outsider when we were at college. I know I am a loner, but I never realised I was an outsider. I had never considered they were related. It was quite a revelation.

His next question was about how I wanted to be after the session. I found this helpful. He said that although it's good to know what I don't want to be anymore, it has to be replaced with something I want in my life. He said that if we don't replace what we don't want with something we do want, then what we 'don't want' could come back into our lives. The problem is that it could return with a vengeance and could ultimately cause more issues.

I asked him which psychedelic to take. He called them 'entheogens'. He said this makes them sound more respectable and stayed with this word throughout the evening. Firstly, he told me about DMT, which is quick and intensive. However, he advised me against doing this for such a significant problem. LSD, and MDMA, he said, are super in their own right. However, he prefers magic mushrooms for therapy work. The therapeutic effect is profound and thorough. The sessions don't take as long as LSD, but they are long enough to work through those past issues. He did mention some other entheogens, but until now, I haven't heard of them.

He recommended we took a break and asked if I fancied trying some cannabis. I shook my head. However, he advised me it would be fine, and I would experience a light head and body effect to help me relax. After a couple of persistent attempts to convince me, I relented. He showed me how to hold a bong half as big as me, pull the smoke into the bong and how to inhale it. All that he told me about exhaling wasn't required. I coughed and spluttered it out. With some encouragement, I had another go, and this time it went better. At least I blew some of the smoke out between the coughing fits.

And then, a short while later, I noticed a sudden lightness come over me as some imaginary weight slipped from my shoulders. Dave was doing this with me when after a while, I noticed his eyes were bloodshot. I asked if mine were too. He laughed and I laughed and we laughed. I could hear his girlfriend chuckling in another room at our laughter. Suddenly, it seemed easier to talk.

He asked me whether I planned to do this alone. I affirmed I was. Then he asked me about the setting. I had to ask him what he meant. He explained that it needs to be carried out in a comfortable place where nobody could disturb me. 'You'll need a sitter, too,' he said. After explaining what a sitter does, I realised I had no one to help me and told him so.

Dave explained that there are good trips and good ones that don't appear to be so. I didn't know what he meant, so I asked him to expand on it. He said that some people call these 'bad' trips. Some inexperienced psychonauts have ended up in hospital panicking when they have seen things that scared them silly. Such events are not necessarily from the drug itself but from a lack of preparation and understanding of the powerful visual effects it has on us when they dig deep into the darkest corners of our minds to show us what we fear. He says it is working through this fear that helps to release its hold on us.

He told me that one problem is that a session lasts for several hours and it could seem like a very long time before the effects start to wear off, especially if you encounter something you aren't ready to deal with. When we see something that disturbs us, it is time for it to be worked through with the idea of not running away. We have to approach it and work through it to understand it to release ourselves from its grip. The answer lies on the other side of the problem. He said that's why all trips are good if approached with an open mind.

At about two o'clock in the morning, his girlfriend said she was going to bed. I said that I should go too. He mentioned I should come back the next evening after I have had the chance to think things through should I have more questions.

And now, I need to sleep with two questions flying in my head. What do I need to ask myself and who can be a sitter for me?

The telephone rings a little after ten this morning and I'm fast asleep on the couch. I force my numb arm to move that's lying underneath me. Finally, it reaches across enough to pick up the receiver. "Yeah," I mumble, struggling to pull my finger out of the cord.

"Here's your psychologist. I just wanted to tell you that you haven't confirmed your appointment for today. I think this is important to attend as you are making great progress. I don't want to see you throw away all this good work you've invested in."

"I've found someone who answered my questions on psychedelics," I reply. "I don't think I need your help anymore."

"I can do that! Why not come by this after-"

I put the receiver back down on the cradle, letting the plunger cut off the signal. I have found some inspiration in taking some control of my life. And if you're thinking about it. Yes, I still have an analogue phone.

It feels like last night's experience helped me to release a tiny bit from my unknown bounds. Like there is a small amount of hope released within me. Not blind hope, but a hope that has potential. That small change is enough to turn my day around to be more productive. I sit in front of the computer and read about various experiences others have gone through with psychedelics, focusing on those who have had 'bad' experiences. I want to know how they worked through it and what happened when they didn't. Reading about this in more depth, I can relate to the fear they must have gone through without knowing what to do. I now realise the importance of having a sitter as they help to keep the tripper grounded in those most challenging moments.

This evening, I visit my old college student companion, Dave. The front door opens. His girlfriend stands there with a warm and trusting smile.

"Come in," she says and stands aside, allowing me to enter the hallway. I see she is holding the bong Dave and I used last night. "I'm joining you today if you don't mind. I don't want to miss out on the fun this time," she says and passes it to me. Still standing in the hallway and with her encouragement, I take it from her outstretched hand.

"Hi, great to see you," Dave says, bounding down the stairs. "Good to see you are making an early start," he says, pointing to the bong.

"Oh, sorry," I say and pass it to him. He lets me keep hold of it.

"Come in," she says, guiding me into the living room. "You need to fire it up."

The living room has a certain haze to it and it smells really good in here. The living room has a collection of chairs, sofas, bean bags, cushions and an old large television in the corner. I was impressed by how many sitting places there were in the living room.

"We have regular gatherings," she says, reading my mind. "Shall I fire it up for you?"

I pass the unlit bong back to her.

"A few more will be arriving shortly, so if you have any questions you want to keep private, now's the time to ask," Dave says.

She flops on a bean bag that almost swallows her petite frame in one gulp. Her arms and bong shoot up in the air to avoid her rapidly rising knees.

"Oh, sorry. I didn't want to intrude," I reply, feeling uncomfortable, knowing their friends are coming around.

"You aren't," he says. "Do you have any questions?"

"Er, yeah. Two," I reply. "I still don't know my problem and I don't know how to find a sitter."

"Hmm, leave that with me. I'll come back to you on that in a day or two," he says, thinking about it.

The doorbell rings and Dave goes to answer it.

"I think I should be going," I say.

"You're not going anywhere," she says, trying to point to another bean bag. "Sit down and join us."

Oh, I don't know what to do. I'll be in the way.

I'm still standing there rather uncomfortably when Dave comes back into the living room with a couple of friends. None of them I know. One has taken a drag on a funny-looking cigarette and passes it to Dave.

"Hi," the first guest says to me as Dave sucks on, what I now realise, is a joint.

"Hello," I reply and raise my hand in greeting. Before I realise it, another hand grabs my arm and pulls me into a bean bag next to her.

"I said sit down," she says to me with a cheeky grin.

"I have nothing to contribute," I answer back.

"If you agree, you can contribute something the next time. How about that?" Dave says and looks at his two friends. They both nod in agreement as if it was the norm.

"So, it looks like you're staying," she says.

What an evening! It's nearly five in the morning, and I've just arrived home. I don't think I have ever, in my entire life, laughed for so long, so hard and so loud. Altogether, there were eleven people. I felt comfortable in their company and they just took me for what I am. No judgement. No criticism. No negativity. Usually, people laugh at me after I have said something unusual. They weren't laughing at me. We were laughing with each other. Oh, that experience was just what I needed.

Giving Up

Nearly a week has passed since I was at his place and I haven't heard anything from Dave about a sitter. I don't want to go around and bother him after all he has done for me. He has already been too generous and I don't want to intrude. That night's euphoria wore off long ago and I now feel as lost as I did before I first went to his place. As each hour goes by and I hear nothing from Dave, my hope diminishes. I don't think I will ever have a chance to receive that much-needed psychedelic help. Maybe as my parents always reminded me, I don't deserve anything good in my life.

Another week goes by and all my hope that he will contact me has disappeared altogether. I'm at my wit's end and don't know what to do. Even the one person I thought could help me deserted me. Who can blame him? Maybe they were laughing at me that night at his place. Maybe it was an inside joke I wasn't a part of. For the last few days, I have been asking myself whether anyone would notice if I were no longer here. The answer is simple. Not really, no. Psychedelics aren't for me. I'm beyond rescuing. That much is clear. It has taken me a long time to realise it. Now is the time for me to accept the truth.

I'm not a drinker, but I've bought a half bottle of cheap whiskey and have gathered all the unused anti-depressants I've been told to take over the last couple of years. Now's the time. I haven't written a goodbye letter. What's the point? No one would be interested in what I have to say and it's not as though I have anyone in my life to send it to. I pour some into a glass and take a swig. As soon as it hits the back of my throat, I cough and splutter, spraying it all over the place. This is not going to be easy. Trying to get used to it, I take another gulp and force it down. It burns to the pit of my stomach. With my free hand, I pop open the entire tub of mixed tablets. I stare at their various shapes and coloured bodies, eagerly waiting to gather in my insides to shut down this worthless piece of shit permanently.

The Opportunity

Okay, now is the time. I throw the tub of tablets into my mouth in one go and panic a little. I've never been able to swallow pills without a drink, so they cling to the sides of my dry mouth. After a deep breath, I convince myself I am ready to swill them down to let them get on with their job. I put the glass of whiskey to my lips as I psyche myself up again to take that necessary swig when I hear a knock at the door. Whether instinct, panic, shock or hope, I spit them out over the thread-bare bed-sit carpet.

I jump up and run to the door, deeply thankful for a reason not to go through with it.

"Who is it?" I ask loudly, without opening it.

"It's me. Open up," Dave replies from the other side.

Grabbing onto the wall in relief, I crack open the door and peep through the small gap. My body is shaking.

"Yes?"

"Can I come in?" he asks. I cautiously let go of the wall and open the door without saying a word. "Boy, you look like shite. What happened to you?"

"Oh, nothing, really," I reply, still shaking. I want to say, 'You could say that I have been considering experiencing another existential dimension,' but I keep my mouth shut. I notice a stray tablet stuck to the roof of my mouth.

"I want to apologise," Dave says, looking at me a little puzzled.

"What for?"

"The last time we met. You said you wanted to go to the next stage and I said I would find some info out for you. We had such a great night that night. I completely forgot. Sorry."

"Oh," I reply. I don't want to take him into the bed-sit with the whiskey and tablets spread over the place. He'll know what I was contemplating as soon as he sees them.

"Is everything all right?" he asks. "We haven't seen you for the last couple of weeks. Did something bother you from our last evening together?"

"No, no, no," I reply. "It was a great evening. I loved it and would love to do it again. I… I didn't want to make a nuisance of myself."

Then he catches me off-guard and walks past me into the bed-sit. He freezes at seeing the mess. My head sinks towards my collapsing chest as my spine gives up its primary function.

"You're not okay, are you?" he asks and turns to face me.

"Just a difficult couple of days. That's all," I mumble. The tablet dislodges from the inside and sticks to the corner of my mouth. I snatch it away and squeeze it in my hand.

"Look, I want to ask if you still want to go through a therapy session. That's why I'm here," Dave says, ignoring what had just happened, although he had seen me snatch it away.

"Yeah… yeah, I do," I reply, my head and body still slumped forward. My legs want to crumple.

"Here, ring this number. This person may be able to help you. The Instructor is a qualified psychotherapist who happens to be a friend of mine," he says and hands me a piece of paper.

"Really?" I ask. I reach out and take it. I read the number as though it's the holy grail of… of… something …. A step forward out of this mess. "Thanks."

"Look," he says as he grips me by the shoulder. "Just ring me or pop around if you need someone to talk to or chill with some company. You don't have to talk if you don't want to. You are always welcome."

"Thanks," I reply, none too convinced he means it.

"Why not come around tonight? We're doing something special. You can at least get a viewer's interpretation of what could happen should you decide to work with The Instructor," he replies.

"Really?" I reply and stand up straighter as my spine remembers a part of its function.

"Really."

Today is turning out to be better than I thought. Now I need to make a telephone call.

"Ralf, what you're thinking of doing, it's not worth it. Tidy yourself up and I'll see you later tonight, okay?" Dave says and leaves me to sort out my mess.

"And? Did you speak to The Instructor?" Dave asks me as I enter his house that evening. Andrea, his girlfriend, sits in the same beanbag from two weeks ago. She's wearing different clothes, so I assume she left it at some point. She waves to me and I give one of those stupid waves back with a cheesy grin, instantly regretting it.

"Here," Andrea says with a friendly smile and passes the bong to me. The last time I was here, I had heard one of their friends call her that.

"Thanks," I reply and sit in the beanbag beside her. I take a pull of the cooled white smoke I have built up in the bong and feel it enter my awaiting lungs. Then after a couple of seconds, I release it slowly and casually wait for its light effect on my mind and body. I pass the bong back to her. "How can I contribute to the usage here?" I say as I pull my wallet out of my back pocket.

"Don't worry. The next time we'll sort something out," Andrea says. She puts her hand on my arm and gives it an affectionate rub. I notice she glances up at Dave, who nods and then smiles at me. That's the second time they've said that.

"So, you still haven't told me how your telephone call went," Dave says. He squats down with his hand out for the bong.

"Oh, sorry," I reply, passing it to him. "The Instructor explained we need to get to know each other first. Once we've agreed that this is the right direction for me, he said he would explain what would happen in the therapy session. Is The Instructor as good as you say?"

"And better," Dave replies. "There are others who are doing similar work to The Instructor. Some cover such a session in a day or two with good results. I find The Instructor thorough. Because of that, you need a couple of days to understand what you will be working through. You need to be mentally ready for the therapy session and to know how to get on with your life afterwards before you even begin. This session will be one of the best you can attend. Just so you know, there will be several participants going through the same ritual, so you're not alone. It's an amazing session. We did this a few years ago."

"I can't wait," I reply and that's true. I would so love to start it today.

I met The Instructor and was so impressed with this psychotherapist's style that I felt a bit of hope rise within me when I left the office. What a gift this person has! I left with a date, location and some homework I need to complete before starting. The assignment will help me understand what I want to deal with in the session and afterwards. Interestingly, the questions I need to answer are like those Dave asked me the first time I visited his place.

All I have to do is wait for a month to participate…

Part I: The Minor Mystery – The Afterlife

Finally, today is the first day of the four-day session with The Instructor. I have been driving for the last three hours on the open roads and all I have to do is hope my car survives this pot-holed country lane as I arrive at my destination. And there it is, Eleusis House!

Twelve cars parked between the farmhouse and a barn. I park my rust bucket in an open space. I grab my overnight bag packed with essentials and the answers to The Instructor's homework questions. The Instructor told me we wouldn't meet civilisation for the next few days. All mobiles are banned and are kept in the main house for security. When I head towards the farmhouse, I see an arrow pointing to an old barn. Although I see an old tractor and some other rusty farming implements in the long grass nearby, I see no traces of active farming work nearby.

Nervously, I walk over to the barn and see a small door ajar that is built into one of the closed massive double barn doors. I hear several voices from the other side and enter. Immediately The Instructor approaches me with open arms and welcomes me into the spacious barn.

"Welcome, Ralf, and good to see you again," The Instructor says to me. "You are not the last to arrive. We are waiting for one more participant. Then we can begin. Please take your name badge and help yourself to a drink over there." I wander over, put my bag near the stairs with the others and then take my name badge from a small table.

After the catch takes hold of the pin and with a quick check to see if my name is the right way up, I glance around the converted barn. It is divided into two and I'm standing in an open half that has been made into a large working room with chairs that form a circle. Hanging on the walls are several camper beds. Do we sleep together in one room? I stand there alone because I'm too nervous about introducing myself and hug my glass of water for some type of non-existent protection.

The entrance door to the barn squeaks open. A colossal man stands in the entranceway blocking out the natural light from behind.

"Am I at the right place?" he booms. The Instructor dashes over and welcomes him with open hands. After a brief hello, he bounds towards the table where I am avoiding everyone else. He grabs his name badge and of all the places to choose, stands right next to me while fixing it to his t-shirt. But this isn't a man; it's… it's a walking mountain. This beast's clothing looks military; green trousers and a white t-shirt bursting with muscle which confirms he doesn't have an ounce of fat. His neck and arms are as thick as my body and the breadth of his chest is as wide as I am tall. As for height, I feel I am just a little higher than his belt buckle. If he decides to slap me on my back as a greeting, I'm through that barn wall without touching the floor.

"Hi, I'm Steve," he says in the friendliest manner possible.

"Ralf", I reply, shaking a finger from his outstretched shovel of a hand.

"Welcome," The Instructor says. The massive guy, Steve, and I sit down next to each other on the two remaining chairs that form the circle. "And thank you for joining me at Eleusis House for your life-changing time here. But before we get started for the evening, I would like to give you a bit of history and explain how I work over these next few intensive days. There are fourteen of you and it is important to get to know and help each other throughout."

The Instructor takes the time to tell us how each day will progress, how we are to discuss things with each other and that the exercises will not only help prepare us for the main psychedelic session on the third day but for afterwards too.

Before getting to know the other participants better, we are taken upstairs into the upper half of the beautifully converted barn to our guest rooms. Each has been fitted with a concealed wet corner. A small and simple pine wardrobe and drawers are for our belongings. The wooden floor is a stunning golden yellow enhanced by the simple white walls broken by an indiscrete picture hanging on the wall. The view from the window is just fantastic countryside for as far as the eye can see. I breathe and smell the fresh air through the gap in the partially open window.

"Sort yourselves out, and we'll begin in ten minutes," The Instructor says and disappears.

I see most people are back in the room as I come down the stairs. The Instructor is standing in a small gap between the chairs with a flipchart nearby.

"Please take your seats," The Instructor says as the last of us come down into the main room.

Some put a glass of water on the floor next to their feet, others prefer to hold them after taking their seat. A sick woman rolled her wheelchair into a gap opposite me. A bag of clear liquid hung from a pole behind her shoulder that is fixed to the rear side of the wheelchair. I have to say she doesn't look too well. The big guy I have privately nicknamed Hercules the Warrior sits next to me. I'm just skin and bone myself. Yet I still try and suck myself in to make myself even smaller so that I am not intruding on his immense bulk that invades my space.

"Remember I mentioned the great Greek Mysteries of Eleusis earlier on?" The Instructor asks. "They're a big inspiration for me. From what we know, this is one important way the Greeks cared for their people's mental health regardless of age, race or status. These powerful ceremonies started around 4000CE when the Greeks held one of two religious festivals each year. For those who aren't sure of the history, Christianity and the other Abrahamic religions weren't even a thought in a scribe's mind when these started to take place. At that time, humankind followed a collection of fictional gods supported by various festivals worshipping them. Just like modern religions do today, using one of the many fictional gods created by man with rituals taken and watered-down from other older beliefs.

"These festivals aimed to release fears, doubts, inhibitions and trauma that had manifested over time. The festivals were open to anyone over a certain age with no criminal record. All walks of life could attend, ranging from the highest to the lowest of society regardless of whether one was a businessman, philosopher, politician, social or manual worker or even a beggar. There was no class segregation allowed and everyone was treated equally. All you needed to do was to be able to speak Greek and pay for the festival. This equalled a month's wage plus payment for the accommodation. Just like you have done here."

I am riveted by what he says and risk a quick look around. We all are.

"The first part of the journey was a physical one that took them from Athens to Eleusis, where this festival was held. It consisted of an eleven-mile or a seventeen-kilometre walk. It took from sunrise to sunset, with many onlookers cheering them along the way. Today, you all arrived here by transport of your means and without the parade. A shame, but that's progress for you.

"For those who had never been to the Eleusinian Mysteries, they speculated what was happening and how it could change a person's life. They didn't know what happened inside behind those closed doors as an oath was given to those who participated in keeping it a complete secret from outsiders. The secret was kept so well that we still don't know exactly what happened to this very day.

"We know there were two yearly festivals, the Minor Mystery and the Major Mystery. For all of you here, this is your first, the Minor Mystery. Still, it doesn't mean it is less important than the Major Mystery, it just means the Minor Mystery prepares you for the next life-changing experience that happens in the Major Mystery. And just like with the Greeks, you need to complete this session before you can attend the next one.

"We do know, however," The Instructor continues, "that a part of the ceremonies was based on some of their gods. The main one is Demeter, the goddess of Wheat. The other is Persephone, Demeter's daughter, and her marriage to Hades, the god of the Underworld. Yet," The Instructor continues, "what we do know is they used a couple of essential entheogens near the end of the Mysteries for the release of a limiting belief or two. They made a type of LSD from a fungus that grows naturally on wheat. This is the same fungus Dr Hoffmann used when in the laboratory, he accidentally discovered LSD. Their second entheogen occasionally used was magic mushrooms, or rather, the psilocybin found in them. We, however, are going to use magic mushrooms for our ceremonies. We grow, harvest, and prepare them for the sessions ourselves here. We are using the ones we grow here because we know their quality, effectiveness and how much is required for each person's optimal dose.

"But before you are ready for your therapeutic session, I need you to explore why you are here and to explore a little deeper what you want from your life. In the Minor Mysteries, stories were told of Demeter in search of her daughter. Persephone was kidnapped and subsequently married Hades, the underworld ruler. However, for today's generation, this story is pretty much unknown outside of Greece and is outdated for the world we live in today. Yet, one crucial point it did focus on is what happens when we die that is still important today as it was then and that is whether there is an afterlife after we die or is this it? Although I think you may find some moments challenging, I aim to ensure you a smooth and exciting transition, I hope you get the chance to peek behind the Universe's Veil.

"For the next half an hour, I want you all to get to know each other and to talk about whatever you wish. I want each of you to remember that if you don't want to discuss anything and remain silent, that's fine. Please listen instead. Respect each participant's personal space. And importantly, regardless of what someone tells you, even if it sounds weird or unimportant, respect the person's comment because, for them, it is of the utmost importance.

"So, without further ado, let's start. I'll start and tell you a little about me so you know who you are working with. You all know my name and have visited my practice and I'm here to help you through your current dilemma. But what happened to me? How did I get here helping others by doing something illegal? About eighteen years ago, I was diagnosed with cancer detected early enough for me to go through chemo. It was the only choice the doctors gave me in those days. I felt too young to die and went through dehumanising chemotherapy. Nowadays, dietary options and other therapies could help, too, depending on what one prefers. However, regardless of which option we take, nothing is a guarantee. Yes, that was in the days when we had forgotten how the modern diet, the use of chemicals added to foods, medications and stress can cause disease. I'm sure you can imagine the words uttered by your doctor, 'you have cancer' can have a severe and traumatic effect on a diagnosed person.

"Cancer sufferers tend to think that after diagnosis, there is a degradation of life, excess pain and discomfort until one dies. What we tend not to focus on is the extra suffering the patient and family go through during chemotherapy treatment and the risk of death should it not work. All this, and more, can often leave us 'cancerians' suffering from some sort of PTSD afterwards. Usually, this side-effect is ignored by the medical profession. Sadly, few patients get back on with their lives again as though nothing had happened. I couldn't. I was a mess. I went through the most horrific chemo and am fortunate to have survived the critical five and ten-year mark. On average, the survival rate for cancerians is less than thirty per cent after ten years of treatment. That's not a high success rate for a lot of painful and degrading treatment. Thankfully, I'm a part of that survival statistic supported by a severe change in diet. My problem was that after the chemotherapy, I developed a mass of mental issues that sent me into a downward and depressive spiral. Sadly, at the time, I didn't know how to deal with those confusing and unprepared barrages of tumultuous emotions. Chemo has some nasty physical side-effects we can never eliminate, which are still true for me, even today." He catches a young man nodding to himself.

"I'll be open with you and tell you that I was terrified of that cancer coming back. Even after I was treated and it had disappeared, I was sure my life was over such that a part of me had given up. I had stopped eating as I didn't want to feed that cancer again. The problem was I didn't know what foods to avoid. I was advised by my doctor that processed foods and sugars had nothing to do with it. However, we know that is not always the case. Sadly, no doctor told me to stop using foods grown or processed with toxic chemicals. But how does one do that? There is nothing on a label that tells me what has been used, so I can't see or trace which of the thousands of chemicals used in agriculture have been tested for cancers and other illnesses and which haven't. There's even no way to know what the side-effects could be when certain chemicals are mixed because none are listed. This issue still bothers me today as much as it did then.

"I stopped going out as I was scared of dropping dead in the street and didn't want to die alone or in hospital. I quit my university place because I didn't think it was worth my while to invest so much time into something when I was constantly thinking I didn't know if I had a future. I was in a rapidly decreasing spiral into oblivion and nobody could help me.

"My doctor wanted to put me on some medication and said suffering from depression was a part of the chemo side-effects and that I should just accept it. But my father told me to avoid that avenue and pull myself together. To begin with, that was all the support I received from him. I felt alone and started drinking copious amounts of alcohol to drown out those ever-depressing thoughts.

"I needed to return to university to pick up some of my things. I planned to avoid all contact where necessary and when I bumped into a study friend, we started talking. It was the first time I had opened up to someone about my ordeal. In that short time, she mentioned something to me that was the start of a life-changing experience. She said she felt she had to tell me, but it was up to me whether I should accept what she had to say. She told me about experiments done in the 1950s and 1960s against depression using entheogens. In those days, they were legal and the results were outstanding, such that therapists made leaps and bounds in progress for the mentally imbalanced.

"When I arrived home, I visited the local university library when the internet wasn't as prominent as it is now. I spent days searching out research papers, reports and books and read them until I effectively knew them by heart. I found one that said they could eliminate PTSD in military personnel and people who have suffered other types of traumata. But I had a new problem; I didn't know where to get such entheogens except on the black market, as they were illegal at the time. My next challenge was to learn how to cultivate mushrooms from spores that I had bought from a student drug dealer I knew. It wasn't a thing he usually sold, such that I had to wait a while before he had them for me. The spores turned out to be Psilocybe Cubensis Mexicana. Within several long months of working from an old book I had found in the library, I had my first batch of fruit and was ready to go.

"The two most significant learning curves I had to go through were how much to take and the type of question I needed to ask. In those days, I knew nothing about the Greeks, the psychology of framing, and so on. I knew only a little about set and setting from what I had read in a book written by Richard Fadiman. The first time I conducted a session was with my father as my sitter. I was lucky that I got the setting right the first time, although my father had as much idea on how to support me as I did.

"I'm not going to go into details of what I went through. I don't want to influence your experiences in a couple of days when you will do the same. Still, I will tell you that I felt I had understood those fears that had been bothering me since I was diagnosed with cancer and allowed those restricting beliefs to leave me. I felt other burdens disappear too. By chance, I discovered in that session, just as the Greeks did, who we are and what happens to us when we die. After answering my father's endless questions, I noticed contentment rise within me and a new release flowing through me that is still with me to this very day. I wanted to go out to meet friends again. I wanted to go back to university. And that I did. But this time, I read psychology. What I love about this second chance at life is that I can now give something back."

"Did you ever retake them?" a young woman asks in the circle.

"Several times over the next years," The Instructor replies. "Over the years, I have worked through plenty of issues I felt needed tidying up. I also wanted to explore the power of the Universe I had experienced in an earlier session, Since then, I have never looked at society the same again. One thing I will say is that I have never done is take them for fun. I disagree with it. There is something sacred inside these entheogens that connects us to a powerful entity, and I believe that should be respected.

"Right, that's enough about me. Who would like to stand up and say something about themselves?"

After briefly introducing myself, I sit down, relieved. It isn't easy to say what I want from this experience as I am still trying to work out what it is. Next up is the Hercules guy, Steve, who sits next to me. He stands up. It is a light relief to have some personal space around me again.

Hercules stands up and is in deep thought. He lets out a sigh that allows his posture to slump slightly. Still not saying anything, he rubs his chin while thinking about something. It's not easy standing up and saying something personal to strangers. But look at this guy. He has nothing to fear. One swipe of that shovel-hand and the enemy would be launched like a missile on speed. Yet, while watching him, I see some concern spread across his forehead and his eyes are filled with deep contemplation. Something is bothering him. Well, it must be. He's here with us. We all have at least one problem we want to deal with.

"I have to say," he starts, "you have all left me in awe when I compare my life with yours. When I consider my childhood, I don't have a reason to be here." He takes great care to look at each of us, including me. "I'm lucky I have never suffered in the hands of my mother, father, sibling or through someone else's unchecked perverted lust. I can't even guess what each of you has dealt with throughout your life. I can't comprehend the pain and suffering each of you is going through to bring you here today."

He reflects some more before speaking again.

"I hate to say this… here, but… but I've been lucky. My childhood was unspoilt by two devoted parents who are still alive today. My close relationship with my sibling has been my backbone since I lost my way these last few years. I know that I've been lucky. I entered my chosen career even though I am suffering from it. I love military life more than words can describe it. This makes it easier for me to be here with you today after what I experienced in Afghanistan. That still haunts me to this very day." He taps the side of his head. "Here."

"Our shift was coming to an end that should have been a standard patrol. We were on the last stretch back to base when something went wrong. We saw a small child watching us from a distance. He waved. We regularly saw kids scrounging in the dirt. Our problem was that we never know whether this was an innocent child or one that had been recruited by the enemy and used as a decoy. We couldn't respond as though they were the enemy. We were there to protect the people of Afghanistan against the enemy. Those we encountered were mainly innocent people in some war they don't want to be in. We have guidelines and follow them as closely as possible. But this time, it turned out to be a trap. The child waved, One of our crew waved back. We should have recognised it was a signal to someone else. Before we knew it, the leading transporter was blown to smithereens. We tried to dodge the shrapnel flying. As we did, a hand grenade landed in our transporter. I was lucky and saw it flying towards us. I threw myself out of the transporter. I had shouted a warning, but there was so much happening... my troop... my friends... to escape... I was the only survivor.

"The rebel who threw the grenade was still holding the pin as he came over to me. That terrorist bent down and rolled me over as I drifted in and out of consciousness. That bastard prised an eye open. 'Look at me,' he spat. 'Look at me.' I did. I can still see every detail and hair in his greying beard that was separated by a snarl on his dirt-encrusted lips. He said, 'Allah has chosen you to live, just like you have chosen to let your infidel friends die. I am here to haunt you for your failure. Wherever you go, whatever you do, I am always with you to remind you how weak you are. Tell your infidel superiors that you are the reason for this destruction. Tell them to finish you off, just like the coward dogs laying around you.' He patted my cheek, pushed the pin in my mouth and walked away. He was right. I had failed my men... Here... here is that pin." He fished it out from under his t-shirt.

"Whenever I hear of another attack and that more soldiers have unnecessarily been killed in this way, it rips me apart. I think it's my fault... and I don't know what to do about it. It stops me from sleeping.... I'm a danger to my lovely partner when I do.... I once attacked her in my sleep, thinking she was that rebel.... I was having a nightmare... Because of that, we now sleep in separate rooms. I can't take any responsible position as it gets too much for me. I get irritated under the smallest amount of stress. I never used to break down in any situation. I mean, do I look the type...? The doctors kept feeding me pill after pill for all these years with no real effect on dealing with the problem. Those tablets made everything foggy and confusing. It makes me feel I had lost even more control over my life. Gradually, it reached a crisis point that my partner considered leaving me for her safety. Not because she doesn't love me, she does because she is still here. But she told me she doesn't know how long she can cope with my irrational behaviour. She finds it hard living with me, not knowing what to say or do. This is my wake-up call that I need to do something different…. It was through a friend that I found The Instructor. This is the only person to have proposed an alternative that is as old as history itself. And once I understood that I knew I had to at least give it a go. This is my last hope."

He lowers himself to the chair. Before reaching the seat, he lets his whole weight collapse but misjudges where the chair is. His arms inadvertently swing out to regain balance. One of them smacks into me and knocks me backwards off my chair and onto the floor. He is at my side instantly.

"Are you hurt?" Hercules asks. He offers his hand out as his eyes scan me for any apparent injuries.

"Fine. I'm fine, thanks," I reply, a little shaken by how much latent power this guy has. I inadvertently grab his thumb because his outstretched hand is too big to hold onto as he helps me to my feet.

The Instructor asks me if I'm okay. I am a little shaken, but other than that, I am fine. I sit back down again with the inner confirmation that I need to find another seat to survive these next few days.

"Okay, I think that's enough for now," The Instructor says. "Let's take a quick break and gather again in ten minutes. We still have a couple of exercises to do before the end of the day."

I glance out of the barn window, and sure enough, the day turns to dusk. My life has begun to take a new direction.

The following day, we all sit around the kitchen table, hugging our coffee cups and wondering what the day will bring. A couple talks animatedly with each other. I am one of the few who are just listening. What I have to say isn't important.

Two people are missing from the table. That's Hercules... er, Steve, he's out running. He says he needs to keep busy, otherwise, he loses control of his emotions and that starts to make the rest of his day more difficult. The other person missing is the young woman in the wheelchair. Her husband has taken her breakfast into her room situated downstairs.

The woman in the wheelchair is called Zoe. She is amazingly kind with her words to whomever she speaks. Last night, she told us that her life had been a battle from an early age. She had always believed that her mother had loved her and that all her mother was going through was one of life's rough patches when someone contacted the authorities of suspected child neglect.

Government officials took Zoe from her mother as she was considered at risk and was put into care before she was five years old. Once in care, she was passed from one adoptive home to another because they couldn't cope with her emotional tantrums. As Zoe says, all she wanted to do was to go back home. She says that the government's decision to take her away from her mother was the start of her childhood life into sordid sexual abuse. This pushed her to rebel against authority. Zoe had excessive emotional swings, often lost physical control and caused indiscriminate harm to whoever was in her way. The start of using alcohol led to harder drugs and ultimately turned to prostitution. Zoe's self-worth continually diminished until she was just skin and bone and homeless. Before she had turned twenty, she was put on her first rehabilitation programme. The problem was that Zoe ran away after the first couple of days and said she had been trying to run away from herself ever since.

Zoe said this lifecycle continued, fleeing from similar centres for the next few years until she met her now-husband. He was also in treatment, yet it was his way of treating her that had gradually encouraged her to think and feel different about herself. Over time she regained some of her self-worth and even started college to learn a skill. She said she had always wanted to be a hairdresser. Zoe had completed her first term when she discovered she had metastasised liver cancer. At first, she didn't realise she was ill other than the relentless tiredness she couldn't shake off. It was Hercules who asked her why she came here. Her words were, "Maybe I have a month left, but there is so much

I'm still angry about and I don't know why. I'm not ready to go until I know what I am looking for. This is my last chance to find it."

"Are you scared of dying?" Hercules asked.

"I'm petrified!" Zoe replied with wide eyes.

How that answer resonated with everyone in the group. Other than me, we all vocalised our fear of death. It's not that I don't fear death. I do. I just didn't think they would be interested in what I had to say.

A sweaty Hercules bounds into the kitchen and booms, "Boy, that's wonderful weather out there." He promptly disappears upstairs to get a shower, I hope. I have to sit next to him all day. The seats have been assigned.

"I trust you have had a good sleep and are ready for today's exercises," The Instructor says as we settle into our chairs. "Today, we will get deep into the detail to understand who we are and what entheogens could eventually do for us. I want you to work through your previously completed questionnaire with a partner. To begin with, I want each of you to tell them your problem and how it affects your life."

"Excuse me," I chip in and raise my hand. "I know I have a problem, but I still don't know what it is. "

"Hmm, when you think about it, it seems you know better what your problem was than what it isn't, didn't it?" The Instructor replies.

"Oh," I say, not understanding what he means and I nod in agreement.

"It's important to clarify what is happening within you and what has made you into this resourceful person you are today," The Instructor carries on as though I haven't asked anything. "And yes, we are all resourceful people. Every one of us." The Instructor looks around and sees surprised faces peering back.

Me, resourceful! Nah, I can't believe that. I've spent my life doing everything to avoid conflict or challenges or taking on any responsibility that comes my way since I can remember. How is that resourceful?

"Ah, I see most of you are quite surprised about this. Let me put this another way. If we think of someone famous and rich, we could conclude they are resourceful and successful in getting where they are. That is the first group of resourceful people. However, there is a second. They are the ones who avoid contact with people, avoid being noticed and avoid conflict of any sort."

He's speaking about me. I shuffle uncomfortably. Some others in the group do, too.

"And you are successful at it. You are just as successful and determined to achieve your defensive aim as a businessperson runs a profitable business or someone becomes famous for something they can do."

This is news to me. I've always considered myself a failure. I suppose I have managed to live to that expectation quite well. Would that mean that if I had rebelled against my low self-esteem and thought of myself differently, I could have been someone more recognisable? Probably not. Who would want to listen to me, anyway?

"Sometimes, we need to shut society out of our lives to control what is going on in our minds. Sadly, some people label us as a failure or lazy or something else that is demeaning, which, deep within ourselves, we know isn't true. If only that commentator took a short while to think why someone is different or recluse or angry and to respect that something is bothering them who would rather be left alone."

Someone glances at Marie. I guess she is in her early forties. Marie is stone-faced, forthright when she speaks and severely overweight.

Marie told us her story last night. Her nightmare began on her way to school. It was her first year at secondary school and she was walking alone on her way home when she was bundled into a van. The kidnapper didn't want a ransom because he wanted her for himself. Only the kidnapper was her father. I've read about cases like this on the internet. In Austria, a man named Fritzl kidnapped his daughter as she walked to school. He kept her as a sex prisoner for twenty-four years, ultimately fathering seven children with her. Words fail me what to say when someone can do that to anyone without suffering any conscience.

And this is what happened to this poor woman. Her father had kidnapped her and locked her in a secluded location. Through the abuse, she fell pregnant, but her father took the healthy babies away and disposed of them. To this very day, her father, who is now in prison, won't tell her whether they are alive or where they are.

I can't even begin to comprehend what she went through. How does one go about 'forgetting' such a traumatic experience? I don't know. She is the only person in the group with one special requirement: no men to sit or stand next to her, no men speak to her and no contact of any kind with anyone, even if it is meant in a friendly manner. This last point goes for women, too.

"Then there are those who at a later age have suffered some serious accident, surgery or a tragic warfare experience that cannot break the destructive and repetitive mental cycle of what happened," The Instructor says. "Over time, we create extreme boundaries and protection systems so that no one could potentially hurt us again in the same or any other way.

"Ladies and gentlemen, do you know how resourceful we have to be this good in protecting yourselves the way you are? We are social creatures by nature and to fight against this natural tendency isn't easy to withdraw ourselves enough from society to create a delicate balance with all the mental imbalances we fight against each day. Just as a businessperson has to improve his product or sales pitch, you have had to enhance your protection strategy to keep the right distance from others. First, you may have stepped back if someone touched you or said something personal. Then you may have snapped at them to help you withdraw further. This may have been the start of creating more elaborate ideas and strategies where you may have justified such actions to overcome any feelings of guilt. Although you may have thought they were working well. Self-isolation never really works for anyone, no matter how hard we try to justify it. Don't get me wrong, being on your own when you want to be, is addicting, but when you need someone to trust and are alone, this is when isolation starts to hurt."

I'm speechless. Some look away from The Instructor to reflect on their thoughts. My throat is dry and I stand up to fetch a glass of water. What The Instructor said was too accurate to be comfortable with.

"A great idea," The Instructor says, looking at me. "Let's have a quick pause."

It's evening and we have finished working through our questionnaire by answering some rather curious questions. For example, what would it give you if you were to keep your problem? What doesn't it give you to keep your problem? What would it give you if you didn't have your problem? And what wouldn't it give you if you didn't have your problem? I have to say I still don't understand what my problem is. It still doesn't make sense after doing all these exercises. The Instructor told me that I have probably created a mental block to something that had happened in my childhood. However, the afternoon work has helped me understand what I want to be once we have finished the Minor Mystery. I'm not aiming for stardom or being a millionaire, although I won't complain if I could have financial security for the rest of my life. Who wouldn't? I just want a simple life and to be free of those unknown burdens holding me back all these years.

Working with Hercules was great. He asked me some great questions, like, if you could be someone different and you could pinch ideas from others to achieve it, what would you be? Or how would you behave differently once your problem has gone? To begin with, I didn't know where to start and after some thought and prodding, he helped me think a little differently. We have concluded that my problem could be related to my parents' hard upbringing. I'm not sure…. My only question is whether I can release whatever it is if I don't know what is wrong with me.

Getting answers from Hercules was easier for me. He knows what he wants but is battling guilt in allowing himself to want that release. He has immense pain after losing his colleagues and friends in Afghanistan and can't find a justification to let it go. The Instructor mentioned that his guilt should be released after the key session tomorrow and that he should be able to pursue his life more freely. Although he will probably not be the same as he was before going on service duty that day, The Instructor says it is a part of life's experience that moulds us into who and what we are today and that is perfectly fine to grow from there.

"I have a question," Arthur, an older man, says to us all. "I'm in my early fifties and last year I needed to go into hospital for surgery. It wasn't for anything special. Routine. It was planned that I should have been out the next day. The problem was the surgeon made a mistake and that nearly cost me my life. I was bedridden for over six months and to this day, I still think I'm just one step away from death every day I wake up. Before all this happened, I was reasonably fit, but my enthusiasm for life has deserted me. I wake up in the morning disappointed to be still alive. After getting up later, I sit in my chair and do nothing except stare into space and wait for death to take me away. My wife tells me to take up a hobby. What's the point? I may be dead tomorrow and don't want to waste money on something that won't be used. How can I imagine the future when I can't even imagine that I should still be alive today?"

"That is a good question," The Instructor says. "Can I ask, if you hadn't needed the surgery, could you imagine how you would be now?"

"That's easy," Arthur says in a more optimistic tone, returning his gaze to The Instructor. "Yes, I can."

"So, just for this week, can you imagine that you never had the surgery and are as fit as a fiddle, such that you see yourself as 'the you' you are?"

"Er… yes," Arthur replies with a frown. I guess he is trying to understand that question The Instructor has just asked.

"That's right. We'll take this further later, so please keep this thought in mind. Now my partner has signalled that our evening meal is ready. After eating, we will return for the last exercise of the day. Right, to the kitchen. I'm famished."

"Good morning to you all. I trust you slept well," The Instructor says the following day. "Okay, today's task is, in theory, a relatively easy one. Before we can even start our therapeutic session, each of you needs to have a powerful question ready for the Universe to answer. This specific question is fundamental to getting the optimal release to your problem. Please note that I use the singular here. Please stick to one key problem and remember that when designing it, to not stray from this simple rule. Your question may have several parts to help us get to the core of the problem, but that's all. Remember, focusing on any secondary issues doesn't help us because the therapeutic session may remove that secondary problem fairly easily. Sadly, the chances are high that it could return more aggressively if the core problem remains untouched. Today does not come to a close until I am satisfied with each of your questions and am willing to stay with you until we have an agreement. Okay?"

A couple of unsure heads nod. This part scares me the most because I still don't know what my problem is but all of these people here know theirs.

"Good. Now, into the same groups as yesterday."

"Right then," Hercules says to me. "Do you want to go first or shall I?"

"Do you mind if I go first? I like your questioning style. It should help me support you when it is my turn to ask you. I don't think I would know what to say otherwise." It's true.

"Fine by me," he replies. "Er… I'm not sure, myself." He thinks for a short while. "Okay… How about… Do you know what the question is you want to ask?"

"No," I reply. I don't.

Herc smiles to himself.

"Now, I will try a questioning method our Instructor used earlier," Hercules asks me. "Is that okay?"

"Sure," I say, a little unsure. The Instructor asked us a lot of weird questions these few days. I wonder which one Hercules means.

"Right. If you knew what question to ask, what would it be?"

"Dunno," I reply.

"Just try it," he says with patience. "Give me a question. Any question."

"Hmm… What do I need to understand to set myself free?" I reply.

"Hey, that's a great start," Hercules says with a big grin.

I notice The Instructor nods lightly to Hercules.

"Okay, that's great," The Instructor says to us all. "Your questions are perfect! All are done before our evening meal too! After we've eaten, I will explain what will happen in our psychedelic session tomorrow. After that, the rest of the time is for yourself. Okay, for those who have an appetite, into the kitchen. As ever, I'm starving."

We trundle into the kitchen. Hercules pushes Zoe ahead of us. He whispers something to her that sets her giggling. This guy is a hero. I would like to be like him and have his charming personality.

This is the morning we've all been waiting for as we gather in the main hall. I risk a glance around and feel as each person looks. Nervous.

"Good morning, ladies and gentlemen. As you may be wondering why we've had no breakfast just yet. That's because today is our big day and we need our breakfast to start the ball rolling," The Instructor says to us as we shift restlessly.

"Today, we will participate in our psychedelic session," The Instructor says. Today is the first time The Instructor looks like a hippy, wearing faded and torn flared jeans with a matching flower-power-type top. "As we discussed yesterday, some of you may realise you think you have already reached your goal; some of you may not. None of you has. Only once we go beyond our conscious rational thinking do we find the answers we are looking for. This is what we are about to do. Okay, what I need you to do is focus on your question. Remember, this question gives the Universe the guidance to help you understand what you need to release.

"Before we have breakfast," The Instructor continues, "please help me push the chairs aside and take the camp beds down. Mattresses are found in the storeroom just over there." He points to a door I haven't noticed before.

Hercules hands me his chair.

"Take this. I'll start lifting the beds down," he says. I set them in a corner out of the way where The Instructor points.

"In rows, please," The Instructor says to Albert, who takes a couple of beds from Hercules. "And plenty of space to walk around them. From all sides."

A young man carries out a bunch of thin mattresses from a cupboard and drops them on one bed. Another participant distributes the pile onto the empty camp beds.

"What about pillows?" a young woman asks.

"Take the pillows, duvets and bed sheets from your rooms to make your bed here and let's do this before we eat," The Instructor says and walks over to Zoe. "After eating, do you want to remain in your wheelchair or would you prefer to lie down?"

"I'd prefer to lay down if you don't mind. My husband is here to help today," Zoe replies.

"Yes, I've spoken to him this morning. What a great fellow you have," The Instructor says.

"I know," Zoe says with a big grin.

The Instructor glances around and is satisfied all is ready. "Okay, you know which bed you've selected. If you haven't already, change into comfortable clothing and then we can eat together. It's important to eat together in a relaxed and meditative manner. Once you've eaten, go straight to your bed if you don't need the loo. There's something else you need to be aware of. I have some extra helpers here today as I can't be everywhere at once. I'm not going to introduce them to you because they will be gone by when your session is over.

"We have male and female assistants to support you, so should you need the loo at any point through the next five to eight hours, a helper will be there to assist. One of the entheogen's side effects is that your legs may feel rather weak, making you slightly disorientated and unstable on your feet. The helpers will ensure you don't stumble on one of your fellow psychonauts," The Instructor says. "Remember, when you have finished the session, please don't talk to others in this room. Get up quietly and go to the kitchen, your room or go for a walk. That way, you can reflect on what you have experienced in your own time."

The participants, including myself, dash upstairs to fetch our pillows, duvet and bedsheet. Zoe's husband comes out from her bedroom, carrying hers to the camp bed. He bends down to her.

"As we agreed, I'll ask you the last time," Zoe's husband says to her quietly. "Do you still want to go through this? It's going to tax you immensely. You know how weak you are."

"I must," Zoe replies. "I'm petrified I don't get to find out before it's too late." She takes his hand in hers. "I need to deal with this... I'll be fine."

"I'm behind you," he replies and kisses her.

None of us utters a word as we gather in the kitchen. We meditate on our respective questions and get into the zone before the psilocybin hits us within around fifteen minutes after taking it. In silence, we finish our breakfast of scrambled eggs mixed with our prescription of dried ground psychedelic mushrooms. They don't taste brilliant.

One by one, we leave the kitchen and enter the newly made hall of beds. Zoe's husband struggles to lift Zoe out of her wheelchair to lay her on the bed.

"Can I help?" I ask.

"We're fine, thanks," her husband replies. "You need to sort yourself out."

I nod, leaving them alone. Hercules is the last out of the kitchen and goes up to them.

"Let me help," Herc says without waiting for a reply. He slips his arms around Zoe. Without any effort, he picks her up, turns towards the bed and lays her down. "How's that?" he asks her.

"That's fine, thanks," she replies and squeezes his arm.

Her husband gives him a thankful nod and bends down to make her comfortable.

I'm on my bed and pull the duvet over me as Hercules passes me.

"Good luck, my friend," he says to me.

"You too," I reply. Nobody has called me their friend before. I smile to myself.

Music starts to play from the speakers on the wall. As instructed earlier, I grab my eye mask and slip it on. My eyes are closed. It's dark. I hear some barely audible music playing in the background. I'm focussed on my question and repeat it like a mantra as I try to relax my nervous body. I hear some footsteps around me. I guess they must be the helpers getting themselves acquainted with the person they are responsible for.

Suddenly, my arms start tingling from my shoulders down to my fingertips. They go hot and cold at the same time. I think the magic is about to begin.

My head feels a little dizzy. I see some tiny sparkles of light in the darkness. They grow with intensity and start to change colour. Suddenly, I'm thrown into a kaleidoscopic tunnel with various brightly coloured lights and shapes flying past me. My body feels like it's flying through a tunnel, up, down, left, and right. I completely forget my question because this is amazing! I never expected this. I wonder how these patterns and images will help me remember what happened in the past.

I see a beautiful young woman with long dark hair whom I don't recognise. In a flash, she's gone as quick as she came. Then I see a woman's gravestone with the same surname as mine. Who is she?

After that, not-so-pleasurable kaleidoscopic colours fly around me as I hear myself crying like a small child. I am riddled with emotions of pain, loss and feelings of intense guilt.

I see an older blue car parked outside a house as I am lovingly held in someone's arms. I see a young man about the age I am now. He is grinning admirably at the car while holding a cleaning rag.

Then everything disappears into blackness.

A car's bright headlights flash up in front of me from nowhere. I hear the sound of a metallic crash mixed with the sound of broken glass. Then everything disappears into blackness again.

I see the young man, but this time he is more sombre looking and is on crutches. He stands next to the woman's grave with the same surname as mine. I'm being held by my mother, who stands next to him. My father is next to her.

'I'm so sorry!' this young man whispers towards the grave. What has he done? Who is he?

All goes black.

This young man reappears, standing at the side of my bed. Although he is staring down at me, he is looking through me. 'You're a drain on those around you, you are,' he slurs with a nearly empty bottle of whiskey in his hand that hangs to his side. 'You're a burden no one can forget.' I guess I'm about three years old as I remember this. 'Nobody wants you. You're a worthless piece of scum,' This young man mumbles. 'You've ruined everyone's life.' I feel myself crying as I look up at him and notice that my eyes are wet under the mask.

Whoever you are, I'm sorry for letting you down. I'm so sorry!

Then it goes dark.

I see myself in a hospital. It's more of a cot than a bed I'm lying in. I don't remember this happening to me. I wonder whether this is just some fantasy I am creating. I'm on my own except for a nurse doing something next to me and then she leaves. My body aches and it is painful to move. I feel my arm is fixed. I turn to look at it and see it is in a cast of some sort. I have a broken arm!

I am swallowed up in the blackness again.

I see myself at primary school in the playground. I'm on my own and am isolated from everyone. It is so silent that not even the birds are tweeting. It's a cold day and I am wearing an old, bedraggled coat. Looking around me, I see the school building and realise I must be in my second or third year in primary school. Something hits me against my back. When I turn around, I see a football rolling to a stop. 'Hey, kick it back,' I hear a child's voice say in the surrounding total silence. In the distance, other kids are playing, running, screaming and having fun. Some girls are skipping. Some girls are throwing a ball to each other. Some boys are playing 'war' in some long grass. A small group of boys still wait for their football to be returned. A disgruntled boy runs up, takes the ball away with his foot and glares at me. He joins his mates with a big silent kick of the ball.

Again, I feel even more alone as the darkness wraps around me again.

I see a beautiful girl I fell in love with at school. My first and only crush. Except she never knew it. I see her long mousey hair and her beautifully thick-set eyebrows. She was in the school athletics club I had joined to get to know her. This must have been the ninth year at school, making me fifteen. I see myself running behind everyone on the racetrack. I'm not just behind.

I'm a long way back. She's smirking at me along with her friends. After the race, I pick up my stuff and leave. Nobody stops me and even the sports teacher ignores me. This is the first and last day in the club. As I walk home, I hear that inner voice repeatedly scolding me, 'You're not worth it, lad. You're a failure.' Lastly, I hear another inner voice say, 'Even your mother would be embarrassed about you if she could see what kind of failure you turned out to be.'

Blackness overwhelms me again.

As the blackness fades away, I see a coffin formed in the shape of a beer glass. It sits in the middle of a pub. The young man I saw earlier lies motionless in it, wearing a hangman's noose as a necklace. The glass coffin changes to a hospital bed. He is connected to a dialysis machine. I see myself playing with some toys on the floor. My mother sits beside him and scolds him for something, but I don't understand what she is saying. He pulls the tubes out of his arm and shouts, 'I don't need this!'

He picks me up and dashes out of the hospital. Next, I see we are in that same pub, but this time without the coffin. He slumps in the chair nursing a drink, surrounded by several empty glasses on a dark round table. He hugs me and whispers, 'I'm sorry. I'm so sorry.' He passes out while I'm still in his arms, sending the glasses crashing to the floor.

I smell the last of the stale alcohol and cigarette smoke as those black curtains instantaneously envelop me again.

I am with my mum and dad at this young man's funeral. Nobody else is present except a vicar going through his monotone routine. What does this dead person have to do with me? Why am I at his funeral? As soon as the service is over, mum drags me away. Dad follows behind while lighting a cigarette. I feel such a wave of loneliness come over me. I don't know why, nor do I know what to do about it.

It all goes black.

I see, hear, and feel nothing for what seems like an eternity. This pretty much sums up my life, my experiences and my adventures. Nothing. Even people I know want nothing to do with me. My parents were beasts to me. They had treated me abysmally as though I wasn't theirs. Why haven't I experienced anything about them yet?

I think my session is about to end because I am still experiencing nothing. No change. Just this empty void. All it is doing is confirming what my father had been saying to me all my childhood life. I'm useless and not worth knowing. I paid all this money and put myself in debt to confirm what I already know.

As I lay on this camp bed, my wet eyes turn into a stream of tears. This quickly turns into heavy sobs, leaving me struggling to breathe. I sit up on the edge of the bed, pull the mask off and wail into my hands. I am truly a worthless piece of shit. What do I have to live for? I have no one. I am useless and entirely alone.

I feel a comforting hand on my upper arm.

'Let it out,' a female says near my ear. Her voice is familiar.

And I do. I let it out. This reassuring hand remains in contact with me, with her thumb stroking me lightly on the shoulder, which I find comforting. Slowly, I take my hands away from my face. They are wet. I look to where I think this person is standing, but no one is there. I feel the reassuring hand leave its gentle grip on my shoulder. I turn the other way expecting to see a helper, but nobody is there.

Quietly, I get up and head to the loo. A helper dashes over to me and slips his arm around mine. It's a good idea as I realise the floor has turned into lava and I almost stumble into it. Carefully, I edge past the other floating coffins surrounding me. Inside I see massive cockroach things grimacing at me. One shoots up without any eyes and stares at me. It has one wide black hole like an open mouth instead. I jump in fright and stagger away. The helper grabs my arm much tighter to stop me from falling into another cockroach-occupied coffin swirling around me on this torrent of a floor. Finally, I get to the loo. It's a relief to sit on something a little more stable. Afterwards, as I stare at the massive swimming room full of enormous cockroaches while planning my journey back, I see my bed floating higher than the others, telling me where it is.

After what I have just learnt about myself, I'm wondering whether I should gather my stuff and head home…. What's the point of staying when I know my self-value is as low as it is? Yes, I've decided. It's time to leave. I head towards the stairs to my room to gather my things, but my helper whispers for me to lie down a little longer. I shake my head, pull away from him and head for the staircase. But when I reach it, it's not there. The stairs are gone. I can't get to my room!

"Where are they?" I ask my helper, who catches up with me as I point to the open space I see. "Who stole the stairs?"

"Come sit down for a minute," the helper says, guiding me back to my bed. I stagger past the other boats floating around me and see motionless eyeless corpses lying in them. I pass one that has some worm-cocoon-thing tossing and turning, probably ready to burst free and fly away like a butterfly. What happened to the coffins full of cockroaches? Did they drown?

I get back to bed and flop on it with some assistance. Resigned, I wait for the time to pass until the stairs decide to come back from wherever they have gone so I can collect my stuff and go home. I glance at the clock on the wall and gather that just over three hours have passed. Or is that four? When did we start? I can't remember. Well, it's three or four hours, so it can't be five or two. The instructor had said that we need between five and eight hours, and I'm not in between. Maybe waiting for a while is the right thing to do and reluctantly yank the duvet over me. I'm not happy waiting because the stairs didn't want to wait for me. Perhaps The Instructor has hidden them on purpose. That's not a nice thing to do.

I lay my head down, close my eyes and then… I'm sitting half-sleep in the back of a car as a child strapped in a child seat. I guess this is because the size of everything around me is larger than it would be if I sat in a car today. In the driver's seat is the young man who had collapsed in the pub and who was standing next to the woman's gravestone with the same surname as mine. He is chirpy and driving the blue car. The young woman I saw earlier, who I still don't know who she is, sits in the passenger seat and smiles lovingly at him. I look outside. It's just darkness. I say a word or gurgle something and this beautiful woman turns to me.

'How are you, my lovely little one?' she asks as she leans over to wipe something from my chin. The car swerves and then carries on.

'Shit!' the man driving mutters under his breath.

'Tired?' she asks. 'Why not take a little break and get some fresh air.'

'Not far now, love. We'll be home in half an hour,' he replies and winds the window down to let the cold night air into the car. I feel it whizzing around my face.

This woman turns back to me, rests her hand on my upper arm and strokes it with her thumb. 'You do know how much we love you, eh? My little cherub,' she says. 'You're my world.'

'And mine too!' he says. I feel their unconditional love flow through me.

Suddenly, the inside of the car glows bright white from the headlights of an oncoming car. There's a massive crash. The car we're in summersaults in the air. Then, thump, it lands on the roof.

All goes black.

I see a hospital ward and lay in my cot with that broken arm. I see this young man's slumped body on a bed near me. I don't know how I recognise it, but he has broken ribs and a few cuts on his face. 'All will be well, son,' he says to me. 'Once mum has had this operation, we can all go home together.' I reach towards him with my free arm and grasp the air with my stubby baby fingers.

'Dada,' I say. 'Mama.'

Here, I notice that he changes his speech from the first person to the second person within these two sentences. 'I was a fool not taking a break', he says while looking at me. 'You were a stupid fool.' His eyes glaze over, but he doesn't look away from me. He continues to say, 'You should have listened to her.'

A man in a white coat comes in, stands near dad's bed and looks serious. Dad glances nervously up at him and instantly recognises what the doctor is about to say.

'I'm sorry,' the doctor says after a short silence. 'She didn't make it. There was too much internal damage…. We couldn't hem the bleeding.'

Dad turns his head back towards me. He stares wildly around the room, trying to comprehend what happened. His eyes glaze over. 'You stupid bloody fool,' he says as he looks through me. 'You worthless piece of shit! You've killed her. The love of my life.' He starts to cry. 'I'm sorry. Oh… my… God…. I'm so sorry,' he sobs as I try to reach out to him.

All goes black again.

I'm at home, tottering around in an untidy living room I don't recognise. I see this young man looking unkempt and slumped in a chair with a whiskey bottle in his hand. His clothes haven't been changed for a while. Neither has mine. I see my arm has healed, although it seems pale and malnourished. I'm hungry. 'You're a worthless piece of shit,' he mutters. 'You're not worth anything. I wish you would die.' and takes another swig from the bottle. 'You don't deserve anything more.' He looks at me and bursts into tears.

The blackness envelopes me again.

It's my fourth birthday today, and I clamber out of bed. Breakfast! I leave my bedroom with just a bed and a chest of open drawers with clothes piled on top. I totter towards the staircase and see something move in another bedroom, so I enter it. This young man hangs from his neck, swinging slightly from side to side. I find a note at his feet.

I open it as I sit on the floor. I can read the words in it.

'Sorry, son,' it says. 'I let you and mum down. Don't be a failure like me. Love Dad.'

That's my dad! He can't be. Mine deserted mum and me when I was fifteen!

I look up as a policewoman with tear marks on her cheeks bends down to pick me up from between the strewn beer cans, empty whiskey bottles and dirty clothes. She carries me out of the house I never knew.

Again, all goes black as I bury my head in her shoulder.

I am in the bedroom I recognise from my childhood and sitting on the sheetless mattress on the floor. I have my old and tatty school uniform on. The oversized shirt is a hand-me-down and the trousers have specks gathered from years of wear. The three old hemlines at the bottom of the trouser legs show how much I've grown since I've had them. These are my only pair. I guess I am about twelve years old.

The woman, I now realise is my adoptive mother, puts her head around the door. 'Get yer arse moving before I give it a reason to,' she barks at me and then disappears.

Reluctantly, I stand up, step over scattered and unwashed clothes on the threadbare carpet and head out onto the landing. Parts of the landing wall don't have any wallpaper from where it has been pulled off at some point, just like in my messy bedroom. Clothes are stuffed into large bags stacked on top of each other. Old televisions, videos and other shabby boxes filled with junk are piled up in every available corner.

I stroll into the kitchen and this woman, who I thought was my mother, sits there holding a cracked and dirty coffee cup and a cigarette in the same hand. 'Well, what yer doin' standing there?' she bellows at me. 'Get yerself gone, yer useless piece of shit! Or I'll give you something you'll not forget,' growls an unshaven man in a dirty vest. He is slouched in another chair at the breakfast table. He stands up and slides his belt off his trousers. This man has beaten and shouted at me for most of my childhood. This is the man I thought was my father.

I dash for the back door fearing for my life. Then I feel a grip around my shirt collar that pulls me out and up into the dark air. Below, I see my stepfather growling at me with the belt wrapped around his furious fist and the belt tip snaps in the air. It is refreshing to breathe deeply into my lungs as I feel separated from the invisible restraint I have lived with for most of my life. I feel dizzy from this amazing realisation I have just gone through. I shoot higher and higher and the scene below gets smaller and smaller.

I see a wisp of shiny dust streams flying around that are coming closer and closer. The wisp breaks into two powerful energy wisps that whizz around me. Then shiny wisp stays in the background as the other flies towards me. As I shoot higher into the dark and starry sky, we approach each other.

A stream of light speaks to me, not in words, but as an energy form.

I recognise it! It's that young man. It's dad. My real one!

The other wisp of energy closes around me, enters and fills me with absolute love that dissolves the guilt and shame about those I thought I have let down. Words fail me how to describe its intensity and its effect on me. I realise this wisp is mum, the young woman who gave me so much love in the car just before the crash. For most of my life, what I thought was, wasn't. And that new perspective lifts a dark cloud away from me. It no longer has any function based on a past that I incorrectly thought had happened.

Just like with dad, mum's energy speaks through vibrations. These vibrations release and empower me to break the incorrect patterns of torture I had endured for all those years and I casually enjoy the sensation of them dissolving away. I try to hug mum's energy field. But I can't. It keeps whizzing around and flying through me such that each time it imparts even more unconditional love within me as my barriers continue to weaken.

Briefly, I see the car that had lost control that had ploughed into our blue car before it flipped us into the air. It was the reason for the accident.

"Dad!" I call out in a frequency. "That accident wasn't your fault. You didn't kill mum!"

Dad's spirit joins mum's spirit. Gradually, they spin so fast that they become one, forming a spinning spiral that shoots into me and... Oh, I feel their powerful love surge through me, freeing me of even more of those restrictive feelings I have been carrying in me for most of my life. They leave me feeling euphoric. The intensity of those feelings explodes into a mass of fine particles that scatter out into the Universe. I watch them disappear and see other energies forming into a spinning ball far from me. They spin faster and faster and then explode into fine particles that shoot to the edges of the universe.

As I float in this vast Universe, I feel as if I am a part of it and that it is a part of me. After all this time, I now realise I have never been alone. Not once. This is such a reassuring sensation that pulsates through the whole of my body that I am shaking from its intensity. Unbelievable, I have always been a part of this never-ending and powerful force of Universal energy. I am it, and it is me, you, and those around us. We are all connected to it.

I lay in this elated state for what seems a long time and languish in it. There is nothing to fear and I am aware of what is waiting for me in the afterlife. There is nothing to fear. No heaven, no hell. Nothing we are made to believe exists here. I begin to understand that what I have just gone through is that heaven and hell are the two choices we have for our stay in this physical life, not in the afterlife. There's just the Universe which is where our spirit returns after we die and return as energy. How many times have I been physically re-born as some living creature, plant, animal, or person on our minute planet or somewhere else within our ever-expanding and vast Universe? I don't know. What I do know, though, is that this isn't my first time. How? Once I acclimatise myself here in the Universe, it feels familiar, like an old stomping ground. Home. My real home. We have spiritual experiences that are happening in our physical bodies.

Wow! Where is all this coming from?

I lay there for a long while and enjoy this new sensation flowing through me as I gradually return to my physical body. I can never go back to how I used to be. All those years, I have been living a lie and have wasted time that I will never get back.

I sense there is some movement around me and open my eyes. I see a couple of participants sitting on the edge of their beds. One participant rubs her face. Hercules turns around and nods to ask if I'm okay. I smile and nod in the affirmative. I nod to him with a facial sign that asks him if he is too. He gives me a double thumbs-up with a massive grin.

I look around and all of us are awake. Zoe's eyes are closed and she seems content lying on her bed. Zoe's husband whispers something in her ear.

The Instructor walks around and looks at each of us. Then says quietly, "You're all back. The remaining time is for you. Either talk to each other somewhere private or if you prefer to find a quiet spot and reflect on what you have just gone through, that's fine, too."

Zoe's husband calls The Instructor over. The three talk quietly.

"I'm ready to go home," I hear Zoe say to The Instructor.

"Please give it an hour," The Instructor replies. "Just to ensure you have most of the psilocyn out of your system."

It starts to rain. Not hard, but enough to create a soothing sound on the barn roof. I stare at the hypnotic drops running down the glass pane. It is as though the inner pain I had carried for all these years is now being washed away. It allows me to feel newfound freedom and an inner lightness which I have brought back from the Universe.

Did I really just meet my biological parents?

That shower turns into a downpour and the noise is drowning out any conversation in a couple of groups that have formed. The Instructor asks them to talk somewhere else. Zoe's husband tries to pull a cardigan around Zoe, who is still lying on the only remaining camp bed.

"I need to go home," Zoe says weakly as she grabs her husband's hand. "Now!"

He nods and calls The Instructor over.

"Isn't it better to wait until it stops raining?" The Instructor asks a little louder due to the noise of the torrential rain bouncing off the barn roof.

"I have to leave," Zoe says. "My time is coming."

"I'll help you," I say to them, understanding her wish. "Where's your car parked"?

The husband fishes the keys out of his pocket and hands them to me. I snatch an umbrella hanging from a hook near the door and dash outside. I press the fob button several times to find the right car. I jump in and drive as near the doorway as possible. The only problem is it's still several meters away. The path is too narrow to reach the barn doors due to several large decorative stones blocking the chance to get nearer. I line up the side of the car so she can enter the rear passenger door with the least fuss. Not able to do anymore, I dash back into the barn.

Her husband stands near the doorway, squeezing the wheelchair grips, ready to push Zoe to the car. She doesn't have a rain jacket. She's going to get soaked before she even gets to the car.

"I'll carry you. It will be quicker," Hercules says to her. He turns to me. "Grab that other umbrella and cover her until I get her in the back seat." I nod and grab the second umbrella. He turns to her husband, "And then we can pack everything in the boot. Agreed?"

"You sure?"

"I'll take that as a yes," Hercules says. He turns to me, "Ready?"

I nod with the second umbrella in my other hand, ready to throw it open. The first one is above me as the rain hails down on it.

Hercules scoops the woman out of the wheelchair. Another participant runs forward with an oversized raincoat and drapes it over them.

"That should help somewhat," Herc says. "Thank you."

I throw the second umbrella open and Herc is quickly on my heels. He walks fast and I double mine as I need to keep one step ahead. Holding two brolly handles precariously in one hand, I grab the rear passenger door and yank it open. Carefully and as quickly as I can with my free hand, I hold the raincoat above them to stop the downpour from entering the car as Hercules carefully sets her onto the rear passenger seat. He fastens the seatbelt around her.

"Okay?" Herc asks her.

Zoe nods. She closes her eyes as she lets her body sink into the seat.

Hercules closes the rear car door and dashes back to the barn. I'm on his heels with the umbrellas and the raincoat flapping in the wind.

"She's fine," Hercules says to her husband as he grabs the folded wheelchair. "Ready?"

The husband nods and picks up her hold-all. I give him his car keys back.

They dash out to the rear of the car in the increasing wind. Hercules is wearing a simple t-shirt and is soaked to the skin before the boot lid opens. Herc talks to the woman as he puts the wheelchair in the boot. He then says something to the husband, who promptly gets into the back of the car next to his wife.

Hercules dashes inside and says, "You drove here, didn't you?" I nod. "Follow me. I need to drive them home."

"Let me get the keys from my room," I reply and dash upstairs. Hercules is right behind me.

As I leave my room with the keys and a coat, Hercules dashes out of his room wearing new clothes. He slips an arm into his leather jacket.

As we run down the path in the pouring rain, he says, "Just follow me." He clambers into their car and I run over to mine.

Hercules drives past me and I follow behind. I look at the dashboard clock. It's quarter to eight in the evening.

The following day, we enter the barn as the sun rises and just as the rest of the group is just finishing their breakfast. Marie pours a coffee for us. That first sip touches my soul.

"We made it to their home through the storm," Hercules says. "How long she has left, I don't know. Zoe said she is so grateful for this opportunity to go through what she has and it wouldn't have been possible without your support. All of you. She says she has been able to deal with her past issues and is now ready..." he trails off.

"I need to freshen up," I say, breaking the atmosphere.

"A good idea," The Instructor replies. "Do you guys want to sleep a while or will you join us for the last part?"

"I'd like to join you," Hercules says. He turns to me. "You?"

"Yeah, I think this is important to close this last part of my past life."

We agree on a delay before starting. We disappear to our respective rooms to get a shower.

And sure enough, half an hour later, both Hercules and I bound down the stairs simultaneously. I'm exhausted, but the cold shower Hercules recommended worked wonderfully. I feel alert and has helped to overcome some of the tiredness.

With a respectful gap remaining where Zoe once sat, we gather around for the final day. The Instructor asks each one of us to explain what happened in each of their sessions.

Jim, a man in his late thirties, has been quiet and reserved most of the time. He puts his hand up to signal he would like to begin. He whispers, "As you know, my girlfriend and I argued one day we went hiking…. After I had said inappropriate things to her, she stormed off, telling me she never wanted to see me again… and that's when it happened…. She slipped and fell to her…. The whole time I've blamed myself for what happened. Yet, in this session… she forgave me…. Not in words…. You know, I don't know how to put it…. She took that pain and guilt and pulled it right out of me. It was like it disappeared. Evaporated… then I see a future before me. The future similar…

we were considering before she fell…. She allowed me, told me or permitted me to live my life…. She told me to meet someone new and to better understand that everyone is different. I mean, it's too soon… to meet someone…. Yet I feel the release she has given me…. I need to work through this new revelation, but…."

"As you work through your new learnings, you may have some more revelations today," The Instructor says to Jim, "and please don't be surprised if this carries on over the next few months. Please remember that some future realisations may be hard on you, so please be prepared to work through them. What you have experienced today is good because you realise and understand what it means to let it go enough to start living the life you were destined for. Okay, anyone else?"

"May I?" Hercules asks, standing up.

Usually, Marie shook like a leaf each time she heard Hercules' booming voice. However, today, she looks as contended as a welcoming breeze on a hot summer's day.

"I just want to say, Jim, I can relate to your experience," Hercules says to the man who had just spoken. "In this session, I met my troop and like with you and your partner, they took my guilt away. I'm glad you said they didn't speak through words but through some form of emotional telepathy. It… was like this form of communication had more meaning than words could ever say. If you know what I mean."

All heads nod in agreement. Mine too. Herc looked relieved to see our responses.

"With that emotional telepathy, they said something else. They 'told' me that as the sole survivor, I'm their representative to experience as much of life as possible. I'm their proxy to do things on this planet that none of them can do anymore. I didn't expect this. But there's something else I'd like to say."

His mobile rang. "Excuse me," he says, looking at the screen. "I know the rules, but I promised to take this call."

Hercules turns away and answers it. "Hello…? Yes…. Oh…. My condolences…. I will. Thanks for letting me know…. I'll call you later when I'm finished here…. Yeah. Bye." He switched his phone off. He turned to the group and let out a big sigh. He sits back down and rubs his free hand over his face. He says, "I'm sorry that Zoe passed away about an hour ago."

The room falls silent.

"We spoke in the car as we drove them home," Herc says after a short pause. "She told us what she had experienced over these few days. I'll not go into the details because that's a part of her private journey. What I will say is that she found what she was searching for…. She said they were waiting for her to join them on the other side. It released that fear of dying and she went with peace of mind."

She was asleep in the car when we arrived at their home last evening. Hercules carried her in and laid her on the bed. Her husband put a blanket over her and made her comfy. We sat with her for a short while to allow her husband to organise a couple of things so she wasn't alone. Once she awoke, Zoe looked around and said, 'I'm home…. I can go now.' She turned to us and moved her fingers for us to move closer. Hercules was nearer, so she took his hand in hers. 'Thank you,' she said. 'Both of you for helping me live my last wish.' Her weak grip loosened after she closed her eyes. It was at that point we took our cue to leave. It was only right she and her husband had their last precious moments together.

We never spoke once on our way back here. There was nothing to say. The silence said everything.

"Her husband," Hercules says as he sits down, "said he is grateful to you all for making his wife's last days something special." He rubbed a tear away with the palm of his hand.

The woman, Marie, who normally trembles with fear when Hercules spoke, steadily stands up and approaches him with a sigh of inner determination.

Hercules stares directly at her, wondering what she is going to do. This fantastic woman reaches out, cradles her hands around his head and pulls him to her bosom. Out of nowhere, Hercules starts crying. His arms fall to his side, which allows him to sink deeper into her chest.

"There, there," Marie says as she strokes his hair. "Let it out." She's looking upwards to the barn roof. I guess this is a part of her release too.

Slowly, Hercules quietens down and pulls away slightly to look up at her. "May I stand up and hug you back," he asks her. Marie nods and slowly steps back. He stands up, watching his movements and her reactions to not scare her. He carefully rests his hands on her upper arms. She clasps her arms around him, pulls herself into him and starts to cry. She buries her head into his stomach. Just like she did for him, he does for her. Hercules pulls Marie closer with one hand and strokes her hair with the other.

I look around and see another couple hugging each other. Everybody is crying to varying degrees. We all understand the release we are experiencing from what we have gone through.

Hercules and Marie pull apart. "You okay?" he asks her.

"Couldn't be better," Marie replies. "Thank you for being my first test."

Hercules looks puzzled. Then it dawns on him. "A pleasure!" he says and gives her a big kiss on her forehead. "Can I just say? I'm not normally like this," he replies with a cheeky grin. Hercules stands next to Marie with his arm resting on her shoulder. Her hand holds onto his waist. "As an ex-soldier, I'm trained to keep my emotions under control. However, with such a beautiful woman, how can I not? I needed that."

A light chuckle of release flows around the room and I smile. That's a nice way to break the ice.

Suddenly, everyone is getting up and hugging each other. Even I join in. He's right. He's not the only one who needs it. We all do.

The last session has come and gone. Everyone else has left and it's just Hercules and me standing between our parked cars.

"What are you going to do now?" Hercules asks. The early evening sun starts its first noticeable dip of the evening.

"I'm not sure," I reply. "I've noted down what I went through over these last few days. Maybe the answer will come to me later after I've had a chance to reflect on this more."

"Have you thought about writing a book about what you have gone through?" he suggests. I haven't and I shake my head.

"Can I ask you something?" I ask. He remains quiet and I take that as my sign to go on. "Did you believe in God before you came here?"

"Hmm, let me think how I answer that," Hercules replies in thought. "I don't think I did. Would a God allow us to blame him for all the pain and trouble we are responsible for? I think not. I've never been religious. After what we have just gone through, I know I will never turn to it. One thing has changed in me, though," he says, "There is more to us than we realise. Maybe this life is a phase we all need to go through…. Oh… err…. I'm struggling to find my words."

"Like a spiritual body having a physical experience for something greater," I interject.

"Just like that!" he replies. "And you know what? I didn't meet God. Yet it is as though there is a presence between everything. Within and around us and…. How do I put this in words? This presence is between everything and… and…."

"And binds us together," I say. "You, me, all other people, our friends and enemies, all creatures and plants are linked through this planet, our solar system and right to the boundaries of the Universe."

"Yeah," Hercules says. "It's this single bond that makes us whole. Boy, we have a lot to be responsible for."

Zoe's Funeral, My Revelation and the Start of a New Future

Herc and I meet up again at Zoe's funeral. I am enjoying my life when and where I can. It's not perfect, but I am so grateful for such a start to my new life because it is better than it was before. It is like being presented with something foreign I know is good, but I don't yet understand how to use it properly. I have made some new friends, I still meet up with Dave and his girlfriend, Andrea, regularly. Not only that, I have been offered a job in a warehouse which I am enjoying and earning my pay. It has given me a sense of value I didn't realise was missing within me. I'm still fathoming over what old patterns I need to change, how to use this new way of thinking and what I want to do long-term with my life. So, this Minor Mystery has given me a fantastic push in the right direction such that I am progressing with my life journey.

As for the book, I have noted what I went through and what has changed within me. I have spoken to some of the participants. Some are free of their bind and are getting on with their life at a good tempo. Some, like me, are making progress, but they feel a little lost with the rapid inner change they have been through. I am thankful to know I am not the only one that suddenly feels as though they have been presented with an opportunity with so much freedom but lack the inner resource on what to do next. I'm not complaining. Please don't get me wrong. It's bewildering and sometimes seems too much of no longer having that massive depressive crutch I have used for many years. I suppose I am a beginner at life without the boundaries I once knew. As a beginner, just like a baby, I guess one needs to gather experience to find out what is right for me. If there is a calling for me, I can't hear, see or feel it. Yet. The Instructor did warn us of this and that if we don't find our direction straight away, not to worry, we are not ready for it yet and that there is something else that needs to be worked through first. The instructor also said not to waste our life until we have found what we are looking for but to use it as a chance to try new things, live that new life, get to know new people, find out who we are and adjust accordingly. Just like a baby has to learn to crawl and then walk before it can run, so do I.

As Zoe's family and friends mourn her death, I celebrate inwardly her transition to the next phase without those woes she had thrust upon her in this one. Somehow it is reassuring to know that, as in the physical world, when something comes to an end, spiritually, it is the beginning of something new. What that is, I don't know. I will find out in my own time, just like everyone else has done before us.

"Remember you thought you were adopted? Are you?" Hercules asks me at the wake. It turns out I am. I've checked it out and have had the chance to visit both mum and dad's graves. They are next to each other.

After my parents died in that car accident, which wasn't their fault, the other driver had caused the accident. He was driving too fast. With the amount of alcohol the driver had in his blood, it is not surprising that he lost control and crashed into our car. The driver clambered out of his wreckage with just a few scratches. Alas, you already know my mother died from her injuries and my father couldn't cope with the guilt that wasn't his. He thought it was his fault and took his own life.

The driver who had caused the accident was given a couple of points on his licence. He received no prison sentence and no fine. The judge said it was bad luck that the accident happened on a bad stretch of road and that the driver wasn't at fault. That sentence was a bit of a joke if you ask me. Then again, it seems like a local politician was apparently driving drunk who had the opportunity to use his official post, power and connections to influence his needs that the rest of us mortals are normally denied. Apparently, through political power, the police were 'reluctant' to investigate, thus allowing such a special person to get off lightly and carry on as if nothing had ever happened. In contrast, our lives were irreparably changed. Apparently, the other accidents this politician had caused over the following years weren't his fault either. That's democracy for you.

Anyway, I was adopted by my father's sister and her husband. I moved in with them immediately after my father had taken his life. From all accounts, the start was relatively good. The family took care of me reasonably well until my adoptive father, my uncle, lost his job. His wife, my adopted mother, or rather, my aunt, my father's sister, only had a part-time job to bring money in. After that, they struggled to survive financially. Gradually, I became the reason for their misfortune which led them to take their frustration out on me. I was the only child in that house, as they couldn't have or didn't want kids of their own. As less money came in, life grew harder, leading to more arguments. Even when my uncle did find the occasional job, he was promptly sacked due to his unreliability. His solution was to disappear to the pub to escape his wife's ear-bashing at home.

Consequently, at home, my stepfather needed to vent his frustrations and released them against me, both verbally and physically. His wife, my aunt, felt bound to have to stay with me at home and started blaming and accusing me of being a harbinger of bad luck to the family. The arguments against each other and me grew louder and more aggressive as time passed. The saddest part of it all is they never once told me of my real parents, the accident and that they had adopted me.

Only my adoptive mother, my aunt, is alive. I haven't seen or heard from her for years until a couple of weeks ago. She was drunk when I visited her at my old, dilapidated, run-down 'home'.

She opened the door and stood staring at me as if I were an apparition. I asked her when she was going to tell me I was adopted. She shuffled inside with a cigarette hanging from her mouth, leaving the entrance door open. Without saying another word, I followed her along the unkempt hallway and into the untidied living room stank of stale smoke and beer. I stood in the living room without taking my eyes off her. She yanked open a stiff cupboard door and rummaged through some paperwork. Finding what she was looking for, she tugged at a large envelope and used her other hand to stop the rest of the stuff piled on top from falling to the floor. It didn't work- They scattered everywhere. With a curse, she thrust an envelope towards me and spat out, 'Now you know you don't belong to anyone. Can you finally leave me in peace?' Snatching the envelope from her grasp, I held onto it with my dear life. I left that house with an intuitive feeling that our paths would never cross again.

There were various things in the envelope, including my birth certificate and adoption papers. There were some news snippets about my mother dying in a car accident, an article about my father's suicide and an article about the politician getting off Scot-free for the accident. This confirms the visions I saw in my psychedelic session.

"Tell me," Hercules says. "There is the second stage called Redemption. Are you going?"

"Already booked," I reply. "You?"

"Me too," he replies. We compare dates and see if we are there on the same dates. We are. I can't wait….

"The third part too?" Hercules asks.

"Oh, I can't afford it," I reply. It's true. I would love to attend, but I don't have the funds. As I said earlier, I have found some work, but it doesn't pay much. Another thing I found in the envelope was that my parents had started a small trust fund for me before the accident happened. I have used most of that to pay for the two courses. Initially, Dave had organised it with The Instructor for me to participate for a small sum until I could pay the rest later. That has been paid up and was worth every penny.

"Ah, and what about your book? How's it going?" Herc asks, changing the subject rather nicely.

I'm struggling. I've written up my notes about the first session we had, but I'm unsure if it's enough. I'll wait until the outcome of the second session to see whether it's worth it.

We discussed The Instructor's fascination with the Greek Minor and Major Mysteries. Still, The Instructor failed to tell us much about it. Not only that, neither of us knew anything about Greek history in the first place. Hercules recommended that maybe some basic information on the Greeks and Eleusis be worth including in the book.

As we leave, Hercules grabs me lightly by the arm and turns me to face him.

"Ralf, can I ask you something?" he asks me quietly. His tone is serious.

I nod.

"Please don't be offended. But I greatly admire and respect how you've turned your life around. It would be a pleasure if I could pay for the third course for you."

I step back and am wide-eyed in amazement.

"What I mean is, it's an unconditional offer. If you want to pay me back sometime later, do so. You don't have to. However, if you insist, I will gladly accept it."

On the way home, his offer ticks through my mind. I said I would let him know what I would do in a couple of days. Attending the third part would bring everything together in living my new life by giving structure to different areas of my life. But to be in debt isn't something I want either, especially as my life is starting to come together.

Once at home, I research the Greek Mysteries and how they would have carried out their secretive sessions before deciding whether to include this information in my book. This is a bit of what I found out.

A Bit About the Eleusinian Mysteries

The Eleusinian mysteries are known through records to have started in Greece around 4000BCE, although when exactly, we are still not sure. Around 392BCE, it reached its pinnacle of popularity. The Eleusinian Mysteries continued until the 8th Century CE, when the Church decided to ban all pagan rituals as the Christians thought the mysteries would undermine their festivals. The Pope was anxious about the ridicule of the mysteries' powerful effects when compared to the church's more sedate services and the many powerful rituals, symbols, clothing and phrases taken from other pagan groups, including the Greeks.

It is still one of the most impressive and longest-lasting religious festivals known today, with the Kemet's festivals coming a close second. Interestingly, when comparing the differences between Christianity's single god and the multi-god religions, monism encourages us to focus on our weaknesses and feel shit about ourselves. In contrast, the multi-god religions tended to focus on releasing those restrictive problems and feeling good with separate aspects of our life so we could get on with our lives with minimum fuss and dance.

Interestingly, at that time, it turned out that the followers of differing poly-god religions were more understanding and tolerant of all other faiths, which allowed some crossover of gods from one system to another. However, the poly-god followers were sceptical of those mono-god worshippers because they tended to be more extremist and closed, or orthodox, to the views of others. The mono-god followers came across as if it was all black and white or all-or-nothing and ostracised anyone who didn't fit in with their one-sided beliefs.

At the top of the list of Greek gods was Zeus, who was responsible for the sky. He had two brothers, Poseidon, who was responsible for the seas, and the other one we are interested in, Hades, the god of the Underworld. Although several other gods were involved in the Eleusinian Mysteries, I want to mention the other two more important ones. They were Demeter, and her daughter, Persephone.

The problem for the girls started when Hades needed a wife for the Underworld. He wooed Persephone to join and marry him. The problem was that Demeter didn't know where Persephone was. This devastated her. Demeter relentlessly searched everywhere for her to no avail. Her dedicated search for her daughter led the locals of Eleusis to build a temple in her name.

The problem for the Greeks was that Demeter was the goddess of wheat and fertility. She stopped the growth of crops and the continuation of nature because she was upset about being unable to find her daughter. Because the land had grown barren with no grown food available, it was making the mortal people hungry. Another problem, according to lore, was that animals were perishing because of the famine and that no sacrifices could be carried out to the gods. The gods felt displaced and wanted their sacrifices again and to do that, the mortals needed rich, fertile land to grow food.

Finally, Zeus told Hades he must let Persephone return to the surface so the crops would grow again and that the mortals could eat and make their sacrifices again. Hades agreed. However, he gave Persephone pomegranate seeds to eat on her way home. These seeds forced a bond with Persephone to the Underworld as Hades' wife. Demeter had no choice but to accept this. This meant that when Demeter and Persephone were together, crops grew, nature flourished, people were fed, and sacrifices took place, keeping the gods happy.

Most of the population at that time were farmers or were in the manual trade, so the intellectual discussions we can have today weren't the norm. However, for those months in the year when Persephone was in the Underworld with Hades, crops and plants died and nature became barren because of Demeter's sadness. This was how the Greeks described how the seasons worked since they didn't have enough scientific knowledge as we have today. This was an excellent way to bring nature's limited understanding to their folk.

The Eleusinian Mysteries, as we know, had two aims for the initiates or participants. The first was to help them understand what happens to us after death and that there is nothing to fear in the spiritual life. The second known benefit was to help release any mental burdens that are hindering them in the physical one. This ensured they made the most of their working, family and social areas of life. I guess giving them spiritual guidance in understanding their problems, fears and mental issues that we would categorise as a form of psychological treatment today.

All participants, male or female, old or young, rich or poor, could participate as long as they could speak Greek and pay a month's wage plus the accommodation cost. Another factor for attendance was that the person hadn't been punished for treason or conspiracy. Even if a participant had debts of some sort, they were protected from being hassled during this religious festival.

Two Mysteries took place each year, the Lesser first and then the Greater. The Lesser Mystery was held in spring and predominantly dealt with death, the afterlife, and the return of Persephone from the Underworld. The Greater Mystery was held in the Autumn, dealing with Redemption and Persephone's return to the Underworld. One must have participated in the Lesser Mystery to attend the Greater Mystery. No, if's and but's.

What was impressive about the Eleusinian Mysteries was that they never used any technology like some therapists use today. They had singers and various people playing specific roles in their ceremonies. However, verbal deliverance was the primary tool used over the days of these closed festivals.

A psychedelic was used near the end of the festivities to work through deeper issues the Ego created based on external experiences. This was either an LSD drink made from a wheat fungus or a drink made from psychedelic mushrooms. Which type, we don't really know. However, investigations guess a kind of Amanita Muscaria based on previous Christian scripts they bought from pagans. As a side note, Amanita was almost constantly in short supply and when it was purchased in batches of threes, they were usually made into a drink. Today, Christian priests still wear such symbolical clothing, including a hat similar to a mushroom to signify its deity to the great mushroom. Looking at some older churches and cathedrals in Europe, it is still possible to see Amanita and other psychedelic mushrooms painted onto walls by being represented through the Rose Window or the three connected circles merged into the walls representing the batches of three Amanitas sold to the church. The mycelium is found in some longer new gothic windows. The mushroom gill patterns can be found on various ceilings in the main halls, underground crypts and other rooms. Because back in the day, as Christianity was being created, the Amanita mushroom was usually in short supply. The priests usually participated using a kidney-filtered mushroom drink given to them by the pagans. This filtered mushroom drink had the toxins removed by the kidneys that caused the feeling of nausea and stomach ache.

When the participants partook in the psychedelic drink at Eleusis, the previous days of preparation, along with fasting, helped them release limiting beliefs and key mental turmoil in accepting what had happened. It enabled them to accept that life isn't perfect and that the way we live our life now is the precursor to our next one until we have gathered an understanding of our life journey, for example.

As far as we know, the phases or stages that followed at Eleusis House for the Lesser and Major Mysteries are somewhat different to the original festivities. I'm skipping ahead here because you will read some of what happens to the other participants and me in the following chapters.

Persephone, Demeter and Hades don't mean much to us today. If we had followed their stories of what the original initiates went through, it wouldn't have had the same impact on us. Our guru or The Instructor or shaman or whatever you want to call this person, it doesn't matter, has restyled it for today's culture concerning our most sensible understanding of spirituality. Not only that, but we also know a bit more about psychology than we did back then, however, but the Greeks also managed to get pretty much most of it right. Due to the availability of various mental tools, techniques influencing our thoughts and ideas through conversation and exercises are more potent than ever.

As I have said before, it doesn't matter how we reach our goal, it is the experience and the journey itself that is where we find our growth and in releasing our past is the most important. If we can reach it without hurting anyone or anything unnecessarily, then we have the chance to give something back to future generations.

The modern version is slightly quicker than the original. Yet, we still need several days to get through the material to prepare ourselves for that life-changing psychedelic learning and release of what we have buried and forgotten. Yet, the one thing I have learnt from my experience with The Instructor is that for some of the other participants who had suffered from an intense and longer duration or more complex forms of abuse is that we will probably have several months or years of unlearning and relearning ahead of us that could cause us to think hard about who we are and why we are here. Another aspect I like is that we were in smaller groups for our mysteries. There could have been at least a couple of hundred participating in the Greek festival. That would have been too much for me.

Right, back to the spiritual game… er… the real-world game… or rather, the world and civilisation we live in that we think are real…. Hmm, I'm not sure how to say that, so let's move on….

Hellenistic Philosophy

Although you will read about some philosophies a little later, I felt it important to mention the Greek Hellenistic philosophy and the philosophers before that time. I want to focus primarily on one aspect, that of the Stoics, how stoicism came to light and how the Romans took this philosophy further.

Stoicism was one of many philosophies that were being sold by philosophers back in the day. Each new philosophy was a conglomeration of several other philosophies at the time. Those successful in teaching philosophy have survived into the history books today. We could say that when Zeno developed Stoicism, it was a mix of scepticism, Socrates' philosophy, Criticism, Plutonism and Pythagoreanism, to name a few.

Sadly, there is no original work existing from Zeno and his immediate followers, but we do have more information from four key Romans who followed the Stoic philosophy. These were Epictetus, Seneca, Markus Aurelius and Musonius Rufus.

Nowadays, when we hear that someone is stoic, we consider them to be emotionless. That isn't true. A Stoic has reflected on what is and isn't important in their lives. So, for example, if we can separate our emotions from things we have, such that if that treasure was damaged or lost, we could deal with it with indifference. This doesn't mean to say Stoics and cold and calculating, but a Stoic technique of thinking through the worst that could happen can help us to deal with it better, should it happen. That doesn't mean we should dwell on it, but to think it through to potential outcomes, to then put it aside and wait until it happens, should it ever occur. After that, we can go back to dealing with the moment we are currently experiencing for what it is.

A good example is that if we think we were in a life-threatening situation, which person would be better to have next to us; a person who remains calm and collected, who can work with the situation or a person that cannot control their emotions and could become an irrational risk to the situation? I know which person I want next to me, the one who has their emotions under control to be next to me. That person, we could say, thinks like a Stoic.

The lovely thing about being a practising Stoic is that it is simple. It gives us a clear guideline to work to and to aim for what gives us control and responsibility in our lives. If that's what someone wants in their life, this is a great way forward.

Naturally, since completing these sessions, I have discovered some other life philosophies which are interesting and help to broaden one's thoughts. However, I have to say that I find Stoicism a great structure for me, what I have control and don't have control of, love what I have in my life and how to remain indifferent to what I don't have and what I have lost within my life. The other aspect I love about Stoicism is that is a philosophy for the mind. In many ways, it helps us to work through problems in which psychedelics and psychology are limited in their actions and uses.

As for Stoicism and the Eleusinian Mysteries that after the sessions, I searched for further information on these subjects, which I discovered and read at a later date, I have provided a list at the back of the book. It isn't comprehensive but it should give one a good start if this is of interest.

Part II: The Major Mystery - Redemption

I enter Eleusis House for the second time and see Hercules quietly talking to Marie. She's back too! I dash over and greet them both.

The Instructor stands smartly dressed in front of us and looks around the group with a confident smile. The Instructor claps their hands together to draw our attention.

"Firstly, a warm welcome to you all. It's great to see each of you again."

Like before, we sit on the chairs formed in a circle in the converted barn.

"In this five-day session, we are going to focus on what the Greeks called 'Redemption'," The Instructor says and continues after a slight pause. "When I first discovered the Greek Mysteries, it took me a while to understand what redemption meant. In today's interpretation, we tend to focus on the religious context of redemption in being saved from evil or when used in the financial world, the act of exchanging shares for some money.

"So, what is redemption? I think the easiest way to explain this is to say it means letting go. Just letting go without judgement, without opinion, without any value, just like when we don't think about anything that doesn't disturb us in any way, shape or form. Doing this doesn't mean it puts us above or below someone or something else and neither does it make it irrelevant. It just is. We all make mistakes, great and small, and we all regret something in life. Why should we judge someone else's mistakes when we can't be perfect ourselves? All we are doing is lowering ourselves to their standard when we think we are putting ourselves above them."

"Does that mean we have to accept people in our lives who have hurt us?" someone asks.

"Not necessarily. Just because you have not judged someone for their behaviour, it doesn't mean you give them free rein to do this to you again. They are operating on a different frequency to you and if it doesn't match yours, you don't have to have them in your contact's life circle. Some people can and will harm you given a chance. But that doesn't mean we should judge them because they had no control over how they were brought up as children, which has affected them for the rest of their adult life. In other words, maybe it's best to ask whether this person reinforces your inner feelings and whether you can share a part of your life with them with trust and respect. Then that may help make answering the question easier.

"Okay, now let's cover the original meaning of the word, sin, and compare it with its other 'modern' meaning, so we know what we will be talking about here. However, I would like to say, should your modern interpretation of the word, sin, be based on your religion and is essential to you, that's fine, but outside of this room. Inside this room, I need you to accept and think a little more neutrally about how the Greeks and others have interpreted it for more than the last several thousand years. Today's interpretation is a Christian adaptation that usually refers to those things we have done or think we have done wrong, either to someone or something else. A risk is that we may be misinterpreting what we feel is wrong based on our current education and beliefs or simply believing some other propaganda without correctly questioning and understanding it. This tends to mislead us into feeling guilty or by throwing us into some other self-destructive emotion.

"Sin's original interpretation simply means 'missing the target'. You aimed for something and didn't get there. That is your sin. Those of you here who read the bible, can I recommend you reread those sections with the original meaning in your mind? You may find the text takes a different meaning."

"And our ultimate goal from these sessions is to release those past burdens and those missing goals so we can get on with life without the past rearing its ugly head all the time. It doesn't matter how you go about releasing your past as long as you find a way. The way I will work with you is with one option of many. However, it is a powerful technique with a great history. Suppose we no longer carry these restrictive burdens based on our inaccurate reflection of our thoughts based on our past actions or instruction. By doing that, we have a chance to live a fuller life with open ears, eyes and an open mind and being, simultaneously full of love. Suddenly, the world looks richer, we start to see different ways to live and enjoy life and we start to see how we can integrate differently for our optimal well-being.

"We live in this very physical body just once. It's the only one we have, so please accept and make the most of what you have. Many moons ago, we consciously stepped away from the animal kingdom and the natural world by putting ourselves above everything else. This, in my opinion, is a great shame that we have separated ourselves from Universal nature by trying to make ourselves more elite than we are. In reality, we are all equal with everything on it, so we should be working in harmony with it too. Our ignorance regarding the damage we are causing around us is showing us that the new world isn't fitting our natural tendencies. We are educated to change ourselves to fit in this system which is becoming increasingly apparent that it is causing us more harm than good.

"We need to find out who we are, to find ourselves and to work with one another to support and grow within our delicate life cycles. Do that, and there is enough love, happiness and nature's generosity for everyone in the present and in return, we can ensure we provide for the next. Ignore that, and we, or rather, the next generations, could eventually lose out. Sounds a bit hard, I know. I believe we have already exceeded the earth's capacity to regenerate the necessary resources to support our future generations. This could be the start of another problem we aren't aware of. We know and shout about the environment, yet we are not doing anything that is significantly sustainable. Okay, that's enough of my political speech. You are here for your release.

"So, are we ready to begin?" The Instructor looks around and sees that we are. "Good. Let's introduce ourselves, most of us don't know each other, but all of you know me. Let's start with a quick introduction round." He looks at me to start.

"Er… Yeah, my name is -," I start to say before The Instructor stops me.

"Please stand up. It will make it a little easier for you to think and speak," The Instructor says.

So, standing up, I continue. "Okay. My name is Ralf, and I'm here without a clear indication of what I want from this session. I mean, it's not as though I haven't thought about it. I have. I've read up on redemption and a few other things related to it. I understand what it means, and I know I have some things I would love to forgive myself forgiven for, but whether I deserve it is another thing…. I will say that when I came to the first mystery sessions, I didn't know what I wanted to work through either, but my subconscious did. I had to trust in it. This time, I'm committed to trusting it. It knows I need to let go of something else to help me to be released from what is still holding me back."

"Is there still something holding you back?" The Instructor asks.

"Since the first time I was here, my life has changed in leaps and bounds, but there are still some areas I just can't make any progress. I don't believe I can…. I don't believe I have the ability and commitment to the next stage."

"Could you give me an example?" The Instructor asks.

"Hmm. I'd love to be forgiven for what I have done wrong, and -."

"Can I just stop you there? That's salvation. We're not dependent on a church because we're free spirits. Consider salvation as a personal aspect that represents a faith you follow. A faith we are talking about here is the Universe that allows you to achieve neutrality where it is integrated within yourself, the environment and the people you see around you. Salvation is too binding and restrictive for independent thinkers like we are here today. We need to think bigger and deeper. Let me put it another way: salvation is a recognised way of deliverance from fictional evil and perceived frustration. Both are internal reflections turned outwards by communicating our limitations to others. This restriction stops us from reaching our full potential and being independent. There's nothing better for institutes than having modern slaves mentally bound to their systems. We're a mixed religious group here today, so I'd rather leave salvation out of this discussion if you don't mind. I'm sure I've already stood on some toes today, so I apologise. Remember, redemption is a function of a person's control over him or herself through radical acceptance. This redeemed life can also be a disciplined life by simply letting go of everything without judgement. It's nothing more than that. The first step in potentially recognising it is usually when we are in the deepest moments of a crisis. What else?"

"Err… I'm writing a book on my life and experiences, but who will read it? Maybe I'm not good enough to be an author and am just wasting my time." I say.

"That's a good point. We need absolute redemption to be freely motivated to complete any task that is of importance to us. It is totally okay that you don't know what you want to focus on. You are attached to a problem that isn't the problem you think it is. Rather, it is the judgement you have made regarding the problem that is causing us some concern. We've all gone through something in our past life that stops us from being appropriately disciplined in achieving whatever it is we want. It may have worked well for you last time you were here and I'm sure it will work for you again once you let it go. Okay," The Instructor says and nods to Hercules.

"Yeah, I have to say I'm struggling with this one myself. Like my good friend here, we've discussed this several times without agreeing on something definite," Hercules says. "In our other session, I was able to release myself from the loss of my crew. I'm still sad when I think of them… and know I'm living their lives through me, which is great. It's an inspiration. But my question is am I doing the right thing with my life, for me? Should I be doing something else? I don't know. I know the military. Other than that, I don't know much more about what I could do."

"Could you give me an example of what you would like to do differently?" The Instructor asks him.

"Since I have left the forces, I've been building my own life around anything that helped me avoid meeting up with ex-service personnel, especially those who are suffering from PTSD. Their war stories and how they aren't coping in the civil world were too much for me. Since completing our first session, I've been toying with setting up some kind of halfway house to help them deal with integrating back into the civil world again. Still, something is stopping me from taking that next step."

"Do you doubt yourself in this potential role?" The Instructor asks.

"No… not really. I'm wondering whether it's the right thing I can do for them. Maybe I should consider something else or I'm going down the wrong path altogether. I have to say this new way of thinking is sometimes challenging to know whether I am doing this correctly."

"How are you different since our last session?" The Instructor asks.

"I lost my troop in an attack and was the only survivor. I felt guilty for letting them down. Since the last session, that guilt has gone and I feel their supportive presence around me…. That's fine. What is bothering me, is me. Life's never easy, and we all make some mistakes. There are some mistakes that I am judging myself against and I am worried about making the same mistakes again."

"Is there a difference between the guilt you experienced before and now?" The Instructor asks.

"Hmm… Previously, it was the effect I had on others. This time… this time it is that I affect myself."

"Wonderful!" The Instructor says. "It's this concept that the Greeks understood fully and you've just hit the nail on the head. The Major Mysteries focuses on the life cycles of the inner torment we do to ourselves. Essentially, we can say the Lesser Mysteries focuses not only on death and what comes after that but it works on the problems that have involved ourselves and how we have treated others. In other words, redemption."

"Yeah," Hercules replies. "I can relate to that."

"Thank you. The next, please," The Instructor says, turning to a middle-aged man. He looks as though he has been ravished by time.

"Hi," he says quietly. "My name's Bill. I'm here with my brother, Ben." He nods to the man sitting next to him, who looks just as old, worn out and tired. "We were both on your course earlier last year."

"Can I just stop you there?" The Instructor asks. "And do you mind if I give some background information?"

Bill glances at his brother and they nod together. He sits down with some relief spreading over his face.

"Last year, I worked with a small group of homeless alcoholics. I do believe thirteen volunteers attended in total," The Instructor says.

Ben nods in agreement.

"Out of the thirteen that attended, eight gave up drinking after the first session. Since then, we've had follow-up sittings with these participants, and to date, they are still alcohol-free. Of the remaining five, one has already come back and redone these sessions successfully and is sober. You two are the next to attend. The remaining two have returned to alcohol and don't want to participate further."

"It works against alcoholism?" Simone, a young conservative-looking woman, asks.

"Better than many people realise. Even the highly respected Bill Wilson initially used psychedelics to eliminate his addiction to alcoholism and -"

"But he created a 12-step programme that connects to God for forgiveness," the young woman interjected.

"That's right. After psychedelics were banned, he created the programme. I was initially without the religious connotations it has today. I don't know why religion was included later, I have to say. Wilson, with the aid of a professional psychologist, tested LSD on himself against alcoholism with amazingly quick success leading to abstinence. The outcome of this type of therapy was more effective in helping restore an alcoholic's sanity and gave higher success rates in giving up alcohol the first time around than any other programme we know."

"You're our last hope," Ben said. "Our local AA hasn't helped us much. I started drinking after my eighth birthday. Would love to know what it would be like to be free from that potent drop for at least a day."

Bill nodded at this statement as he kept his gaze towards the floor.

"Thank you for being so open," The Instructor says. "I think this brings me to an important point that if a person doesn't release their past issues in these first sitting or two, it doesn't mean they are a failure. What it does mean is that they have suffered several types of traumas in the past. It's that collection of traumas we need to work through that starts with the most intense and each worked through one after another to regain control of their life again.

It doesn't matter what the addiction is. It doesn't have to be drugs like cocaine, heroin other illegal substances. It also includes legal medication, foodstuffs like sugars, wheat, processed foods and drinks, tobacco and alcohol. And not only foodstuff. Addictions include repeatedly doing something, sex, gambling, socialising, shopping and so on. The role of addiction is that helps drown out some or all of the past events for the duration of its high. Sadly, for those with an addiction, that moment of pain-free bliss doesn't last long enough, and it can encourage the addict to partake in more of that substance to feed that high and switch off those inner voices and images.

"Please never judge an addict of any kind because they are behaving correctly to their understanding of their inner world and its issues. Please respect and not judge their internal battle because no matter how hard you try, you will never understand the turmoil they are going through. And importantly, help them, talk to them, give them a taste of non-judged humanity and most importantly, if they don't want to join in, give them space. Would you like to add anything to that, Bill, Ben?"

Ben and Bill shake their heads while still gazing at the floor.

Right, who's next?"

"Hallo, My name is Helga," says a prim middle-aged woman. "I'm from Germany and still have a problem with the past of my country. Please, first, I want to thank you," she says to The Instructor, "for taking away those troublesome thoughts I had of what other people think of our history. I no longer judge myself for the past of my family when an idiot makes comments to me. I can walk away from them now. What I cannot do is release myself from the past and I am my worst enemy, as you say…. I want to experience my life without that blocking to allow myself to enjoy life. Without all the guilt and shame I put on myself. I know I can't change the past and I know I can't change what my grandfather did. We are from a different generation and I know my grandparents had different expectations. I still have that connection to them and their past. I am here to release that shame I have of me."

"Thanks. We will do all we can to help you there," The Instructor finally says. His attention stays with her a little longer, giving her a reassuring smile.

After a couple more have spoken, a young man stands up who is bursting with energy.

"May I?" he asks with enthusiasm. "Hi, I'm Tom. "I've done this a few times now. I have dealt with my past several sessions ago and am making progress with my life in leaps and bounds. So, why am I here for another session, you may ask? Simple. It was explained to me when I had completed this the first time around. In our life, we still come across problems and issues that can still knock us for six. Sometimes, we may find our thoughts clouding over due to the hustle and bustle of everyday life. I don't mean that it goes back to as it was. Erm… Let me put it like this; before I started these sessions, my mind was like an untidy house. I mean, really unorganised and full of useless stuff constantly bothering me in some way that was no longer needed. Regardless of which mental room I went in, I couldn't use it.

"Once I completed the two sessions for the first time, it gave me a less cluttered and tidier house. Since then, I've moved on with my new life. The best way I can describe each new session is like redecorating my mind – new paper, paint, carpets, new furniture and giving the room a new function. You get my drift. As with anything in life, some things may get too much and after some time, some untidiness begins to show itself in my daily life. Thankfully, the inner mess I have today is nothing compared to the past. I look at it as if it is a bit like having a messy desk that needs to be sorted out. This is what these follow-up sessions are. I return once a year to deal with new issues that have cropped up, so I can get the most out of my daily life. It's worth every penny. Not only do I learn about what I have gone through, but I learn from your experiences in how you deal with your past events. We all have different ways of understanding and sorting out our problems and your perspectives help broaden mine."

"Thanks, Tom." Who is next?" The Instructor asks.

"Marie is my name. I attended my first session with these two wonderful boys," she says, glancing admiringly at Hercules and me. "Before my first session, I had an absolute fear of people. Men especially. I couldn't abide them being near me, let alone being touched. After my last session, the one person who had put the most fear into me through those last days of that old life of mine was Steve." She means Hercules. I still call him this name. Yes, I even say that to him openly. This is his reminder of how others could see him and helps him to adjust his personality when he meets someone who could be unsure of him. Marie turns to give him an apologetic look. "I mean, look at the size of him. He could crush us all in one swipe with those mighty arms. It was that inner potential that scared me silly. Yet, there's another side to him I couldn't see. I couldn't recognise that he has a big heart of gold and stands up for what he thinks is right. It's those qualities I now see what counts."

I nod to myself.

"Marie, how have you dealt with other men you meet?" The Instructor asks.

"Oh, in some ways, better than I could have ever imagined. I feel more relaxed in the company of men I know and trust. My radar is still on. Yet I know there are men out there who would protect rather than harm me. That was something I couldn't acknowledge before."

"And how do you react when someone is a bit different or a potential threat?" The Instructor asks.

"Ah, if I have some doubt, I remain reserved until I am a little surer. Maybe that person is having a difficult time or something that may have distracted him that I'm unaware of. So, in these cases, I keep my distance. I still know how to do that and am slightly more subtle than I used to be. If I'm alone and feel threatened, I have no problem asking others for help. A few evenings ago, I was walking home as it was getting dark. Someone was walking behind me, which left me feeling unsure. Nobody else was nearby to approach, so I went to a house with a light on and knocked on the door. I explained that I thought a man was following me and asked if I could come in. I was welcomed straight away. After watching that person safely through a window, I saw the man walking further down the street. I may have been wrong about him and felt foolish for misjudging him. But you never know. It isn't perfect, I know. I still avoid certain areas with no street lighting, bad streets, enclosed areas, and so on, but I think most sensible women do that, don't they?"

"Amazing progress, Marie, and yes, I think most sensible women do that. Can I ask what you want from this session?" The Instructor asks.

"I feel bad for how I have treated myself and others…. I feel bad for how I have openly misjudged them. I need to let go of this so I can be more open in my inner thoughts, too," Marie says.

The Instructor goes around the rest of the group until we have all introduced ourselves. After that, he gives us some mental exercises in creating a secure Inner Room. We learn how to use this inner room to work on our problems more effectively.

At the start of day two, we are buzzing and looking forward to what The Instructor has planned. We settle down and The Instructor speaks.

"In our daily life, as we discovered yesterday, we come across all sorts of problems that need solving. We also know we have missing information that stops us from making a decision which we recognise as rising emotions like fear, anxiety, anger or shame. For example, a child thinks of a simple plan or strategy to protect themself from some mental or physical harm. It turns out to be effective, so this child decides to use it again by developing it into a more complex solution for the next problem they come across in their life. This ever-growing and complex solution shows itself in a style of self-protection such that the growing child may even take on another personality to achieve that. The other problem is that their 'solution' could become so over-wielding and complex or they take on differing personalities that could take full control of their lives.

That doesn't mean that you haven't developed other reasonable personality procedures or alter-egos that allow you to socialise and integrate at some level within society. Another way of considering this is if you can create new and straightforward solutions to non-threatening problems, and you have, then you can rid yourself of limiting beliefs that hold you back through fear or some other emotion. All you need to do is understood them for what they are not. Let me rephrase that, what you think is the problem, isn't the problem. It's your judgement of the problem that's your problem.

"I want us to go back to that simple problem of yours we discussed yesterday, and I want you to start looking at it differently. I want you to see how differently you think these years of misinterpretation have affected you and your life. Once you have done that, I want you to mentally relive that experience in a way that is new to you. I see a couple of you looking a little worried. Just trust me for the moment and please remember this is why we have chosen a simple problem to work with rather than your main one. This is so you can learn to change things without the risk of something triggering you. We will carry this out safely such that you should experience a release and maybe a revelation too. The wonderful thing is as soon as you realise you can do this once, you can do this again and again in any situation you are faced with. Suddenly, with this simple technique, the future looks more promising in having more control over your thoughts and neutralising them, doesn't it?

"Ok, put all your drinks on the floor and close your eyes. Let's get into the right frame of mind. I think we are ready to begin with some timeline work."

At the end of the second day, we compare notes on what powerful inner resources we have discovered and how we have implemented them into our perceived past problems. If I had known I had these resources all those years ago, I don't think I would have suffered as much as I had, if at all. The Instructor says that now we know how to do this, we have an excellent basis for defining a more fantastic and independent future. The Instructor also noted that even though we know how to deal with most issues. It doesn't mean it will work for all problems, especially intense ones. But having the option to pick ourselves up with a way of knowing how to consider what to do about it, implement it and carry on makes a big difference. The way I see it is that it is better to have an occasional off day than to have the occasional good day. Something like this should be taught in schools at a young age. Imagine how many long-term issues and reoccurring incidents we have relived in our lives that could have been avoided with such learned skills if we had known how to do this from an early age.

We've just finished breakfast at the start of our third day and we are all buzzing from our experiences yesterday. I slept calmer through the night and even dreamt of unwrapping a couple of other problems with the techniques we learned yesterday. Whether they have been solved, I'm not sure. The exercise we were given yesterday was to recognise a simple problem from a safe distance, find the resources we needed and deal with it from a safe distance. Once we recognised those resources, we replayed the problem from different perspectives until we were content with the outcome and all from a safe distance should something didn't go to plan so it couldn't harm us.

Once we were content with the outcome, we tested it out as if it were to happen sometime in the future. This was done in groups and each member tried to activate that past trigger to allow the participant to practice their new behaviour until it became second nature. It was scary being picked on to begin with. Still, after a few times experiencing the same trigger from other group members, those initial worries melt away by reforming an ever-weaker trigger. Knowing I have this powerful tool available for removing or at least dimming down the overactive emotions, I know I can remain calm enough to protect myself, even if I can't get rid of them. And it is reassuring to know I can always turn to The Instructor for more help if I am unsure what I should have done differently.

It's near the end of the day and The Instructor asks us to take our seats.

"Today, in my opinion, is a special day. Today is the day before we take part in our psychedelic session. I think it's important to discuss what could happen and answer any questions. Okay?"

Simone sits rather pensive and doesn't take her eyes off The Instructor. The Instructor gives one of the most beautiful, disarming smiles I have ever seen. Even though it isn't aimed at me, I trust what The Instructor is about to say.

"Let me say that we will learn to get into direct contact with the Universe, the 'I'. We as a species have been doing this for thousands of years and are all still doing it today, even though you may not be aware of it. We receive everything we think of, wish for and demand by karmic representation. That means you receive it by perceiving what you think you deserve, regardless of how great or devastating your visions are."

"You mean the bad luck I have gone through my whole life is down to my way of thinking of who I am and what I deserve?" Simone asks.

"Exactly that!" The Instructor replies. "Across the board, we use the words Spirit, God, consciousness, Soma, Mental, The All and others to describe what is out there and within us. Suppose we start considering the beginning of the evolution of our relationship with spirituality with gods many thousands of years ago in the Savanna. The most simplistic aim has remained the same, yet the metaphors have increased in numbers until they became a fixed form until the creation of independent man-made religions. Over time, the names and locations of the metaphors may have changed. Even some metaphors are still going through changes as we speak."

"Really?" Hercules asks. "It might not be relevant, but could you give me an example?"

"Sure, just the one. Let's refer to Christianity and those who have read one of the many translated bibles. Most of us have heard of Lucifer. Many link him to the Devil. That's a relatively new concept that is only linked to Christians. The Latin word 'lucifer' means the Bringer of Light or the Bringer of Dawn. That interpretation includes all religions that use the word, including Christianity. The problem for Christians began when the bible was mistranslated from its original language. After a while, the Christian readers of the translated book started to link it with Satan even though this once-used word is linked to Rabbi Jesus or Rabbi Yoshua, depending on what you want to call him. Fortunately, today, we know what this word means. Still, it will take a very long time before Christians and the remaining outdated scholars start to read the word correctly. Suppose we are ever in doubt about what is written in the bible, we do have an option and that is to go back to the original stories from the Egyptians, Kemets, Mesopotamians, Romans, and Greeks and read those instead. If, on the other hand, this is too much, there is always an approved religious dictionary that explains the meanings of people and places within the bible. This is quite helpful.

Simone shifts uncomfortably and stares at The Instructor with a hint of distaste.

"Simone, for the moment, if you will, please put aside your religious beliefs, just like you did for the Minor session. Such limiting beliefs determine how we think and behave without providing any real understanding or discussion of what they are trying to inform us." The Instructor says to her. "Later, you can decide whether keep or readapt them however you want. It may help bring you closer to yourself. Okay?"

Simone nods rather nervously.

"Good. What we are going to talk about today are the Universal laws. At my last count, there are around ninety different Universal Laws out there that I am aware of. It's great to know them all. However, some are a conglomeration of others which makes our lives easier. To do that, I want us to focus on just seven Universal principles. By the end of the day, we will have learnt and practised them enough to recognise the Universe is supporting us every minute of the day to help us to represent what we deserve within our lives. Right, my new-born Hermetics, our first principle is The Principle of Mentalism: The All is the Mind. The Universe is Mental."

Eh? What is this crap? This is my very first thought.

And I thought that discovering my inner resources blew me away. Still, these laws have given me a completely new concept in thinking about how easy it is to take our thoughts and actions toward the extreme rather than remaining impartial. Without The Instructor's help, I would have never even been able to comprehend such a new way of thinking on my own, even though I still have a long way to go to fully understand them.

The Instructor said that understanding the power of intention through the words and images we use to describe our perceived inner worth and value determines how we portray ourselves in front of others. Each word or image created is an active prayer or chant to help us tell the Universe who we think we are. The

Universe listens to our mutterings and accepts them as our goal by literally giving us what we have just asked for. The Instructor says that we must take great care with the use of our spoken words and thoughts throughout the day. We need to consider how we want to represent ourselves in this life, even in jest or irony. Otherwise, we may become something we would rather avoid. The other problem is that the Universe doesn't necessarily deliver immediately, meaning it may take a while before we receive it. In that lapsed time, we may have forgotten what we advertently or inadvertently asked for. This could cause us to have a range of confusing emotions about why something happened, possibly leading to other problematic comments and restrictive thoughts, thus leading to a more confused physical representation we are subconsciously or verbally portraying.

This evening, as each person prepares to discuss their question with The Instructor for the psychedelic session tomorrow, most of our conversation focuses on supporting Simone with her increasing confusion about her religious beliefs. What she went through today has shaken her core faith. Albeit reluctantly, she has accepted that not blindly accepting what has been written and translated in the biblical texts is necessarily right. This, at first, seemed radical for her, yet when The Instructor gave Simone some more information on the bible concordance, this is a religious dictionary put together by all Christian faiths to understand what certain metaphorical words, names and locations mean in the bible, it seems to be helping her to understand that faiths do not take each word literally and that they are aware of mistranslations. If it's promoted by the many flavours of Christianity, then why not use it? But like things in life, when misinformation is ingrained and is followed by the masses, how do you correct that information without upsetting those that have realised a mistake but have had to commit themselves to it? Is it better to save face by sticking to the untruths than to admit a mistake?

Simone said that after these sessions, she would like to learn how to dissect the original bible and other translated biblical texts to better understand the content. Simone also thinks this is her way to her God. What surprised her the most is that she never knew the biblical stories were rewritten versions of much older stories. The Instructor told her not to forget about the various African and indigenous religions, as they are also a source of great metaphors, too.

Simone is not the only one suspicious of this Universal approach. Herc is, too, although he isn't religious. He tells me he understands that our mental attitude can affect how we respond to situations. But speaking to a higher form within us is something he is still struggling to comprehend. He struggles to understand that we can receive what we want based on whom we think we are rather than what we think we deserve because that is admitting a lack in our life. If we admit a lack within ourselves, that lack becomes a part of our life. Just as we have created the world's many systems as it is today through thinking creatively, we also create the life we think we deserve in a system chosen for us by our guardians. Our choice is whether to stay in the chosen system or to become the person who fits within a more suitable system for our experiences.

Tomorrow, the fourth day is the big day. The psychedelic session. Although I have done this before, I am so nervous. It's now my turn to sit with The Instructor for a one-to-one to determine whether I have my question formulated correctly…

Today is the start of the fourth day as we solemnly gather in the kitchen. The simple breakfast cooks gently and the dried mushroom portions are weighed according to each participant's needs. Over these days, the kitchen table has provided endless chatter. This morning, however, a nervous silence fills the room.

I stand in line behind Hercules and feel like I am hiding from what is to come. I know he can do nothing for me. My life is my responsibility and no one else's. For the mushrooms will find a way to work through to release the burden that is still holding me back.

At the table, we sit opposite each other. Herc tips the small pot of ground mushrooms onto his food and mixes them. He scoops up a portion of this potent potion and raises it as a salute.

I do the same with mine. With closed eyes, I put the heaped breakfast spoon with mushrooms in my mouth and let my top lip wipe it clean. That bitter taste I am now familiar with lingers on my tongue, even after a swig of water.

Since we all know what to do, we enter the main room and make our way to the beds we set up last night. I see a group of The Instructor's helpers shuffling around in a corner near the entrance. They are here to ensure we are taken care of through our sessions. I recognise Dave. He acknowledges me and I nod back before I sit on the bed. He introduced me to psychedelics and The Instructor. I am eternally grateful to him for that. The smaller barn door opens and his girlfriend, Andrea, slips in. She sees me, smiles and gives me a thumbs-up for good luck. Suddenly, a wave of confidence comes over me that I am in good hands.

I lay down, pull the duvet over me and partially grasp the eye mask, but it falls on the floor.

"Wait," Hercules says. He picks it up and gives it to me. "Good luck. See you on the other side."

"You too," I reply. I take the mask and pull it over my eyes. All is dark.

I hear the others shuffling around their beds as they get themselves ready. The room is quiet after a short while, except for the light background music. I hear the lights being switched off.

The whole time I am repeating my question mantra to myself. My mind is clear and I see nothing happening in my mind's eye. Some light footsteps pass around me. Earplugs are pressed into my hand.

"No, thanks," I reply. I want to experience this session as it is.

"They're under the bed near your left hand should you want them," says a female voice I recognise.

"Thanks," I reply. I concentrate on my question again as I try to relax my body.

And then I notice the first whisps of light swirl in my mind. The mushrooms are starting to take effect. The thought 'The Universe is the Mind' comes to me and quickly disappears.

Before I know it, I am flying down a dark tunnel at a great speed. It's blacker than black. The blackness rushes past me and is occasionally enhanced by other intense colours whizzing past me. Sometimes the streaks of light twist and turn. Sometimes they split into different paths as I shoot down one of them without hesitating.

From nowhere, I see my real mum flash by. I shoot through me, sensing a blast of disappointment. Then I am back in complete darkness.

The following bits happen so fast that I can't quite remember the sequence. I see dad, my real dad, and I see my adoptive parents scowling at him. They're arguing… about me. Then a stream of people appears before me and disappears as quickly as they arrive. There are a lot of them I don't seem to recognise. Some I do. I remember the neighbours, teachers and I guess some school kids who have now grown up. These must be people I must have met at some time in my life.

And as I see these people, I feel shame, guilt, isolation and loss. But I don't know why.

The tunnel I'm flying through slows down to a gradual stop. The colours grow lighter, brighter and more intense. I know this can't be true because if it were, I would notice it through the eye mask I'm wearing. I'm hovering in space and basking in this wondrous light around me. It feels good on my skin and within my soul.

My soul, I have one!

Then, I drop into an unseen void at an astonishing speed that makes my stomach churn and have a wave of sickness flowing through me. I mean, it is a painfully intense sensation of feeling sick. I wrap my arms around my body, turn onto my side and curl into a foetal position. It's soothing but doesn't help the pain. All my attention goes into my stomach, where the will to throw up mixes with an intense sensation of loneliness and, boy, do I feel isolated. I sense I'm unwanted, rejected and a waste of life. Here I am, trapped in my mind with nowhere to go. I see many people getting on with their lives but shielded from me. All of this is happening without me.

A wave of anger flows through me as I try to get out of that restrictive force holding me down. I shout at it, kick and hit it, but nothing. The worst thing is that nobody notices me from the other side. They are just getting on with their lives. They laugh, talk, dance, walk and even work on something, except me. I give up and start to cry. I am lost and rejected, and nobody cares about me.

My adoptive parents were right. Nobody loves me. Nobody needs me. I'm useless and worthless.

The shield turns black, leaving me in the deep darkness of despair. I lie here for what feels like an eternity. Alone, I curl up even tighter and hug my relentlessly aching stomach.

Within the black background, a shape appears, but to begin with, it is too blurred to make out what it is. This object grows larger and gradually, I start to see some definition. I see, dad! He's relaxed, calm and content. I call out to him, 'Dad,' He doesn't speak to me, but he breaks up and takes the form of a spirit. He whizzes around me. Each time he flies through me, I understand his story even more. I relate to his pain and guilt when his wife, my mum, died in that car crash. The accident wasn't his fault, but he took the blame. He couldn't cope and stepped out of the game. I feel his love for me. Oh, this feels so good, but the pain in my stomach keeps me from releasing my burden. I see dad and my stepmother together for a fraction of a second. I remember the last time I saw that they were brother and sister. His sister disappears. Dad smiles knowingly at me.

As his spirit disappears into the blackness surrounding me, I call him to come back.

Some people I recognise appear around me. They drift in and out of the background. When they disappear, they turn into energy similar to dad. They swish around in the background. I've always believed these people were judging me and finding mistakes in me, but they weren't. They were concerned about me. They didn't care about finding my faults. Instead, they saw the harm I was under, but they couldn't interfere. They couldn't help. I mistook their helplessness and guilt as their ill judgement against me. I feel my body jolt at this realisation.

I turn over onto my other side as the stomach pain hasn't eased off. I remained curled up in a foetal position. Another wave of blackness rides over me.

Maybe I'm sweating. I feel damp and the duvet feels clammy. I feel like I am lying in wet dirt. I can smell it. Slowly, I see the shape of a small, dark and dirty room. It's the shed in my adoptive parent's unkempt garden where I was often locked up and imprisoned as a child. Looking around, I recognise the unused gardening tools, uncleaned flowerpots and a bag of composted earth in the corner. The floor is covered with dirt. It is damp and cold.

From behind me, the shed door opens. It's my stepmother. She starts screaming at me, but I don't understand the words she's using. Such awful energy emanates from her the penetrates the pit of my stomach, which forces me to curl up even tighter. Something hits me and I flinch away from the stinging pain. Oh, my stomach aches so much. I see my adoptive parents at the door, blocking my way out. She is screaming. He is lashing out with his belt. I try to crawl away from them to avoid their blows.

Then their torrent of abuse slows down and my adoptive parents gradually fade into nothingness.

I roll onto my other side and remain in a foetal position. The stomach ache eases a little. I notice the dirty floor I am lying on grows softer and warmer. For a while, I lay there and enjoy this new secure feeling the earth is giving me as it gathers around me. I feel comfortable, warm and protected. It's a sensation I can't consciously remember experiencing in my past. I suppose I had this security and comfort before the accident, but I can't remember.

Gradually, the earth I am lying on builds up around me, ever higher, protecting and keeping me warm. My feet are already covered, and the ground edges up my thigh. That lovely sensation flows up my spine, shoulders, and chest. I feel its warmth gently moving around my neck, triggering goosebumps over my body.

Oh, wonderful!

As the earth clambers over and around me, I lose my vision as any remaining fear of the oncoming darkness melts away. Ah, that's tranquil.

I lay submerged in complete darkness. I can't see anything. I realise I cannot move my limbs either. The earth has encapsulated me. It's hugging me along with the darkness that has a calming effect on me. I feel at home here. It's as though I belong here. I am at one with it like I am in my mother's womb. I allow it to feed and nourish me as it absorbs the remaining traces of pain, loneliness and sadness from my body. A symbiosis that makes me feel whole. Complete.

Mum appears before me. She looks so calm and serene. I feel her unwavering love for me. Her unconditional love had never left me. I had lost it. She says nothing verbally, but I understand her message to me. Completely. Her spirit breaks up and whizzes around me. As she enters me, I feel a new level of calmness that deepens my reassurance. I also know it is time to shake off that past and embrace the present.

The ache in my stomach changes. First, it starts by softening along the edges, making its way to its centre. Then it expands into something more comfortable that is warm and soothing. Energy circulates in my navel, where it starts to spread through my body, my legs, and my arms. Here I am, lying under the earth, being nourished by it in preparation to grow.

The Universe is feeding me as I sprout out of the earth. I am a bright green seedling full of potential life as my whole body starts to writhe and twist upwards toward the heavenly Universe. The sapling I am, I recognise as oak.

As I grow, I am being tested against the differing weathers of time; the wind, the rain, the cold and the heat and I feel myself growing stronger. Looking around me, I see other growing saplings swaying in harmony with me.

I grow into a stable and strong acorn tree, I come into flower. The acorns form as the blooms wilt.

I hear voices and twist my trunk towards them, I see the surrounding trees change into the people I know. They surround me and lay their hands on my rough yet welcoming bark. Their warm and trusting touch sends warmth through my trunk. My branches shiver with this flow of energy, making the leaves flutter, which allows the acorns to rain down. The circle of people makes a small gap in the circle. I see mum and dad right before me. Their hands are held out towards me, beckoning me to join them.

I recognise the growth of harmonic solitude by being the tree through how strong and secure it is. Yet I feel it is time to leave stability for the next phase. My body appears where the tree once stood. I stand tall in the circle of people as they take their hands away from me. My parents are still a little further away from the rest of the group, so I approach them and reach out to their waiting arms.

As I reach to take their outstretched embrace, they turn into a spirit and fly up around me like a tornado. The faster they whizz around me, the softer I become until I dissolve into a spirit. This allows me to join them by letting go of the last piece of resistance holding me back. We three whizz around together, up, down and around like a freestyle roller-coaster. Not a word is spoken, but I know what they are telling me through their vibrations. I know what they feel for me. I know what I need to do to start living my life.

Hovering in the air, I watch the people below merge into a spirit and whizz through the air, shooting towards me. We merge; mum, dad, me and the people become one. I am the Universe and the Universe is me. They are within me. You are within me. We are one and we are there for each other.

Gradually, the other spirits disappear into the farthest points of the Universe. Finally, mum and dad's spirits separate from mine. Oh, how I want to be with them again. I realise how much I have missed them. Yet, I know it is time for them to leave and let them continue their journey as I have to carry on with mine. Deep within me, I know they have never left me. Nor will a part of them ever leave me, just as their parents never left them. We are our family's history.

I begin to understand what the words mean rather than just being a phrase one uses when one thinks one has understood the power and intensity of that spell. It is me. I am One, and I am 'I'. It's time to go back to 'me'.

I feel the bed and damp duvet wrapped around me and gradually open my eyes. Not seeing anything, I slip off the mask. It's still dark. I glance up at the ceiling, and I'm sure I see one last glimpse of mum before she disappears altogether.

"You okay?" I hear a voice whisper.

I nod and smile. I'm fine.

And I'm free from those bounds.

For the next half an hour, I lay there just reflecting on what I have just gone through. Then, I have the urge to close my eyes.

Some stars and lights flash before me. I see Hercules. He is smiling and holding a book. There's a title on it. As I try to read what it says, it all disappears. I open my eyes and smile to myself. Hercules is telling me I have to write the book. I know what to write.

This book.

For the rest of the afternoon and evening, I left the building and took a long walk alone to reflect on what I experienced. That was a life-changing lesson I have just gone through. Most of us have heard the metaphor of trying to explain the colour orange to a blind person. That's a doddle compared to putting such a psychedelic experience into words! And no, I don't know how to explain any colour to a blind person. Only when we've gone through intense moments like this do we realise how insufficient our language is to explain something that happened in the fourth dimension.

The following day the room is buzzing! The Instructor is grinning at us, knowing what we have gone through.

"Good morning," The Instructor says. "I trust yesterday was something out of this world."

"Oh, yes!" came a voice above everyone, agreeing with him.

"Super!" The Instructor replies. "Who would like to give the group a taste of what happened? I don't want to know about the trip. Just your realisations."

Marie sits between Hercules and me. She's holding our hands and has a firm grip. I can also tell you what a wonderful feeling it is to be wanted. I return it with pleasure.

"May I start?" Marie asks, standing up. The Instructor nods. "You know my history and some of you have seen the change within me from the first session I took part in." She squeezed our hands to let us know she meant Hercules and me. "If you don't mind, I'd like to keep this as simple as possible. I'm still processing what I went through last night and…. Well… what I had gone through in my childhood set me up as a victim. A role I remained in for most of my life. I realised it had protected me in the past, but as my problems grew more complicated, so did my projected solutions. In effect, I unwittingly enhanced the role of victim to… err…. I suppose I tried to protect myself by remaining the victim by selecting certain painful emotions to influence those around me, so I could tell the world what catastrophe had happened. I guess once my adapted process stopped working altogether was when I started to drive those away I needed the most in my life. And then what did I do? I made it even more complicated by reliving the past more intensely, shutting myself off altogether to justify to myself the loss of those I needed around me so I didn't suffer hurt or disappointment again. All I wanted was to be hugged and for someone to tell me they love me and will protect me and that everything was fine. Everything is fine. I realise that now…. I wasn't using the right resources…. It wasn't the right way forward for me… and now it's gone. Yes, gone! Just like that. I've been playing the role of a childhood victim with its restrictive procedures and beliefs for almost all my life. Yet within less than a day, it's gone."

"What's it given you instead?" The Instructor asks.

"Freedom…. Clarity in my mind…. Trust… and I'm filled with so much love I had bottled away." Marie cried softly and kept hold of our hands. "I…. I suppose it was always there, but I had buried it to play the victim role even better. I think if I hadn't, then 1 would have been even more vulnerable otherwise, wouldn't I?

I lay my other hand on top of hers.

"When I first met these two," she nods towards us. I instantly disliked them. Ralf came across as distrustful," Marie says, nodding to me. "And Steve was just too intimidating," she says, nodding toward Hercules. "How wrong I was. I saw my problems in them and interpreted my challenges as theirs. I couldn't have two more open and caring men in my life. That is what they are!

I am grinning like a Cheshire cat. As I snatch a glance at Herc, so is he.

"You are something special, too," Herc says to Marie.

Marie lets go of my hand to give him a massive hug.

All I can do is grin.

"You are something special," Herc repeats while hugging her back.

"And what about you?" Marie asks Herc as she sits back in her chair and takes my hand in hers again.

"To begin with, I was quite sceptical before this sitting. I spent a lot of time wondering how it would help me. I felt compelled to attend and even though I chose something to work through, I can openly say I came here without really knowing what I needed to focus on. Hmm… What did it do for me? I have to say it blew me away. It was…. Look, this might sound a bit batty, so please accept that I'm still working through this, okay?"

Murmurs of agreement went around the room.

"I… er… entered the Universe…. Ahem…." Hercules says with concern as he scans the faces staring at him. All are taking him seriously. "I experienced the Universe, and…. No, I think I will leave it there."

"Please," The Instructor says, "carry on. This is the ninth veil you have just gone through. This is important."

"Very well… I think I met God."

The room remains silent.

"Not the almighty we are led to believe. I met something that has been around for billions of years. An energy source, but not a person… I first thought I saw this energy around planets within our universe. After a while, I realised the energy source binds the smallest particles together… that joins itself to other bound particles, making them bigger until they form something. So, the way I see it is that to make anything big, like the Universe, first, we need to start with the smallest building blocks and build up from there. If I remember my physics from school, we have protons and neutrons that are held together with an invisible force. I think it was that force I saw." Hercules says and then reflects on what to say next.

"Through the power of the mushrooms, I could see that force binding those atoms together. Each contains the Universal laws which they follow. They continue to follow the laws through us and everything else as they remain bonded. They follow their defined path… and since we are made up of the tiniest of various building blocks, it's what makes our lives unique to each other."

"Will you go to church now you have discovered him?" Simone asks.

"Hmm… In my opinion, there's no point. Why do I need a middleman when I can approach this energy directly whenever I wish? I mean, I now know how."

"But he is our Lord," Simone replies.

"He is not a gender. It is a mental gender," Hercules replies while still in reflection. "It's only our physical bodies that determine us and the energy's gender. Our spirit is neutral."

"And that energy is love," Helga says.

"Thank you," Hercules says and smiles at her. "You've given me another missing piece I couldn't quite find."

"Steve, could I propose a question for you to ponder?"

"Sure, my brain's frazzled as it is. Why not finish it off altogether?" Herc replies with a cheeky smile.

A murmur of laughter ripples through the room.

"You said you met God. What would you think if I told you that you had met yourself, your soul, your spirit?"

Herc sits there, trying to comprehend what The Instructor has just said. So am I.

I notice Simone chewing on her bottom lip. She's wanting to say something but is struggling to find the words.

"What I mean is, you, or rather your spirit, is incredibly small that sits in a tiny part of your brain that drives you like your physical body drives a car. The windows are the eyes, the pedals, the steering wheel and the mechanics drive the vehicle around like you drive your muscles to move your body. We can also say the engine is the heart of the car.

Just like a driver decides the destination and direction to go in a car, your creative mind decides what you want to do and where you want to go. The physical body does that for your spiritual self. A car has a horn to let people know where you are and lights to let people know where you are going, just as your Ego is your interface to the outside world through communication. But your Ego is a separate entity to you. It doesn't belong to you. Your job is to regulate and control how it drives you to communicate to the outside world, just like you do with the lights and horn. Getting the signalling wrong or giving it free rein to communicate how it likes could land us in trouble by saying, doing or reacting to things we should otherwise externally ignore and internally observe, just like with a car horn and lights. Now please ask yourself, what if it was you who gave you the release you needed from the problems that you have been using to hold yourself back? Couldn't you say that in the session, you had an undisturbed opportunity to recognise yourself and understand who you aren't? Without Ego interference, did that free rein over yourself help you determine how you think you are? By releasing those non-attached Ego-based limiting beliefs the right thing to do that was originally based on an event that had died as soon as it had happened? Remaining where we were, isn't self-preservation or protection. That's self-imprisonment. That's suffering from Ophiditis or Self-Ophidism. In other words, poisoning yourself with the venom you had created based on that event by improving its effects on you over its lifetime."

The room sits in perfect silence.

"No, that can't be!" whispers Simone. Either The Instructor ignored it or didn't hear her.

"Okay, Steve, would you mind if I ask someone else their thoughts?" The Instructor asks.

"Go ahead," Hercules replies. "That left me pretty speechless. There's still more I need to understand."

He isn't the only one who has more to learn. I do, too.

"Thanks," The Instructor replies. "Okay, who's next?"

The room remains silent. I guess, just like me, the participants are chewing over that some of us may have met ourselves as a spirit and that each of us has released ourselves from our perceived 'non-reoccurring but reoccurring' problem that our Ego created for its control over us. So, those other spirits I saw flying around in my session, was one of them me? Or were they different mistrusting variants of me I recognised as a demented self-reflection in those who cared and didn't know what to do?

"I would like to say I had one problem when I came here, "Helga says. "I have carried guilt for what my past generations did in the war. In the first sitting, I learnt it wasn't my problem but those of my elders. It helped me, but I still felt bad. Here, I learnt that it isn't my personal history I carry around I feel guilty for. It was someone else's. That is good. I learn this is a history from a generation I do not belong to. I can let go. I also know many catastrophes are happening today; death, murder and torture and I still can't control it. It is sad, but it is not my history. I can control how I interact in representing my fatherland and the people. I know deep down we are a good nation. We have learnt from the past that we will never divide people for their beliefs again. Depending on where we are on the line of duality is our interpretation. Many people tell us what is good and bad in their eyes, yet it is not always true, but we must decide for ourselves what is true and work for a better good."

"How are you different now?" The Instructor asks.

"Released from a past that isn't a part of me," Helga replies. "The Germans have an atrocious history; the British and the Americans have an atrocious history. That is the same for China, Russia, Japan and many more countries. I can live with that past. It is what we do today that defines our past for the future."

I spoke about my experiences and so did a couple of others. Yet, there are two other participants I feel necessary to share, with their allowance, naturally.

Ben stands up, straightens a fold in his trouser leg and then coughs. Both Ben and his brother have said very little over the days.

"I'd like to take the test," Ben says to The Instructor.

"Are you sure?" The Instructor asks. "It's nearly ten in the morning.

"That's never been a problem for us before," Bill says, remaining in his seat.

The Instructor heads for the kitchen. He returns with a clear bottle of Vodka and a couple of empty glasses in his hands.

"Here you are!" The Instructor says. "As we agreed earlier."

"Is that a good idea?" Simone asks, looking shocked.

"Name me a better test?" The Instructor replies.

"But it should have worked within this session," Simone says.

"Only by testing something out, just as you will, is the only way to find out if we released it," The Instructor replies.

"I saw God!" Simone replies, unable to control her emotions. "I saw him. It wasn't me. He spoke to me! That's all the faith we need."

"Spoke? In words?" Hercules asks.

"Yes…. Oh, no…. Not words…. Through his love." Simone replies in agitation.

"Do you accept your god is you?" Hercules asks.

"Why? Oh, I.... Yes.... No! But what The Instructor said. That can't be right. He's around us," Simone replies.

"And are you not his equal who is within you?" someone else asks her.

"Wasn't this session to test your interpretation of whether God exists?" Bill asks.

Simone mumbles something, but I can't hear it.

"Can I ask," Bill says, "whether you met any other religious icons? Jesus or Mohammed or Buddha, for example?"

"I just met God," Simone says, unsure if she should be disappointed.

"I'm just wondering how you will be different in your church community the next time you join them," Bill says. "If The Instructor is right and the god we met is ourselves, then what is the god the church has been shouting about all these years? Fiction for the masses?"

"Oh, my goodness! I'm not going to tell them I doubted my belief and came here to find out," Simone cries out.

"Ah, you admit you are here to test your faith!" Bill says softly with a small friendly smile.

Simone slaps a hand over her mouth.

"Now you've confirmed the existence of God within you. What now?" Bill asks.

Simone starts to cry.

"Oh. I didn't want to offend you," Bill says. He steps towards her with concern strewn over his face.

"I'll go to Hell!" Simone shouts at him. "I'm doomed!"

"If you think you will, then you're already in it," The Instructor replies. "Remember what we spoke about in communicating with the Universe? 'For what you ask is what you receive.'"

"May I ask you something?" Bill says. He kneels next to Simone and rests his hands on his thigh. "We test the faith of many things every day. It doesn't matter whether you worship a personal belief, an item or a God. They're the same. I turned to drink as you turned to God in search of the answers we don't know how to find within ourselves. Can you imagine, throughout my adult life, I have been asking myself what it would be like to live without the pain I carry? Every morning I give myself a chance not to drink as you give yourself a chance not to sin in the religious sense. The best I have managed is no more than a couple of hours before the pain seeps back into my life. This is the same test I've failed for the last forty-odd years. This time, I want to pass it."

"How can you compare God and alcohol?" Simone asks. "They're two completely different things."

"Except they help us to get us through another day," Ben says from his chair.

"They're both man-made spirits doing the same job," Bill says.

Simone scowls at him.

"Simone, my intention isn't to hurt you through our discussions over the last couple of days. You have helped me understand the comparisons I've made throughout my life. I hoped I could give you something back. I'm not offended if you disagree with me. By opening up on your battle, I can thank you for helping me open my eyes to what is happening inside me."

Simone stares at him. I think she trying to understand what he means without losing her already confused state of her religious beliefs.

Bill says to The Instructor. "I think I have said enough. May I?"

"Sure," The Instructor replies and tips some vodka into each glass. Ben and Bill take them.

Bill swirls it, brings it to his nose and smells it. He wrinkles his nose and lowers the glass to his thigh.

Ben stares at the full glass. He raises it to his mouth. But before the rim touches his lips, he pulls it away.

"This is tempting," Ben says. "But I do like what I'm thinking."

"What's that?" his brother asks.

"Nothing. I'm thinking nothing," Ben says with an ironic smile.

"I'm asking myself, 'what if?'" Bill says, still staring into his glass.

"What if, what?" The Instructor asks.

Bill raises the glass and tips the contents down in one gulp. He screws his face up as the alcohol hits the back of his throat.

A few gasps fly around the room.

"Would you like another?" The Instructor asks.

"No… no thanks," Bill replies. "That did nothing for me whatsoever."

"None?" Ben asks.

"None."

Ben throws the shot down in one with his eyes closed. He smacks his lips, but no 'ah' leaves his mouth.

"It's a bit of an anti-climax," Ben says to his brother. "There's nothing for it to work on."

Bill turns to Simone and says, "There you are. We've both tested it and have broken our faith in alcohol. The difference I can see between us is that my faith never really worked for him. All it did was provide me with something to hide behind when I didn't know what to do. All it did was hide the pain of helplessness. Now I need to search for something new in my life that I can comfortably live with. Now, that's a scary thought. I guess you are still confirming whether your faith is working for you. Maybe you are considering whether you can now take it to the next level. I can appreciate that can be scary too."

"What do you mean?" Simone asks.

"Well, let's consider that you did meet yourself in yesterday's session. As The Instructor implied, you have learnt how to communicate inwardly instead of externally. With this new understanding, how will you take your spiritual life to the next level?" Bill asks.

"Huh, I hadn't thought of that," Simone replies and goes into thought. Her arms remain folded tightly across her chest.

"What an interesting discussion," The Instructor says. "Ben, Bill, can I ask whether this has worked in eliminating your alcohol addiction?"

"I think so," Bill says, holding onto his empty glass. "That insistent and abusive shouting and screaming in my head has gone. I hear a calmer and more supportive voice within me. That's it. There's nothing to drown out."

"Hmm, after noticing its tastelessness instead of the bitterness, I'm not sure," Ben says. "Like my brother, my internal dialogue has changed. It's more relaxed. I didn't know I had one as calm as this. But… and I don't understand why I wanted to drink this again…. Even knowing I don't need to drown anything out, I feel a part of my routine is missing."

"That's right!" The Instructor says. "And how are you going to act differently after today?"

"That's a good question," Bill says quietly.

"Isn't my God the same God as everyone else?" Simone asks.

"Can I say something?" Hercules asks.

The Instructor scans the room and nods approval to Hercules.

"I'd like to call God something different. Do you mind?"

"Go ahead," Simone replies.

"I think there are two ways to think about this," Hercules says. "We know that the Universe is mental and mental is the mind. Everything I experienced yesterday is within the limitations of my mind's capacity, which I am beginning to believe is vaster than we realise. That is if I don't set any restrictive and limiting boundaries. The perceived size of the Universe, so to say, is my tiny spirit's perspective glancing up at all those neurons firing in my brain. For the spirit, me, or I, wouldn't it look like a mass Universe from where it is located? However, in reality, it is only my inner world I see and participate in. If so, would this fit in with your belief that we are all made in God's image because what we see is what we want to recognise within our interpretation of our internal Universe? Maybe by having such a potent experience we can't believe or are conditioned to believe that we could never deserve to be a part of god and the Universe. So, instead, we decide to meekly comment that we are made in its image.

"Secondly," Hercules continues. "If I am wrong, maybe there's a portal within our minds that connects us to an external Universe from which we all originate?"

"But!" Simone interjects.

"Please let me finish. I'm struggling to formulate this.... So… if there is a mental portal to a unified Universe, our spirit or energy can take any form it wishes through physical birth. Suppose an animal were to take a psychedelic. Would it meet its own powerful spiritual energy that looks like itself? If so, does that mean the animal belongs to this Universe through its resounding spirit, just like we do? Hmm, can I take this a little further?

"Oh," Simone says. "Animals don't have souls."

"We are all animals. Anima means 'soul' in Latin," Helga says. "If they don't have souls, neither do we."

"And thirdly," Hercules continues, "this portal joins us all together right up to the edges of the Universe. Then is this an energy shared by all?"

"And the energy doesn't judge. It observes. It gives us our wishes and desires, matching who we think we are," Helga says.

"Exactly!" Hercules replies. "You've helped me understand something else I was struggling with."

And this fantastic conversation continues…

Through lunch, we swap more stories from our bewildering experiences. After lunch, we gather in the great hall again.

"Okay, I want you to re-work through your future goals just like we did a couple of days ago. Get into pairs and use the provided script to work on how you will achieve your newly perceived goals. Okay? Great. Let's get started," The Instructor says.

I partner up with Hercules and lay a five-metre length of rope out. Herc marks his present position on the line. To his left is the past, and to the right is his future. The last part of the rope is short, as we are only working on our future goals.

Later, as we are enjoying our evening meal, I look around and notice through the buzz we are all tired. We've all worked on our future with the resources we think we need based on experiences from the past. We've rehearsed potential issues that could naturally crop up in our lives and worst-case scenarios, too, so the chance of surprise is minimised. It's impossible to cover everything, I am aware of that. However, a new level of awareness is present and that makes this moment easier to enjoy. I'm exhausted. The one thing I am looking forward to today is my bed!

"Today, the fifth day, our last day, is our Universe day," The Instructor says to us on this sunny morning. "Today, we are going to start communicating effectively with the Universe.

Remember, we learnt that all our thoughts and conversations are acted upon by the Universe. Well, we will use what we learnt to start consciously communicating our desires with the Universe for what is rightfully ours."

"Cool!" I say quietly. Hercules nudges me with a wink. Previously, he was sceptical about this. However, since his psychedelic experience and the discussions we had yesterday until the early hours of the morning, he is committed to the Universe's principles. I think just like the rest of us.

"Let's do a quick practice run. For this round, choose something simple. We can choose something a little challenging after that. Once you are back home, you can work on something even more challenging and in your own time. Okay. You are working alone on this one." The Instructor switches on some new-age music playing in the background. "Firstly, close your eyes, and let's come into the present...."

After finishing the session with a final meditation, I open my eyes and feel great! I sense I have learnt a lot more compared to the last time we did this. Not only that, it makes much more sense after going through what we have through our psychedelic sessions. My restrictions are no longer there, and I am open to this new way of thinking, which, I am sure, will change and develop over time. I still need to practice it to make it a part of my routine, but we all have to start somewhere, don't we?

"Fantastic!" The Instructor says. "Any questions?"

"Yes, I have one," I say. "Although I understand the seven principles, I'm still coming to terms with what they mean and I feel some are linked to each other more than I can comprehend. "Would I be pushing the boat out if I said that all are strongly linked together?"

"Spot on!" The Instructor replies. "They are, in fact, all linked to each other. Mentalism, correspondence, vibration, polarity, rhythm, causation and gender. We find each in all. Remember, 'All is in The All', and 'As above; so below. As below, So above', for example, are interrelated. A polarity goes from one end of the spectrum to the other like a pendulum does over time. How they swing depends on what is happening in our lives and how we react to it. Ultimately, the aim is to remain neutral through observance. I am aware we can't expect that straight away with everything we come across for the first time. We need to be aware of such polarity changes to know what we still need to understand, accept and release. If you have a different interpretation of what I have just said and it helps you find your neutrality, use it. But please remember, finding neutrality can be a life-long exercise for all."

"When we put everything together that we have been through over these days," Hercules says in deep thought. "Am I beginning to understand what is meant by the phrase 'The All is Mind; The Universe is Mental'? I know I have discussed this before, but are we a complete network within ourselves, a hologram of perceptions seen in each other? What we recognise within us is what we recognise around us."

The Instructor stands there with the biggest grin possible stretching across such a friendly and trusting face.

It's just before lunch and an excellent end to The Instructor's version of Major Mystery. I appreciate how it could have been all those years ago as the Greeks who had walked out of the Major Mysteries to have the old self symbolically die and return to their homes re-born. They must have felt that they had a new chance to live a fuller life again, to be free from those old burdens where those intoxicating and worthless thoughts never seem to leave us alone. It must have been seen as a magical and powerful gift from the gods by family and friends when seeing the participants change for themselves. For those who had never attended the Mysteries, it must have provided a considerable attraction where hope to release a burden could become a reality.

I say goodbye to the incredibly inspiring brothers, Bill and Ben and to the others who are going home today. Hercules, Marie, and I head into the city, nearly an hour's drive away and visit a charming Bistro to enjoy a lovely meal together. In the evening, starts the third course. This time, however, no psychedelics.

I am looking forward to this.

At the Bistro

"Can I ask?" Hercules says quietly so the other patrons sitting at another table can't hear us. "Is there anything else you would add to what we discussed earlier we felt better not to say in the group?"

Marie and I are happily eating with full mouths. We nod to Hercules and wait for him to ask his question.

"Hmm, let me start," Hercules says, getting the hint. "I understand what we have gone through and the results each of us has experienced. What I can't quite understand is how all this is meant to come together…. I mean… we have had two amazing psychedelic experiences that helped release the past. We have learnt how to still our mind, about the Kybalion on how we are connected to the Universe. How do I bring this together to live my life? Are we mentally free that everything automatically falls into place and we get on with it? What I mean is, is this what I am feeling here and now the norm from now on, or am I missing something?"

"Hmm! Maybe I can help!" Marie says as she swallows her food. She takes a quick drink before continuing. "Sorry! Let me explain. This has fascinated me almost all my life, but I could never get my head around it until today."

We both turn towards her with interest. I take another bite of my delicious sandwich as I wait for her to start her explanation.

"By having had the chance of going through these wonderful experiences, we have met our spiritual selves or that of what we once interpreted as God. We have had the chance to recognise what we thought was bothering us isn't what we thought it was. What I love the most is we have learnt to know when we judge others, we are recognising internal thoughts of ourselves externally. That is our judgemental and destructive Ego taking care of itself at the expense of ourselves.

We both nod.

"God, or rather our unconditional self, radiates unconditional love without judgement or punishment or praise. Recognising it is one of the challenges we have."

"Does that mean I have to accept all my enemies within my life?" I ask.

"Ah, that's where self-love comes in. We need to decide our emotional and physical boundaries for ourselves because there are people who will feed and drink us dry to exhaustion if we don't set and respect them. We can love those who don't respect our boundaries for their mortal being and not blame them for the childhood mistreatment that made them the way they are. Still, we can protect ourselves by stopping them from using our energy and contribution to feed their inferiority, which over time, weakens us. You have the right to avoid those who can't respect your boundaries, just as they will avoid you when you don't provide them with the feed they need. It doesn't mean being nasty to them. One can excuse yourself and walk away while still radiating love for them. It is important to remember that these respectless boundary breakers have a different internal fight when we compare what we were going through. We must respect them and give them space to work through their battle independently. They want others to do it for them, but as we know, that's not possible. They need to work through their pain to release their past, just like we do. Everybody needs to be protected from being hurt by others and everyone deserves a chance to release themselves from their past burden. This Universe is here for everyone. It's our giver constantly giving us exactly what we think we are."

"What do you mean, the Universe is our giver to what we think we are?" I ask.

"From the moment we wake up to the point of going to sleep, the Universe is listening to everything we say, think and do. In return, it shows and gives us exactly what we have become through our inner thoughts and reflections of ourselves."

I look blank at her.

"We think we can work through an issue, release it and become who we want to be through meditating, but it doesn't work like that. I certainly thought like that when I first started meditating. All meditation is, is to still the mind. Anything else is active mental work."

"That's it?" Herc asks.

"As we have learnt, meditation, like any other mind-calming method, is just a tool to help ignore the Ego's independent and oft-destructive thoughts for a while. It helps us to get a perspective and realise how we need to regulate our Ego by being its filter. As The Instructor said, once we 'still' our minds, we are spiritual. It can help us to reach that peace of mind while meditating and the effects should last a bit longer. It helps us to understand what we need from the Ego so that we can relate sensibly to the outside world. It is that open mind we need to carry with us through the day. It's that open mind that lets the Universe give us what we are thinking or asking because this is, mentally and physically, what we are emulating. If we live and think of good health and live as though this is true, we recognise what we need to improve our health and we have a better chance of getting healthy through our chosen way. Even the smallest, and perhaps that slightly sarcastic thought or comment murmured against us is understood as our requirement because, at that moment, it became a part of our focus. Our self. That focus is the attraction we see of ourselves through others. That attraction, albeit fleeting, lands on our lap at some point. and the Universe gives us exactly what we think of ourselves."

"Are you saying that each time I give myself a hard time, even as a type of self-punishment, it is understood that I want it in my life?"

"Essentially, yes," Marie replies to Hercules' question. "Because that is how we see ourselves within our inner mind. We reflect externally what we see internally. We are the Universe. The Universe, or rather, we give ourselves what we wish for, whether we want it or not.

"Hmm. Remember The Instructor spoke about karma. Is that what this is?" Herc asks.

"That's a bit more complicated," Marie says.

"How do you mean?" I ask.

If I understood The Instructor correctly, we could consider karma as two things. The first is that we create our karma through cause and effect. The Instructor said, 'today's cause is tomorrow's consequence.' I understand this is what I do today, and then I will meet its consequence tomorrow or sometime in the future. The second version is similar to the first but from a different perspective. And that is I am living the pain in this life for the pain I caused to someone or something else in the last life."

"But what about if someone doesn't believe in reincarnation?" I ask.

"Then I suppose, like any belief or religion, they will find out afterwards, won't they?" Herc says with a grin.

"That gets me thinking," Herc says. "What did I do in my past life to experience such a tragic and painful loss of my friends?"

Wow! My mind is spinning. I ask myself, what did I do in my past life to deserve losing my parents and being fostered by a family that punished me?

"Why am I having to find a way to deal with it?" Herc asks, beating me to the same question I had in mind.

"Redemption," Marie says. "This karma we suffer from a past life is a chance to learn from those past mistakes we didn't manage to learn from. I suppose we need to understand the consequences to make sure I can consider whether it would be worth doing again. We will, after all, return to this Universe to play the game again, but with different consequence criteria. As I understand, what The Instructor said is that we can only progress to the next Universe level once we have learnt through both sides of an experience."

"For example?" I ask. This conversation is beyond my comprehension.

"For example, we kill animals to survive, just like other meat-eating animals do. We eat them and use the remains for tools or clothing. That's part of the game and spiritually, we accept it. But we are the only species that pollutes, tortures and kills for fun. Love is a Universal bonding, but some can't come close to that by using violence to satisfy their immediate needs. This abuse goes against the Universal karmic laws and must be paid back later in another life. The karma waiting for the person's next life is probably similar to what their victims are going through in this one."

I glance at Herc, and Marie notices.

"Yes, Ralf. I have been asking myself what I did in a past life to deserve this in my present life."

"Sorry, I didn't mean…."

"What about karma where masses of children are abused in families, religious institutes and war?" Herc asks.

"As I understand it, that's the population's karma," Marie says. "We've grown to ignore our children's safety in many aspects. Some are willing to leave their innocent children with someone they think is respectful or trustworthy. Some of these trusted people abuse that position to take advantage of those children for their perverse satisfaction, leaving many parents in denial of what they have allowed to happen to their offspring. This, sadly, manifests further confusion for the abused child they will experience in later years. I think another problem is that we don't know how to educate our children enough to allow them to protect themselves in awkward moments. If you think about it, how many people shout about such horrible things as buying products that have knowingly been made by enslaved children? Or where parents support a religious institution to attend services, fund it and yet allow their child to sacrifice its innocence in the hands of a priest to release the child's parent of its sins.

"Let me put this inbred contradiction another way," Marie continues. "One popular demonstration that is taking place internationally is 'Fridays for Future.' People demonstrate against the use of products that cause environmental damage. That's all and good. Yet these same people are wearing clothes or freely using products that damage the very environment they tell others to protect. They buy some kind of coffee or other sweet beverage in those single-use non-disposable paper or plastic cups that are thrown away afterwards, causing more harm to the planet than would have been generated without the demonstration. Then we consider how did the demonstrators get to the protests that are against pollution and the use of fossil fuels. To this very day, I have never seen many bikes parked near where the demo started. I do see roads clogged with vehicles that happily pump those very fumes they are fighting against into the air for others to breathe.

"Whether the driver buys fuel from a tank station or recharges a battery from home doesn't matter. Toxic fumes are still pumped into the atmosphere that we breathe. Such demonstrators want the world to change but don't want to lead by making that first sacrificial step."

I nod in agreement.

"And this is precisely what we are doing with the Universe. Those demonstrators are protesting against something but are not considering implementing a replacement, so the old demand remains. Instead of disappearing, it grows in intensity since this is all we are thinking about. Remember what The Instructor said? If we want to give something up, we must replace it with something we want. Otherwise, what we tried to give up without a replacement will come back with a vengeance. That is the Universe giving the population its consequential wish.

I remember The Instructor telling us that.

"So, how do we live the life we want or deserve?" I ask.

"That's where I'm struggling too," Marie says. "That's why I want to do this next course."

"Stoicism," an older man says, sitting at the table behind me. "Sorry for interrupting. I've been practising this fascinating philosophy since I was a teenager and am still living that life. Let me say that regardless of your life philosophy, there are no guarantees in life. Nothing owes you anything. All you can control in your life are your thoughts and actions. Nothing else. It's these thoughts that come into play that help to determine your actions in preparation for their consequences or, as you said earlier, karma. If you believe in stoicism, it is an interesting and helpful part of working with your life's lessons regardless of whether you want them.

We three stare at him in bewilderment.

Part III – The Way to the Philosopher

We sit expectantly on our chairs in the training room in the same barn where we have all been through the modernised Greek Minor and Major Mysteries. I look around to see several new faces and a couple I recognise from the group who have just completed the Major Mystery.

"Welcome to you all," The Instructor says. "This session will show you how to live practically with what you have learnt, to recognise what qualities you have and how to use them and to work through any thoughts and actions that may still hinder you. As I have said often enough in both the Mysteries, there is more than one way to get where you want to go. I'm just showing you the oldest systems that are still shown to be the most reliable.

What I am about to go through with you is practising a philosophy that can be used for daily life and therapy. It doesn't mean you have to agree with it. However, in my opinion, stoicism is still one of the most practical philosophical systems out there. Whatever new tool or philosophy you discover you find helpful, use it. However, this system I am about to show you was the way of thinking and living for the Greeks and Romans that lasted for several hundred years. We are not just going to cover Stoicism, but we will consider some other Hellenistic philosophers, Socrates and Pythagoras too. We will focus on some modern philosophers that have built on the Greek Stoic philosophy. I would also like to say that this philosophy is still being practised today and is steadily growing in numbers.

Let me say that if today someone is considered to be a stoic, this is usually considered a person who is cold and emotionless. However, it's not true, thankfully. It's about thinking through issues and emotions to help determine what is important to us and how to react accordingly, should we need to. Even the most ardent Stoic feels pain and frustration like we do. Still, they have gathered a collection of tools to help them along the way in accessing those emotions and thoughts. These range from having a reply ready for those who like to say the obvious or have an action in mind or have a technique on how to process extreme emotions, events and things that are out of our control. With such mental preparedness, it does make life easier to enjoy this 'festival' we are in when we are better aware of what is happening around us. This doesn't mean being in the past or future all the time. It means thinking through the events you know you are attending and considering what could happen. It doesn't mean you have a reply for everything, but you will have a head start. And then, once you have thought about it, you forget it and get on with your life by being in the present.

If you are struggling with the meaning of 'stoic', let me put the word 'stoa' or rather 'stoa poikile' differently. Translated, it means 'porch' or rather 'painted porch' because that is where the philosophical discussions notably took place with Zeno, the founder of this way of thinking, Cleanthes, Chrysippus and other philosophers.

"We will also find that the Romans took stoicism further than the Greeks and we will refer to four important Roman figures after Zeno's time. They are Epictetus, Seneca, Marcus Aurelius and Musonius Rufus. We will also work through this philosophy as a psychological tool, just like we did with some bits of it in the Mysteries. We will link it to a modern but slightly less effective psychological tool called 'Cognitive Behavioural Therapy', or 'CBT'. Many modern psychologists say that the Stoic philosophy is the first psychological tool created. It is a great tool the Greeks have created, but I disagree. It isn't the first psychological tool they popularised."

"What's the first?" a participant asks.

"The Mysteries," another participant replies.

"That's right," The Instructor replies. "As we are aware that in the Mysteries, we still don't know what other psychological tools were used on the participants in preparation for the entheogen's work. However, we have a reasonable idea of what could have happened based on how other indigenous tribes worldwide have treated their folk in similar moments of need. Once we look at what happened across the world, we can see there is a pattern carried out between each tribal medicine man with their patient.

"Some say the Greeks developed another powerful tool to help their people, the Hermetic Universal laws we covered in the Major Mystery. Okay, back to modern psychology and the great work of Albert Ellis, who determined the first wave of cognitive therapy called Rational-Emotive Behaviour Therapy, or REBT for short. Although he only linked some of his work to the Stoics because of its false reputation as a cold and emotionless system because of the risk it could harm his new technique and a cold and soulless system. As Marcus Aurelius said, the philosopher's role is the 'physician of the soul'. And how right he was and still is. CBT is now passing through its 3rd wave, mainly thanks to Aaron Beck. However, much of it today reflects more from Eastern philosophy than Western philosophy, which is good when considering its relationship with nature and not its practical use. One thing we need to remember is that Stoic philosophy takes us through and beyond those spiritual and theoretical boundaries and that it shows us how to live through our daily challenges, how we integrate, do business, accept our fate and enjoy what we have because we can't always control what we have in life.

"Right, before we get into the details, I want us to consider what we have control over and what we don't. I like to start here because using Epictetus' thoughts helps us to reflect on what we can do, what we need to accept we cannot change and know which is which. In your notepads, make two columns and head them 'what I control' and 'what I can't control'. Under each section, note down what you think you have control over and what you don't. Okay, away you go.

"Right, that was more surprising than most of you thought, wasn't it?" The Instructor says. "As we see, we have less control of things than we thought. For example, everything you think, say and do are the only things you can control. Sadly, we know from our past that even this can be a challenge for us sometimes."

"Surely, we can control what other people do, can't we?" a participant asks.

"Not really, no. If this were the case, then psychedelics would be legal worldwide, the current poisons wouldn't be allowed in foodstuffs and we would all live comfortably without having to financially scrape by. Bringing this example more to home, I would be unemployed as a therapist because if everybody did what the other person wanted, we wouldn't have the issues we currently have. On the other hand, I guess I would have other problems to help out with because everyone would be exhausted doing everything others wanted!"

"I control my body and what I eat, so what don't I control with it?" another participant asks.

"It is categorised as an external. An external is what you can't influence. Can you stop yourself from not digesting the food you have just eaten? Can you stop yourself from gaining weight after eating a lot of carbs? Can you stop cancer from invading your body? No, you can't. You can choose what and when you put something into your body to support it, but after that, there are no guarantees.

"But I can control how my body moves."

"To an extent, you can. For example, you can clap and turn your head to a certain extent. But can a person move their limbs faster and more accurately than we already do? Not really. We can fine-tune it with plenty of practice, but that's it. So, no, you cannot control your body beyond its basic design we are given allowance over.

Everything in life, be it your career, relationships, wealth, health and so on, you have no control over. You can maybe influence someone else's decision through action or statement, but you can't control it. Just like death, you may be able to delay or enhance it slightly, but ultimately, you cannot influence the exact moment you die. Maybe it is easier to consider that the body doesn't belong to you and that it's on loan, then all you can do is service and repair it with what nature has given you. Accepting whatever you have been given in life is an opportunity to work with it, love it, take care of it and learn from it. Waiting for things to change or paying for a superfluous change is a wasted opportunity to empower your inner value, growth and learn with the things you have.

Okay, next, we need to understand how pathological passions can cause burn-out and even drive us crazy if we are not careful."

"If I can't change my body, then why do I eat to keep it healthy?" a participant asks.

"Even with eating healthy, there is no guarantee you will not fall ill, although the statistics are on your side. There are no guarantees in anything in life. But by eating healthily, you are reducing the risk of falling ill, that's all. The other question to ask ourselves is, what is healthy? If we compare what we are encouraged to eat by industry and what we ate thousands of years ago, we should ask ourselves why there are such big discrepancies that nobody is picking up. Is this modern diet intentionally eating up our valuable time and resource by feeding our hard-earned money into the medical industry or are we designed to live such a hedonistic and epicurean lifestyle, such that this is part of our plan for us to suffer at some later point in life when most Stoics and others tend to avoid this phase?

"Okay, that's a great place to stop that subject. The next thing we will review is how the pathology of passion can be mentally destructive. For example, passion is things like desire, fear and aversion. We know that when a person starts a business linked to their passion, it is a great start, to begin with, but after a while, that passion dies. When that passion dies, so does its quality and the love the person once radiated for their subject. This is where the phrase 'do what you love', becomes an issue for us. However, another thing we are aware of is that if we take the original quote from Steve Jobs, 'love what you do', it gives us much more flexibility in being independent of what is happening around us. In every aspect of a job, family, career and so on, there are aspects nobody enjoys. Still, if we tell ourselves that we are loving what we are doing because it is the only moment that we are going to have, it makes the task something worthwhile. We don't need to be chirpy or overemotional about doing the role, but we can remain more indifferent. Just like we do when considering other emotions we have under our control. This is, in itself, a superpower because when we remain indifferent to what we cannot control, this can give us a new inner balance and a fuller perspective to get through pretty much anything life can throw at us."

"Right, the last action of the day, which will also be your first action for tomorrow before we meet up, is to reflect on Pythagoras' *Golden Verse* and to consider how the day has gone and the second part is on how to review your day as it starts. Pythagoras believed in taking control of one's life and thoughts by recognising what has not gone to plan and what has. He also considered those things we haven't done that we had planned to. Not to worry, we will cover in detail tomorrow how we deal with goals, deadlines and activities we don't manage to achieve. Let me read out the Golden Verse and as I do, I want you to reflect on your answers within:

Nor suffer sleep to close thine eyes
Till thrice thy acts that day thou has run o'er;
How slip? What deeds? What duty left undone?

"Epictetus said something similar and more direct: 'Where did I go wrong? What did I do? What duty is left undone?'

"The second part is to help you consider your structure for the next day. Remember, your day won't flow exactly as you have planned, but you will be surprised how near you are to it as the day progresses and how much work your subconscious has already done for you before you have even started your first activity:

As soon as ere thou wakest, in order lay
The actions to be done that following day.

"Upon awakening, I do like to reflect on my day again to review what I plan to do and I highly recommend you do the same too. Do this exercise on your own, reflect on how your day has gone today three times and then how you intend to structure your day tomorrow."

"Could you give me an example?" a participant asks.

"Naturally, I can't include everything, so, for example, I get up at six in the morning, before I drink my coffee, I meditate on my day and consider some challenging aspects of what could happen. Afterwards, I get on with the day and do my fitness routine. Next, I go grocery shopping, if I need to. Once everything is packed away, I go to my practice and work with clients. At lunchtime, I try to do something for myself and make it unique as often as possible. In the afternoon, I write up my notes, meet a couple more clients, prepare for these group sessions and then head home. At home, I check on the mushrooms. My partner and I cook our evening meal and enjoy each other's company. Before bed, I meditate and reflect on my day and plan for the next. That is just an example of one day. Okay, time to start your reviews…."

"Right, good morning to you all. I trust you have reviewed your day for today. Doing this review on the course is relatively easy. However, each of you has your own smaller routines and challenges that allow you to experiment a little. Practice planning and reviewing them over these days. It won't become a habit here, but it will help you get into the routine once you return home.

"Today, we are going to consider in more detail what externals are and how we can be indifferent to them. Being indifferent to the things we cannot control helps us to put things in perspective. Perspective helps us to realise where we are in life. The great thing about observing our emotions when somebody has said or done something is a great tool in realising what has happened, even if we think the effects of someone's decisions are disastrous. I have to be careful what I am saying here because it doesn't mean we are cold and emotionless. We aren't. We accept what is happening around us and continue to work with the results we have received. Again, this doesn't mean we have to accept criminal activity, we don't. The criminal has put value into something stolen or damaged and has willingly paid the price to be characterised as untrustworthy and unreliable. Most people don't like being labelled as such and avoid such actions. However, for some, this can be a prestigious label. I don't want to get into the ins and outs of labelling, however, whatever we do, buy, say and so on, we sacrifice a part of ourselves to become that person and we need to be aware of whether there is some worth in that sacrifice."

"What do we sacrifice?" a participant asks.

"Time. We sacrifice a part of our life for whatever we want to get in return. Even with something simple as receiving praise from someone, we sacrifice a part of our life to acknowledge it. How many people sacrifice the most valuable asset they brought to this planet for a remark from someone they don't know? Practically all of us. This includes comments from work colleagues, friends and family. It isn't easy, but we need to remain indifferent to their comments too. Maybe they are trying to support us but depending on how that support is done, it may harm us in the long run. The only person suitable to honestly know the best thing for you is you."

"But what about when I was blinded by events from my past?" another participant asks.

"Rarely do we trust ourselves when we know something is bothering us, so we irrationally and blindly listen to others to base our decisions on those external comments. In other words, we casually pass our responsibility from being in our control of our life by putting it in the hands of others. So, if something goes wrong, we think we are not at fault because we were told to do or think something by someone else. We are totally responsible for that decision and its outcomes."

"I made mistakes in the past," Hercules says. "So, how am I a reliable source for me?"

"We have all made mistakes in the past and we will all make mistakes again in the future, but you stood by your decision and remained responsible for your role in the event. Nobody is perfect, so we need to be fully responsible for everything we think, say and do. That's why you are here listening to this philosophy. You take what you need to help you fully control your life without hurting others. You can still help and give opinions to others when requested, but remember, you are taking the responsibility to support someone in their decisions, even if different from yours, not to make them.

"Right, I have digressed a little there. Externals. These are the things we can't control, but we may be able to influence. More people sacrifice a part of their free lives thinking of something that could go wrong. In the end, however, that fantasised disaster either never happens, or if something does happen, it turns out differently from what was considered. Remember what I said that there is no good or bad. It's a personal judgement of what is or isn't. That doesn't mean we can't plan for some eventualities or the future. We can and we do. But we can't do anything at this moment when something related isn't happening. All we are doing is wasting our valuable life that we will never get back and I find that a great shame.

What does all that worry do? It makes us depressed, restricts our thinking and stops us from enjoying something at that moment. Easier said than done, I know. What we can do is consider what judgements we have made and what could be missing to make a decision. If a decision can be made, we could think it through until we have some ideas of what could work and what couldn't. But after that, it's a waste of the only resource available by staying fixed on something we have thought through."

"We could justify our thoughts for an event that has occurred," a participant says.

"That's right. It's not the event that happened that bothers us, but it is our judgement of the event that happens that bothers us. And that is where we need to start asking ourselves appropriate questions. I want us to be aware of what they are and how we recognise them as judgements."

"But what if someone is really cruel to us, shouldn't we let them know?"

"An interesting question, but the answer is a clear no. And why? That person in their mind did or said something for their own perverse reason. From their perspective, it was an acceptable thing to say or do against you. Maybe they were thinking they were helpful. We could bite back, but that would feed their inner demons even more by making them happier inwardly. We don't want that. What we want to do is smile and say nothing."

"Say nothing!"

"Saying nothing can be a very powerful and protective communication. Saying nothing allows you to consider at a more leisurely pace and away from this person what was meant by their actions or words. If they were right, you can reflect on them, accept them and change something accordingly. However, if they were wrong, their judgement made an error and it is no concern of yours. You can't change or control it. By saying nothing, you will not be feeding them their confirmation of what they are thinking about you. Not responding makes them focus on themselves a little harder because your lack of response hasn't fed their Ego the way it needs feeding. They may even ask themselves questions like, did they hear me? Should I repeat it? Why are they not responding? What did I do wrong? Do I need to be harder against them the next time? I'm angry because they didn't give me what I need, and so on.

"I suppose you could say something. If you like, thank them for the super feedback and you will consider it later when you have time. Or you could say that if they need help finding more faults the next time, you are available because you felt some were missing. Make a joke of it and show how relaxed you are, even if you are fuming on the inside. It's the fuming they need, not the humour and niceties. So, don't give them what they are prodding you for."

"What if they are provoked even more to hassle me further?" I ask.

"As with any idiot, agree with them again and thank them for bringing this to your attention. Then walk away. If you can, agree on something they haven't said. For example, I agree with you that we should have a break from each other. Let's give it a year. And then simply walk away. It helps later if they try bothering you again. Remind them of the agreement, even if they deny it. It is now in the open and is easier to uphold."

"Is that what you do?" a participant asks.

"My opinion, which is a Stoic opinion, is why should I be bothered about something a person I don't know has said to me? Even if I find it painful, which can happen to the best of us, it's not worth holding a grudge because once we die, there is no longer a grudge. We don't know when we will die, maybe my time is this afternoon, tomorrow or next year. Why should I carry that grudge when I know it will come to an end when I die? Life is short. Let's not sacrifice our one precious commodity for a person's limiting beliefs we know nothing about. Let them take their grudge to the grave and let us take love, peace and happiness to the grave. As Aurelius said, the best revenge is not to be like your enemy.

"Right, now for the wonderful negative meditation technique. What I want you to do once you have stilled your mind is to think of something precious or important to you. Once you have that in mind, think about the worst that could happen. Once we have that, detach ourselves from it and observe it so we can be indifferent to it. Next, if you have a favourite vase, for example, describe it as a lump of clay formed into a water holder. Or your car is a lump of metal that moves you from A to B. By neutralising it, it helps to find your indifference to whatever it is you hold precious when something goes wrong or breaks."

"Does that mean I will never feel emotions should something happen?"

"Sure, you will probably feel a lot of emotion, but as soon as we remember what that object is without the grandiosity attached to it, then it helps to let go of what happened and move on. We can't change it anyway. We may have some extra actions that have come out of what happened, but that's fine. We are here to learn. So, what can we learn from it?

"For this exercise, choose a subject that has some value to you. Afterwards, you can work on something more valuable once you understand how this works. You are on your own for this round and let's say we discuss this in thirty minutes."

"One of the last things we are going to cover today is virtue," The Instructor says. "As we have often discussed, we are not using the modern religious meaning of virtue, but its original meaning of what is good and bad."

"I thought there was no good and bad," a participant asks.

"That's right, there isn't when we consider the Universal rules of duality. We should consider what is a good and bad virtue to help focus our efforts in the right direction for our remaining life. We still have an ego, we still have opinions and no matter how you look at life, we all have beliefs. If we have all these effects happening within us, we need to work with them as best we can. For this discussion, I want you to continue considering duality as we covered in the Major Mystery. Let's put unity aside since very few of us will ever reach that level. We are here and we should consider what we see, hear and feel with neutrality so we can neutrally reflect on what is happening around or within us. By considering virtue as living your life to the full without judgement, criticism and by taking complete responsibility for oneself, then we have a great playing field in front of us. We arrived in this universe with no expectations, but that doesn't mean we can't define our path how we wish. Experiences define our direction in getting the most out of life. My experience with cancer guided me down the psychiatry and spiritual path. Your experiences will guide you too. This is the nearest we can get to the freedom of choice without the direct interference of others."

"Are you saying we don't freely choose our life direction?"

"To date, pretty much all you have achieved based on what you have chosen to do is primarily based on the ideas of others. They tell you in school to work hard and get a job by working for someone else. Some parents tell their children which career direction to take or which goals to have. So-called experts tell you how to invest your money and they tell you what and how to spend your money. In many cases, we trust them implicitly but look how often they are wrong. How many people hate their job, how many have lost their life savings or have gone into liquidation or have fallen ill due to trusting others' advice?

"But how many have considered what is okay to eat when reviewing the chemicals used in foods and see how they are processed? How many have changed career directions because the advised job wasn't giving what was expected? How many people look at money as the primary driver and focus on the next thing to purchase rather than enjoying what they already have? This isn't your virtue; this is someone else's virtue you are living who is happily taking your money for their gain. I have said this before, but we should consider how much of our only limited resource, our time, is worth the sacrifice. Many things are. Many more things aren't.

"We can choose to play a music track repeatedly, but we can't do that with our time. We play each part of our life once and then it dies as quick as it came. We may think we are playing it again, but the day, time and environment are completely different. We are different, too. We only have one chance of that moment and that is now. That is the moment we are living this very second and moving flawlessly to the next. Once that moment is gone, it is gone forever. Remember when we covered death? We said that we were dying all the time. The time you had together for breakfast up to this point is long dead. This sentence you are hearing me say with that part of your life has now died, even though you may be reflecting on what I have just said. For most of us here, more of our life has died that is behind us rather than what is ahead of us.

"When we sacrifice our life to survive in a part of this civilian system, we work and we earn and from our life over seven days, we are permitted just two days to enjoy our life in relative freedom. For the other five days, we sacrifice it to a living mini money-making business god. This god gives us something in return through our dedication of a higher sacrifice to that overseer. A part of this is receiving payment to be primarily used in item exchange to decorate our external life, whether for the self or the benefit of others. The other is creating a misperception of yourself, your values and ideals based on a money giver's interpretation of what makes a good person and what doesn't. That third-person's preferred one-sided view, if taken literally, can restrict how you live your free time in numerous ways.

"If I don't have money, I will be bankrupt and end up homeless," a participant says.

"That's true. Do you get the most out of your job? Do you need and use all the things you have bought with your earnings?"

"My job stinks. And no, I don't use most of the things I buy. I bought them to help me feel better about my miserable situation."

"Are you saying we should do what we love and live life frugally?" another participant asks.

"Ultimately, that choice is yours. What I am saying is, are you happy with the use of your living time sacrifice concerning what you get from it compared to the amount of time you have left on this planet? Are you content with the financial binds you have committed to anonymous industries? Are you content with the marketing strategies they use to convince you to behave in a way you wouldn't have normally done? Are you happy that your doctor can no longer diagnose you because of the undeclared thousands of chemicals used in our food and non-food products? Are you satisfied that those unknown chemicals may result in you having to sacrifice more personal time to gather more money to pay for treatment or even have your life cut short? Are you really happy to trust a faceless and emotionless money-making machine to meet the expectations they want you to achieve?

"Are you?" someone asks.

"I've been bitten by industry through cancer I had endured. Now I read all about what we are consuming and the potential side effects it could have on us. Whether for our bellies, lives, mindsets or external expectations, only we are responsible for what we eat. These industries do not care as long as we worship their products for the exchange of money. Sounds extreme to some, I guess. But let's look at it another way. If you were earning money from others, whether you are a businessperson or politician, it doesn't matter, and the product could be making them ill, you could let it bother you or say that it is not your responsibility to tell others about the potential dangers because it is the purchaser's responsibility to find out themselves, although you trusted the designer to make the product safe. If businesses and politicians are willing to do that because corruption is happening somewhere, where does the responsibility lie?

"With ourselves.... Everything?"

The Instructor smiles and nods.

"So, virtue. What do you want and how do you get it without harming others? Easier said than done after all the conditioning we have gone through, I know. So, before you start resigning from your jobs, let's consider what we can do, even in situations we are not content with. Not everyone will have the chance to live their dream life and not everyone can have the luxuries of retiring early, but we can make the most of what we have.

We have heard the expression 'do what we love', but actually, it's a mashed-up sentence from Steve Jobs 'love what we do'. Why? Because we know from experience that those who do what they love as a career usually quickly end up hating the subject altogether. Whereas, if we love what we do, regardless of what it is, then we can enjoy the process for what it is rather than the result it could give us. We can even hate the subject, but if we love what we do, it is certainly the right step in holding out in that job or activity we don't like or want. Maybe once we start loving what we do, we could find out that the job has some benefits we haven't noticed before. The time used at work is a third of our daily life we invest in the job we are doing and a third of the remaining time is available for use as we see fit. The other third is for sleeping and recovering.

"If we find ways to love what we do, it doesn't matter if it is the most menial job or the most demanding role ahead of us. If we love what we are doing now, then we have a greater chance to take that love home with us. This is much better than those other emotions we have gathered through the day than those unsatisfied thoughts that eventually ruin our free time with daily thoughts that leave us exhausted. It just gives us the potential to snap at the family or whoever is nearby when we take the destructive emotional part of the job home. Because we have the choice, isn't it better to choose wisely how we want something to affect us? It doesn't mean to say any job will not have its moments, but if we look at it as a part of our growth and learning process, it can certainly help us to have a different reflection on our life outside of work that gets carried into our retirement. Remain neutral. Remember, you can moan with a colleague if you aren't moaning internally. That's fine.

"Virtue can lead to happiness, but what is happiness? Some say it is being in the present and taking the moment for what it is. Some say it is harmonising with nature and some say it is altruism in giving to others regardless of the receiver's background. I say it is all three. Why?

"If we really want to, we can always find fault in someone else. I am sure the very first time you came to the minor mystery, most of you had some distrust in someone else based on your inner thoughts about yourselves. But there is another issue I would like to focus on and that is the lives of others. We all have problems and we all project something onto someone else. Some of us play 'the grass is greener on the other side' quite often and we wish to be in the shoes of others. But how many of us would really like to swap lives with someone else because we think they are doing something we wish we could do ourselves? The problem is, rather than considering the person's whole life, we tend to focus on one aspect we think is important. So, my next question to you is, who would swap all their problems for all of someone else's? And this is our next exercise.

"I want each of you to stand up and tell the group all the problems you have or have had in your life—the really bad parts, the frustrating parts and the problems that don't seem to go away. If you wish, include those imagined problems as well as the real ones and don't hold back. As you are listening, ask yourself whether you would be willing to give up your problems in exchange for theirs. Okay, I'll start as I am sure some have thought how great it would be to have the great life I have helping others. Ready…?"

Wow! That was an eye-opener. We all have different life problems that hold us back in some way. I had always thought I was the only one who had it in a bad way. Having listened to the others, I think I will keep my problems, thank you very much! I know them and they don't seem all that bad after comparison.

"Okay, we have come to the end of considering philosophy as a thinking tool, especially Stoicism, on how to help us to think through our mischievous thoughts that occasionally creep up on us, review emotions and how to deal with them. They help us to focus on our lives and how to live life fully with what we have. Naturally, we may have set a high goal to reach, but don't worry if you don't think you are achieving it. Nobody is the perfect stoic. Nobody is the perfect philosopher and there has never been a perfect sage. My opinion is to have a high standard and to do your best to achieve it. Those moments we trip up or lose our composure are moments for reflection and improvement. That is all we can ask of ourselves.

"If you decide to tell others about your new philosophical beliefs, which I advise against, say you are a 'practising stoic' just as we are with everything in life. Nobody knows everything. Some may say stoics are emotionless. Let them think that rather than argue otherwise because you know you are not emotionless. Anyway, arguing isn't for Stoics. As you know, it's not worth the effort to try to convince someone of something they know little about or are convinced of their way of thinking. And lastly, if you do lose your indifference to something, please remember to review it at a suitable time to find out what was bothering you and to adjust your behaviour accordingly."

"Can you give me an example?" a participant asks.

"Let's take money, for example. Most of us want more without knowing how much more would be acceptable. So, when we get more, we are still unhappy because we could still have even more, which is still an open problem. Maybe it is better to imagine you have no money and you have to scrape by, just like the majority of the population. If you can remain happy and content with what little you have, then at some point, should you receive more money, then the chances of remaining content are much higher.

"Can I consider other philosophies or do I have to stick with the Stoics?"

"You can choose what you like. This is just a recommendation. The four big stoic names are Epictetus, Seneca, Markus Aurelius and Musonius Rufus. However, over these last few days, we have included the philosophy of Pythagoras, Critics, other Greek philosophers and some more modern philosophers like Spinoza, Descartes and Hume. If you come across some philosophy that helps you to be virtuous, happy, keep in touch with nature and be indifferent concerning your life experiences, then consider it. Although we have touched on it, it may even be worth reading up on the history of philosophy, how philosophic thinking has changed over the years and what key points are still valid today. Schopenhauer's or Spinoza's viewpoints, for example.

"I have a question, if I may," Hercules asks. The Instructor nods for him to continue. "Hmm, I'm not sure how to ask… okay… We've done intensive work with psychedelics, have learnt the power of the Kybalion, we have learnt how to meditate and are aware of how to rationalise our emotions through philosophy. Can I combine them or do I have to keep them separate? What I mean is, can I still use psychedelics with active meditation for working through any issues I have with the philosophic models we have learnt?"

"That's a good question," The Instructor says. "With entheogens, we switch off our Ego to work at a deeper level quickly and effectively. You can also philosophise your visions and learnings while participating in that session, just like if we choose to use active meditation instead. Keeping the principles of the Kybalion in mind helps to rationalise and remain neutral when we have experienced indifferences. Let me explain what I do. Daily, I work through problems or lack with active meditation and philosophical thinking as per Pythagoras' morning and evening questions. This helps me in the majority of cases. I have a friend whom I trust and discuss some deeper challenges now and again. I also have my partner to discuss and work things through if I am not sure, which is always my starting point. If you can, I recommend you find someone you can openly trust and talk to. If not, remember the technique for working through issues alone. One thing I do yearly is to use psychedelics to help tidy some things I may have consciously overlooked, and that's it.

"At the end of today, you will re-enter the real world with real problems. You are now at a wonderful starting point where you have enough tools to deal with everyday problems. So, Steve, combine as you see what works for you. If you find another tool more effective in dealing with whatever may come your way, use it. There's no right or wrong. The tool is the messenger, nothing else. Any other questions?"

No one asked anything else after Hercules' question.

"Right. That's it for this part of the course. I hope you have enjoyed this as much as I have. You have learnt a lot and I recommend you read further as we haven't managed to cover everything. Also, practice the exercises further until they become second nature. A personal note from me is to thank you for having faith in me to learn how to deal with your mental troubles. I am still reachable if you need me. However, until then, enjoy your new life with your newly gathered and much-needed resources. Remember to enjoy those oncoming crossroads in life because it is these moments that take you to the next level on your life-long journey and being completely responsible and committed to your decision is important for the type of consequence you receive the next moment."

I have to say, these last days have been astounding.

The Bistro

After the course, Marie, Herc and I head back to the nearest city to discuss this further. This is accompanied by a good strong coffee and a lovely sandwich in the same place as before.

"How do you feel after this philosophy course?" I ask them both. I take a sip from my much-needed coffee.

"Full of hope!" Marie says. "I have new tools to help keep my thoughts rational. It's interesting, I could never calm my mind down, but this has shown me how to think and has given me something to help me reflect on the key things to help me remain neutral. I see why he did this part of the course last."

Hercules, and I both nod in agreement.

"I feel there is a life ahead of me," I say. "Only I'm still not sure what I will do with it."

"What about your book?" Hercules asks.

"Oh, I'm going to carry on with that idea. I think it's good to document how it has changed my life. But I'm not sure what else I need to do afterwards. I want to do something worthwhile and find out what that is." I take a bite of my sandwich. "What about you, Herc?" I ask with a full mouth.

"For the first time in a long time, that's an easier question to answer. I intend to help veterans who suffer from military trauma. I can't do what The Instructor did with psychedelics, but I can support and guide them to consider the other tools we have learnt."

"What about yourself?" I ask. "What are you going to do for yourself?"

"Oh… I thought that was about me. That's where I want to direct my energy."

"Maybe you are right," I reply. "What I meant was, what are you going to do for yourself, just you?"

"Well, I need to build up my partner's trust in me and I can only do that through being that person she needs in her life. I need to give her the confidence that she is safe with me. I want her to be a part of my life, day and night."

"Cool!" I say. "Let's raise our cups to our new lives."

We chink them together and toast the start of our new beginning. Our rebirth has started to become a part of reality. As an active part of the Universe, our life is now taking a different direction. I have the tools, resources and the Universe behind me that gives me exactly what I ask for. I am ready for what life can throw at me.

The Beginning, Not 'The End'

More than a year later, Hercules, aka Steve, Marie and I meet up. Herc has started actively helping ex-service personnel who suffer from PTSD. He helps them through the day using meditation using a few other techniques The Instructor has shown him. For those who want to go further in releasing their trauma, he recommends a visit with The Instructor to determine if they are suitable and trustable for the Mystery sessions. The problem is that psychedelics are still illegal here and each person needs to be vetted properly.

The first thing we noticed about Marie is that she has lost so much weight. She has a bounce in her step and looks so radiant. She is helping troubled women through an established charity. These women have undergone some form of abuse from a partner, parent or in someone else's hands, usually more than once. Just as with military personnel, some women suffer the worst form of PTSD from such terrible and cowardly treatment. Marie helps the women build a stronger and more independent relationship with themselves, believe in themselves more and live with less fear. When she thinks they can cope and are responsible enough for the next stage, she advises, just like Herc, to meet up with The Instructor. She tells me that some have taken part and have worked through their past trauma with great results.

As for me, Herc asked me to help him set up his help centre and I'm now one of his key team members. I left my hometown and have temporarily moved into the spare room he was once using. His lovely girlfriend has been a great support and has accepted me with open arms into their home.

Herc is funding this project through private sponsors because the government rejected his application for support. They showed no interest. The only option the government offers is telling traumatised veterans to visit a doctor to access various types of medication that seem to cause more problems than help. Politicians are willing to put these brave soldiers through absolute hell for some resource or egomaniacal point and to put them through hell again with numbing medications for whatever reasons that don't make sense to man or beast.

Is this a conspiracy theory or are we educated to make us believe it's a conspiracy? I believe the government supports the pharma industry and its need for financial backhanders more than those who voted them into power. It is these voters who can't contribute anything more than the enforced taxes we have to pay that lose out the most. And that's wrong. Maybe a public vote isn't as influential anymore to a politician as the inner authority or egotistical megalomaniac thoughts they experience when they receive a significant back payment from some industry influencer. I think we are now in a world where we can no longer truly trust the government's advice but we have to take on the responsibility ourselves to find out what works and what are marketed profit-only schemes.

If psychedelics were legal, we wouldn't have as many people suffering from PTSD, nor would people with other mental illnesses fill up institutions and hospital beds, scaring the locals and putting unnecessary pressure on our policing services. I don't think we could reach a mentally illness-free world with how industry controls our consumption of undeclared chemicals. Still, after a couple of generations of proper governmental regulation, our health options could be much, much better and cheaper than it already is. In the future, maybe a politician's abilities should be rated against levels of fear being produced by the government. The higher the fear the civilian experiences, the more incompetent and greedier the politician has become. Today, fear is the key to mass industrial manipulation for profit. Without it, it would be a great start in creating a more peaceful and calm society.

Anyway, I'm moving out of Herc's place next month. I have met a wonderful girlfriend who is one of Herc's ex-military colleagues. She has completed The Instructor's Eleusinian Mysteries and the stoicism training and has since started a business unrelated to psychedelics. Also, with this new inner freedom, she is loving life. Even with me, I'm besotted with her! She is helping me to grow in other areas of my life and she tells me I am helping her grow, too. I don't know if our relationship will last, but we have agreed we will live and enjoy each other's time and company until we know otherwise. I can live with that and contentedly so.

The other thing Herc, Marie and I are doing is helping The Instructor during other group mystery sessions when the participants have taken their psychedelic dose. It is an honour and humbling to watch those nervous participants take the first taste of those special mushrooms and enter into another dimensional portal and come out different on the other side. Most participants are entirely released in the first round and don't need any more sessions. However, some need another round or two to remove those extra blockages. As The Instructor says, that is okay because more layers need to be worked through one at a time. Occasionally, a participant can have a battle getting through a session and will never do it again. Fortunately, this doesn't happen so often, but as we know, no two sessions are the same, and this way may not be for everyone. That is fair enough. Although it is a powerful one, it is only a tool, after all.

My main project has been writing this book and since you are reading it, it's finished and released. I am sure there will be some strong resistance to the subject of psychedelics. With the book, too, because I am sure some readers will say that it doesn't go deep enough. That is my fault. It is a difficult subject to put in words that I am not skilled enough to give it the justification it deserves, so I apologise to those it offends.

Still, if this book helps one person discover a new tool, psychedelics or otherwise, that helps them to get their life back, then the risk has been worth it. I know it's a risk to communicate to the world what potential psychedelics can offer, especially in a country where psychedelics are forbidden in favour of anonymous pharma industries and corrupt politicians increase their profits at the detriment of medicinal and potentially life-inhibiting side effects.

The last thing I want to do is to update you on some of the participants' progress from the Minor and Major sessions:

Jim had carried a mass of guilt due to the untimely death of his girlfriend. He completed the Major Mystery with us and said, "I still remember what happened and I still respect the consequence I caused. I have grown to respect that we all have some history we may not understand. I'm still single as I don't feel ready for another relationship. Yet, I am open to whatever happens in the future." What a great new start for him.

Arthur is a middle-aged man who suffered a near-death experience while in surgery. The consequence was that it had stopped him from living his life because he had feared imminent death. A short while after completing the Minor Mystery session, Arthur focussed on his health and fitness. He has dropped his excess weight and goes to a gym most days. He says he doesn't need to do the major mystery.

Zoe's husband completed the Minor Mystery session a few months after her death. He told us that this helped to deal with her loss. He says that in the session, Zoe told him that she is back home in the Universe and preparing herself for her next adventure. She told him to enjoy life as it is the only one we get as the person we are. Nobody is perfect, so enjoy what you have. She told him we may even discover a quality we never knew existed and would be a shame to waste it by wishing we were someone else.

Simone had doubted her blinkered religious tendencies and wanted to test her faith. When I spoke to her last week, she told me she had left her church because it was frowned upon to question it. However, Simone has joined a different religious group that is more open and critical to other interpretations and spends her free time reading other texts to help her understand the hidden meanings found in the bible. Also, Simone confirmed that The Instructor was correct about the bible's mistranslations and had guided her towards the Sinai bible too. Apparently, this is an older version of the King James version, but that doesn't mean much. As Simone said, she found at least thirty different versions of the bible. As she said, if any, which is the correct version if she has so many to choose from? I suppose that much be similar to choosing a god to worship when there are more than three thousand currently worshipped. I understand why The Instructor pointed her towards the Sinai bible since there is much more information in there than in any of the newer translations that have been left out completely. Her research continues and she would like to write a book on the different bible variations and how they can be used as a useful psychological tool instead of being used as a historical timeline or for selective oppression.

Simone told me that The Instructor provided her with a lot of extra information, including sources, contacts and other reading material to start her on her way.

Previously, Simone hadn't participated in the philosophical session because it conflicted with her religious beliefs. Why? In Christianity, it is encouraged not to question anything in the bible or otherwise, whereas philosophy questions everything. However, she tells me she will participate later as she wants to understand that the philosophical way of thinking may help her research further. I hope these changes in her life bring her towards her goal and she finds what she was truly looking for.

Helga is back in Germany and is rightfully living a life without any historical guilt. Her old problem has been dealt with and her country's history belongs to a generation she wasn't a part of. Helga said the one thing she can do is to ensure the past doesn't happen again with the government trying to separate the people through conflicting opinions without backed information sources. She is involved with protests when she feels her government responds to something that could reflect a return to those older and darker days of mass population control. Helga has my respect for standing up for what she believes.

Tom had his life in order and is still enjoying it. He still takes psychedelics but no longer does it with The Instructor. He said he has learnt how to prepare himself by getting the right setting and knows how to put his question forward to what he calls 'the Universal Spirit'. He was content with life when I first met him. However, I don't know why he initially participated in his first Minor Mystery session. Nevertheless, it is a superb continuation of his personal growth and understanding of the Universal powers.

Ben and Bill are the two that interest me the most and we are still in regular contact. Bill managed to overcome his drinking after that second session I attended. Ben still struggles with alcohol more out of routine than anything else. One thing they are doing is enjoying their inner peace a little more. Being in their early fifties and with no work experience, they occasionally help out at a shelter for the homeless and help support other alcoholics where they can. Ben tells me that one lovely aspect that these sessions have given is mental quiet. They still have an inner voice, but it is a friendlier one they can work with. I can relate to that. This is a huge step forward for two painfully shy people who have had nothing to live for, for many years.

The Instructor knows I am writing this book and reminds me that successfully breaking an addiction using psychedelics is around 70%. In contrast, the success rate with Alcoholics Anonymous is between 5% and 10%. Yet, psychedelics are illegal! You know what I have had to say about that. I'm not getting on my high horse again to complain about our government that still wants to keep hold of racist idealism and pharmaceutical industry profits in preference for the population's mental health...

And that's it. I could not reach the remaining participants or they didn't want to participate in the book. I respect that.

My book has been released. How do I know? You are reading it! As I have said earlier, I hope you get something out of this from what I have experienced here. However, I appreciate that I have intentionally (and I guess unintentionally on some occasions) left a lot of information out. There is no one answer to anything when healing ourselves from our past. I think we need to research and work with experts who know what other options are available should one option is not as helpful as one initially hoped. By working with an expert, the expert can ask questions and guide or provoke the mind to think differently. The expert knows nothing about what you need to release the problem. Only you do. What they can do for us is recommend different tools or prompt us with questions we need to be made aware of. Even doing nothing is doing something and an expert shaman should know when the right place to use that tool too.

Good-Bye

The present is all we have. The past is just a collection of dead memories of a life we once lived. Our present defines our past. Our future is a blank canvas that should not be painted by the past but to help create our freedom based on the release of our past. The future is fantasy and other than some planning on what could happen or what we want to achieve, we have no control over what we come face to face with. All we can and should do is make the most of the present and enjoy what we can while we can. That includes the things we hate or make us emotional since this is an experience we can learn from. And that's the wonderful thing, too, no two lessons are the same.

Instead, we sacrifice this most precious piece of time for the most fearful fantasies that, in the end, do not happen. And if they do, there is usually another way forward to the one we planned over the previous days, weeks or even years. One door closes and another opens. Finding and recognising that open door can be a major challenge for some. I appreciate that saying something as simple as this can be difficult to swallow when a life's work or relationship is about to be lost somehow.

As I have learnt, it is perfectly okay to live through the pain and keep the memories. Just as it is perfectly okay to have a part of them in your heart and to use that experience to live your life in the fullest and most free way possible. We are educated to earn and to yearn to be surrounded by luxurious things as some status symbol of success or achievement that has been defined by someone we don't know. And it is that someone we don't know welcomes your hard-earned money in their bank account for their product that will most probably be forgotten relatively quickly. Still, if we can live without those yearned things and enjoy what we have at this very moment, because we may never manage to achieve more than what we have, we are certainly not wasting our time on a fantasy that expects us to sacrifice more of our limited personal time that defines our short and undefined life on this planet. Unless we want to, of course. Not every sacrifice has the same value. Ultimately, only you can decide...

Afterword

Since finishing the book and using the extra information I received from The Instructor, it encouraged me to dig around for some more supportive information. This is, by no means, a complete source. Please consider it a starting point if you wish to review some of these materials and tools further:

Redemption:
Hallucinogens and Redemption by Marlene Dobkin de Rios, Charles S Grob, John R Baker, Dr Phil.

Mistranslations:
Regarding biblical mistranslations, there is a fair bit of information out there. If you wish to research this further, there are several textbooks on the subject, and I recommend you search out what you are looking for. However, to start the ball rolling, here are a couple of links.

The Sinai bible is an important source of reference that is often overlooked:
https://www.codexsinaiticus.org/en/

This is not of interest to me but if anyone is interested in comparing the differences between the Sinai and KJV bible, there is a lot of information available. Here is a simple discussion on the subject:
https://restlesspilgrim.net/blog/2016/01/10/sinai-vs-kjv/

Lucifer:
Wikipedia is a good starting point.
https://en.wikipedia.org/wiki/Lucifer
This link focuses on the mistranslation of the Latin word 'lucifer.'

The Instructor spoke a lot about the contradictions in the bible. This is not of interest to me, but it is interesting to see how many conflicting pieces of information there are within this book: http://www.lyingforjesus.org/Bible-Contradictions/?fbclid=IwAR0EycBZ17ya6EpsMJqokK_1Tg0 Pcuc0oMKleQ3cIs9PYMZ1kAAuuOyvLZ0

By going back even further to the Greek scripts before the bible's protagonist and antagonist were even considered: https://www.abarim-publications.com/Meaning/Lucifer.html#.XpA4ivj7Tb0

This link goes on to explain other mistranslations from Hebrew into English: https://www.franknelte.net/article.php?article_id=218

I have chosen one aspect of the Bible's misinterpretations. However, there is plenty of information out there on the others. This work includes how psychedelics were used within the church in its heyday and how they are overlooked today. Some material is still found on the walls, doors and artwork within churches and other books. A great starting point is:

The Psychedelic Gospels by Jerry and Julie Brown.

Regarding Hermetics, *The Kybalion* by the Three Initiates is a brilliant short book to read on the seven. Universal laws and I have reread this several times since completing the Major Mystery. I have included *Summum. Sealed Except to the Open Mind* by Summum Bonum Amen Ra because some may find the more modern English easier to read.

The Instructor mentioned other works of Neville Goddard, Krishnamurti, Alan Watts, Eckhard Tolle, Ram Dass, Almaas, Vadim Zeland, Blavatsky, Florence Scovell Shinn and others. I haven't included a list of their books because they are too numerous. I think it is worth checking them out on the internet or at your local bookshop to find out which ones appeal the most to you.

Meister Eckhard:
His works are an excellent read for all. In the 16th century, this bishop went against the pope to explain God and spirituality rather than being used as a tool for control and manipulation. His work is still reflected upon and highly respected today.

Active Meditation:
After the course, I discovered the Silva Method in getting into the Alpha. The Instructor tells me his system is similar to Silva's method.
http://www.silvalifesystem.com/free-lessons

Eleusis:
For further information on the Eleusinian Mysteries, there is a small but excellent collection of information regarding Eleusis and the Mysteries. This is by no means complete and in no particular order:

The Road to Eleusis by Gordon Wasson
Mysteries of Eleusis by Margaret Doody
Bronze Age Eleusis and the Origins of the Eleusinian Mysteries by Michael Cosmopoulos
Eleusis and the Eleusinian Mysteries by Goerge Mylonas
Sacred Mushrooms: Secrets of Eleusis by Carl Ruck
The Rites of Eleusis by Aleister Crowley
The Eleusinian Mysteries and Rites by Dudley Wright

YouTube:
The   Sacred   Way:
https://www.youtube.com/watch?v=A4LOEZMGMJ8

Eleusis: The   Great   Mysteries:
https://www.youtube.com/watch?v=iaprpVwW-QU

Albert   Hoffmann   –   LSD,   and   the   Road   to   Eleusis:
https://www.youtube.com/watch?v=_nx2hJ7ue_c

Time-Line and NLP:

The Instructors instruction on Time-Line fits nicely with the book from Tad James, *Time Line Therapy,* which works well on the subject of NLP. Because I have no experience with NLP, I will not recommend anything from the mass of information out there. I will say that NLP was initially developed by Bandler and Grinder and maybe it is worth starting with their material. Maybe you prefer something more appealing from another expert. I don't know what to recommend, this field is amazingly large.

Alcoholics Anonymous:
Regarding the AA (Alcoholics Anonymous) and its history, I was surprised to find out The Instructor was right about the ineffectiveness of the AA. The Instructor recommended reading the book *The Sober Truth* by Lance Dodes and Zachary Dodes. I appreciate that the AA has helped around five to ten per cent of attending participants and has managed to find a life without alcohol. Full respect for them. I guess, like any addiction, if one doesn't feel ready to quit, then no programme will help.
Philosophy is still my weakest area in all that I have learnt because there is so much material to read. I do, however, recommend a few books, starting with the Greeks.

Pythagoras:
Pythagoras' Verses is a great booklet on his philosophy on life and is reflected in Stoicism.

Stoicism:
Stoicism can be a challenging read without any background knowledge, so it might be worth reading *The Practicing Stoic* by Ward Farnsworth first. This doesn't cover everything, but it does help to get an overall understanding before reading up on the big four (Epictetus, Seneca, Rufus and Aurelius). On the last day of the course, The Instructor mentioned some criticisms of stoicism. I couldn't remember exactly what The Instructor had said, so I focussed on a couple of points I thought were important from the book by Farnsworth in the story above. Naturally, I am not a philosopher and cannot put those points across as wonderful as he did.

I had trouble reading the material from the big four and searched for several sources to help me understand what they were saying about how to live a stoic life. It isn't easy and it was a relief to read that even the most stoic of stoics is or was never a perfect stoic. Introducing this into my life is a conscious effort that I review twice daily. In case you are asking, does this stop me from living my life? No, I am living the life I deserve, the quality of my life is amazing and the love I have for those around me is immense. I know we all have a history and we all say and do stupid things we thought were right or intended to make us happy. If we can learn from it and do or say it differently the next time it could occur, is a steady way to make progress in our journey. If we are not careful with our thoughts and actions, they can eventually work against us and could eventually lead us to a life of isolation and bitterness. Who would have guessed that philosophy is the psychology of the mind?

The Rules of Being Human:
The Instructor brought up some work written in Sanskrit called "The Rules of Being Human". I have dropped hints about this in the story. However, I think it is worthwhile including them all.

After the session, I searched the internet for more information. The text in capitals is a translation from Sanskrit. The following text is helpful notes to understand the rules better. Here are the nine rules:

1. YOU WILL RECEIVE A BODY.
You may like it or not, but it will be yours for the entire period round.
2. YOU WILL LEARN LESSONS.
You are enrolled in a full-time informal school called life. Each day in this school you will have the opportunity to learn lessons. You may like the lessons or think them irrelevant and stupid.
3. THERE ARE NO MISTAKES, ONLY LESSONS.
Growth is a process of trial and error and experimentation. The 'failed' experiments are as much a part of the process as the experiment that ultimately works.
4. A LESSON IS REPEATED UNTIL IT IS LEARNED.

A lesson will be presented to you in various forms until you have learned it, then you can go to the next lesson.

5. LEARNING LESSONS DOES NOT END.

There is no part of life that does not contain its lessons. If you are alive, there are lessons to be learned.

6. 'THERE' IS NO BETTER THAN 'HERE.'

When you're 'there' has become 'here', you will simply see another 'there' that will again look better than 'here'.

7. OTHERS ARE MERELY MIRRORS OF YOU.

You cannot love or hate something about another unless it reflects something you love or hate yourself.

8. WHAT YOU MAKE OF YOUR LIFE IS UP TO YOU.

You have all the tools and resources you need, what you do with them is up to you. The choice is yours.

9. THE ANSWERS LIE INSIDE YOU.

The answers to life's questions lie inside you. All you need to do is look, listen and trust.

Some may argue there are 10 or 12 rules. It doesn't matter if you like the other rules, include them. I started with these nine and agree with the other three if you wish to search them out. A helpful book on these (ten) rules in approaching this further, if you are struggling, is, *Life Is A Game, These Are The Rules* by Cherie Carter-Scott.

I am sure I have overlooked some information you found interesting in this book. A quick search on the Internet will, I am sure, bring you the necessary information you need.

Symboles

Pli vallée (vers le haut).
Pli montagne (vers le bas).
Ligne de pli.

Plie dans cette direction.

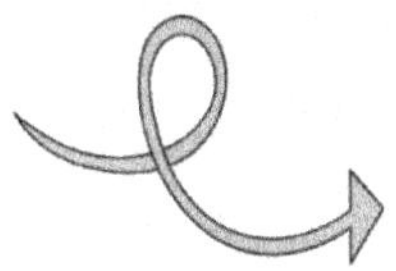

Retourne.

Plie en zigzag.

Montre le résultat après chaque étape.

Feuille carrée

Feuille rectangulaire

Feuille pentagonale

Toutes les feuilles ont deux couleurs pour mieux différencier chaque étape.

Feuille pentagonale

Tu auras besoin d'une feuille en forme de pentagone (une feuille de papier à cinq côtés) pour réaliser l'un des modèles de ce livre. Ne t'inquiète pas, il est très facile d'en faire une à partir d'une feuille carrée. Voici comment procéder :

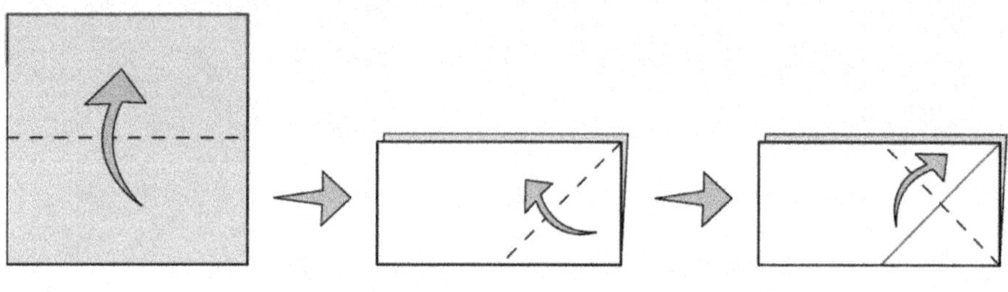

Étape 1

Plie la feuille de papier en deux.

Étape 2

Plie le coin inférieur droit en diagonale vers le haut, puis déplie-le. Répète l'opération avec le coin supérieur droit.

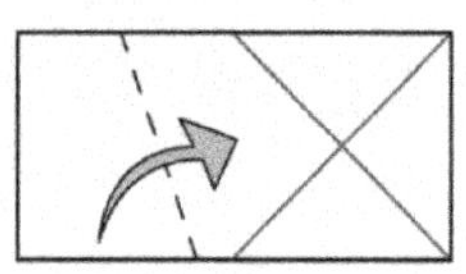

Étape 3

Rabats le coin inférieur gauche au point où les deux plis que tu viens de faire se rejoignent.

Étape 4

Plie le même coin vers l'extérieur comme indiqué sur le dessin.

Feuille pentagonale

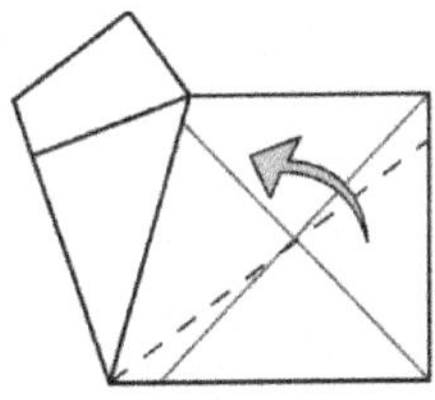  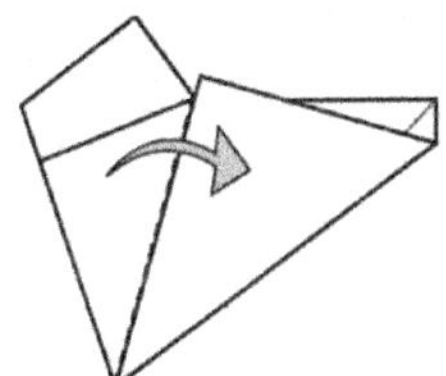

Étape 5

Plie le coin inférieur droit le long
de la ligne qui va du coin inférieur
gauche au point où les plis de
l'étape 2 se rejoignent.

Étape 6

Plie la figure vers l'arrière le
long du bord du rabat que tu
viens de faire.

Étape 7

Découpe le long de la ligne
indiquée sur le dessin.

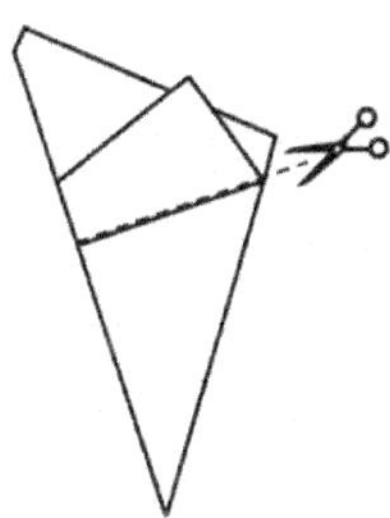

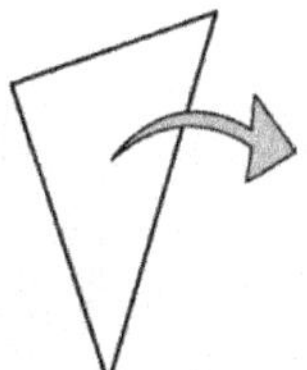

Étape 8

Déplie le tout.

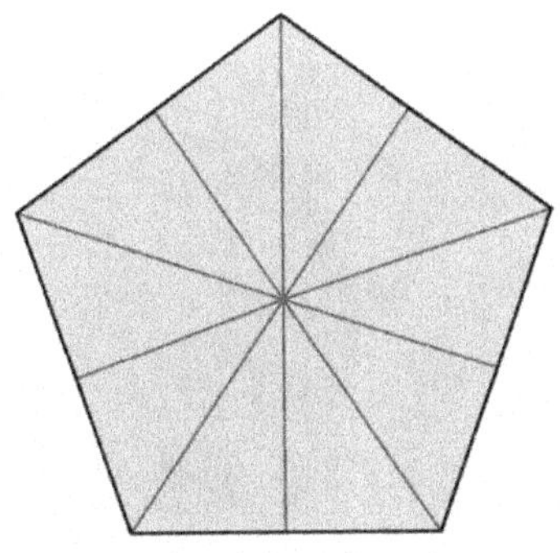

Feuille pentagonale

Feuille de houx

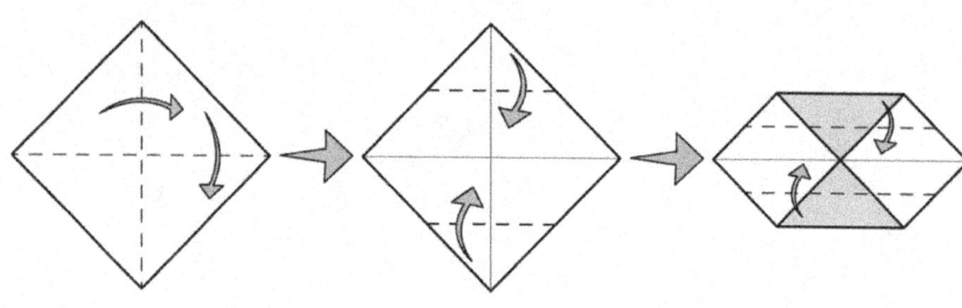

Étape 1

Plie la feuille le long des deux diagonales, puis déplie-la.

Étape 2

Rabats les coins du haut et du bas vers le centre de la feuille.

Étape 3

Rabats les bords du haut et du bas sur la ligne horizontale de l'étape 1.

Étape 4

Plie la moitié gauche de la figure en diagonale, comme indiqué sur le dessin.

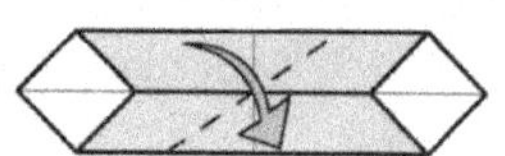

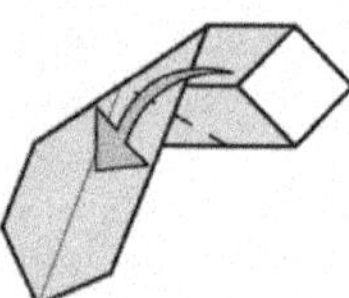

Étape 5

Rabats le côté droit de l'autre côté, comme indiqué sur le dessin.

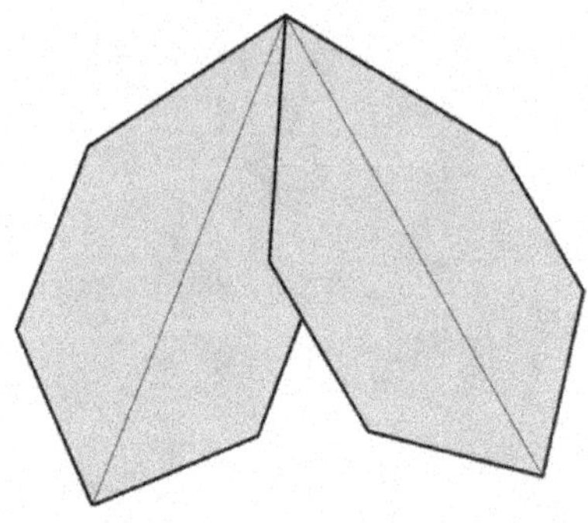

Feuille de houx

Bougie

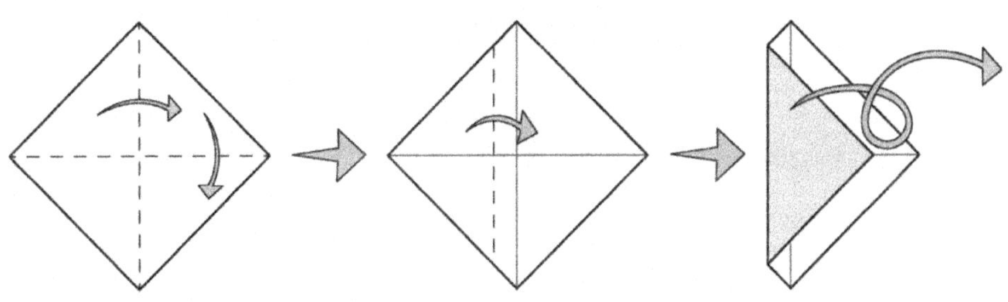

Étape 1

Plie la feuille le long des deux diagonales, puis déplie-la.

Étape 2

Rabats le coin gauche vers l'intérieur en laissant un petit espace entre ce pli et le pli vertical que tu viens de faire. Retourne ensuite la figure.

Étape 3

Plie la figure sur elle-même encore et encore comme indiqué sur le dessin. Rabats ensuite le coin inférieur vers le haut.

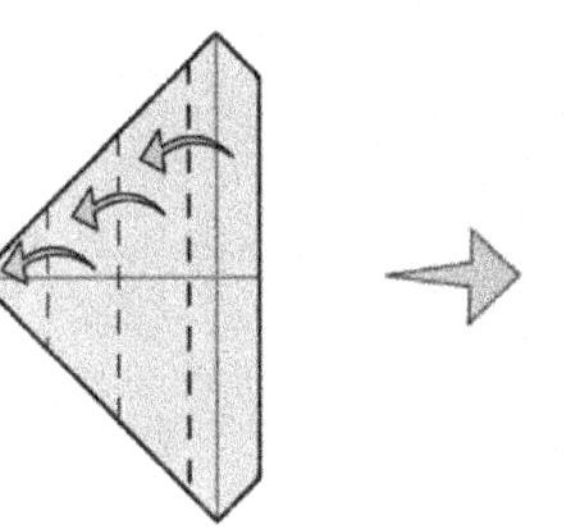

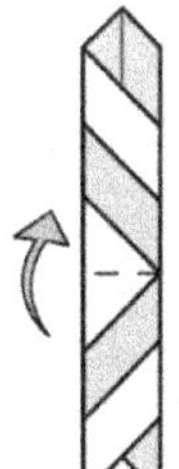

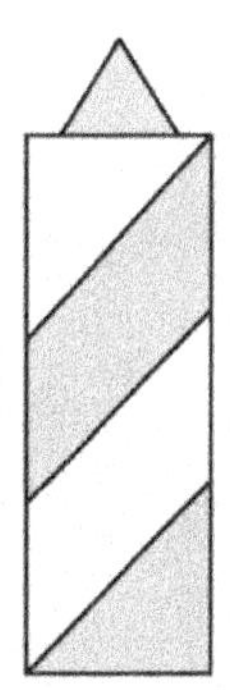

Étape 4

Plie la figure en deux, puis rabats les côtés du coin supérieur vers l'arrière, comme indiqué sur le dessin.

Sucre d'orge

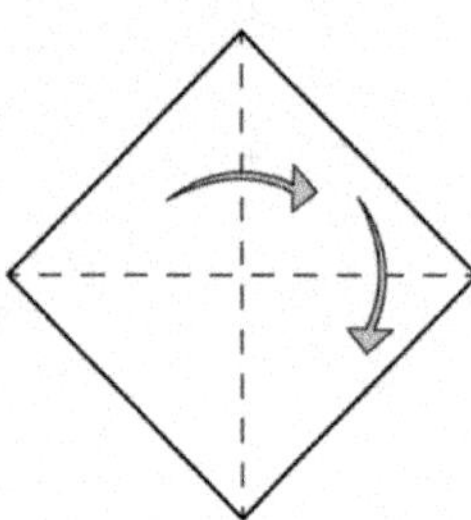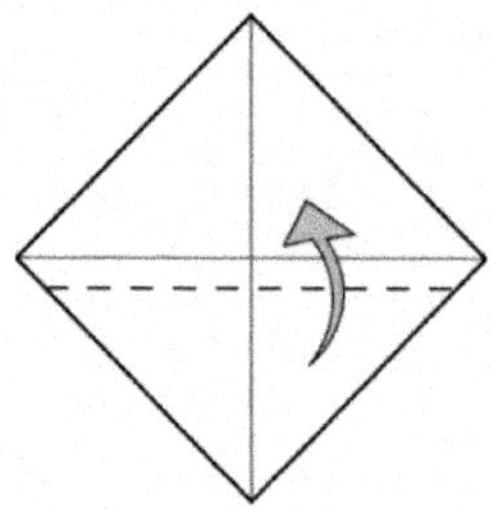

Étape 1

Plie la feuille le long des deux diagonales, puis déplie-la.

Étape 2

Plie le coin inférieur vers le haut en laissant un petit espace entre ce pli et le pli horizontal que tu viens de faire.

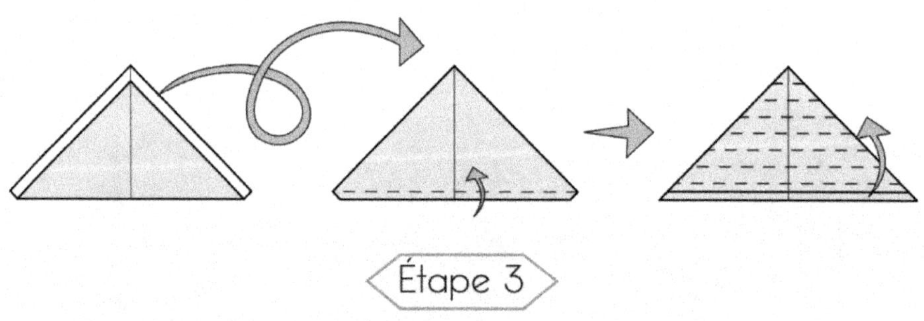

Étape 3

Retourne la figure, puis plie-la sur elle-même encore et encore comme indiqué sur le dessin.

Sucre d'orge

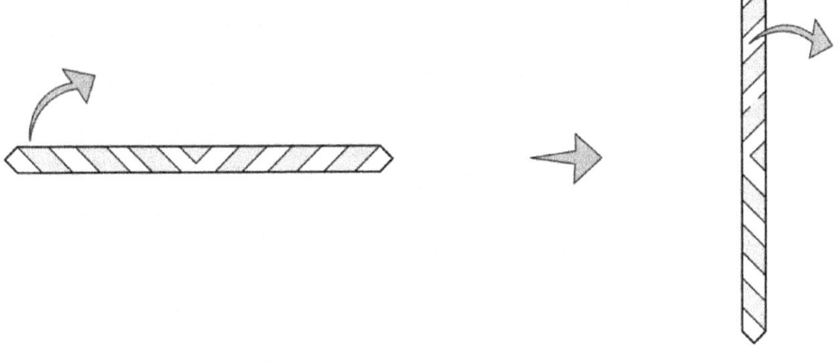

Fais pivoter la figure comme indiqué sur le dessin et plie son sommet en diagonale vers le bas, de sorte qu'elle se retrouve à l'horizontale.

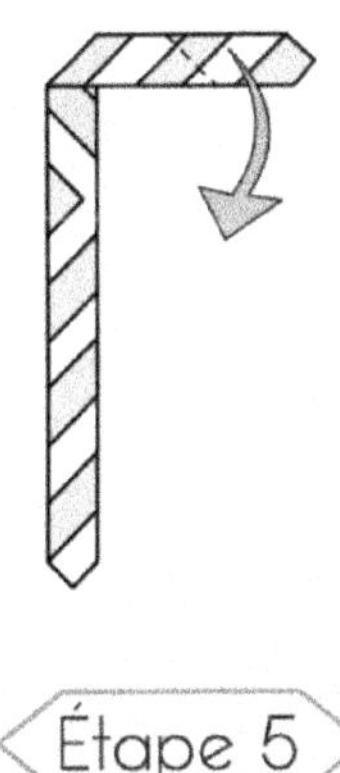

Étape 5

Plie la pointe de cette même section en diagonale vers le bas et vers l'arrière, comme indiqué sur le dessin.

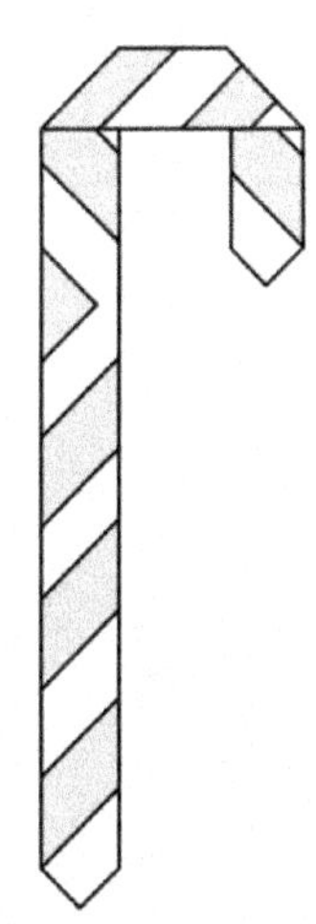

Sucre d'orge

Sapin de Noël

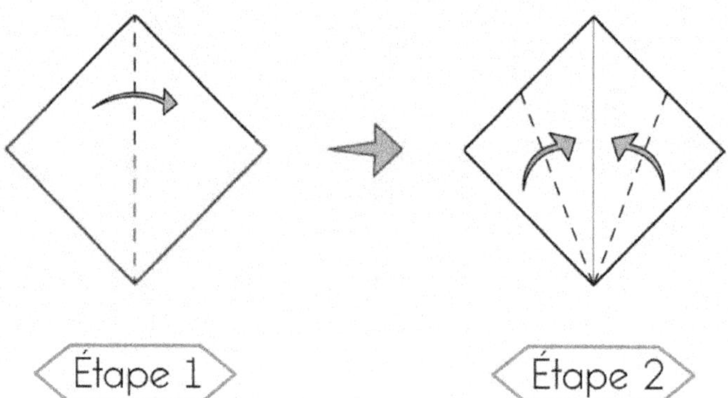

Étape 1

Plie la feuille de papier en diagonale, puis déplie-la pour former un pli.

Étape 2

Rabats les deux coins latéraux jusqu'à cette ligne médiane verticale.

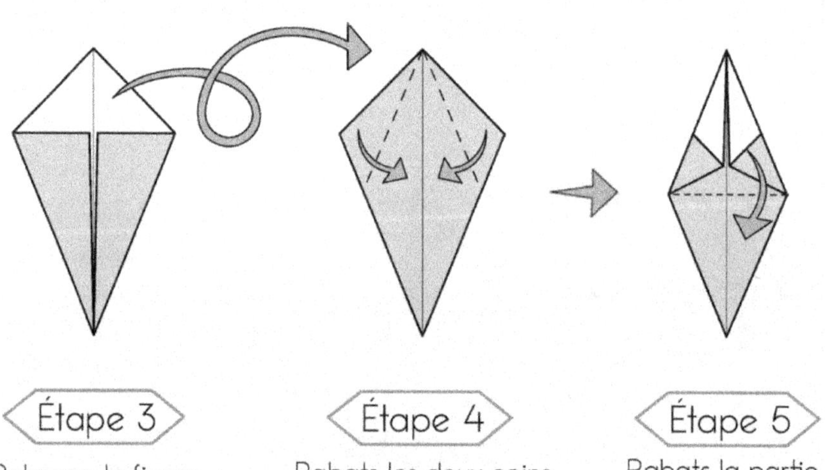

Étape 3

Retourne la figure.

Étape 4

Rabats les deux coins latéraux jusqu'à la ligne médiane verticale.

Étape 5

Rabats la partie inférieure de la figure vers l'arrière.

Sapin de Noël

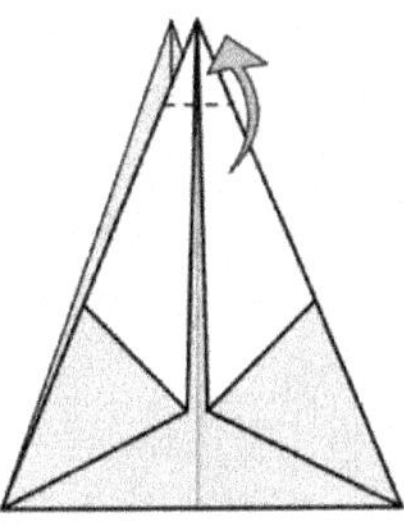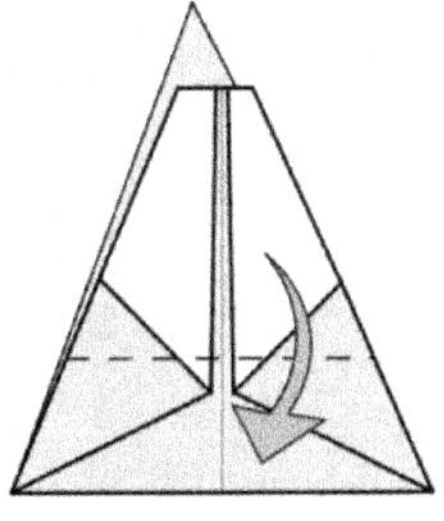

Étape 6

Plie la pointe de la couche supérieure comme indiqué sur le dessin.

Étape 7

Rabats la partie supérieure vers le bas comme indiqué sur le dessin.

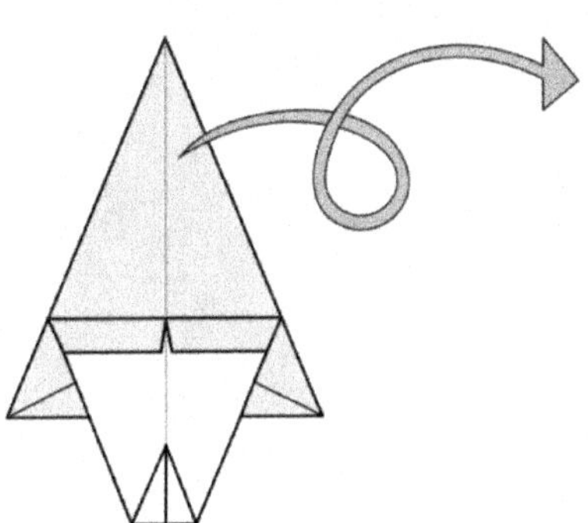

Étape 8

Retourne la figure.

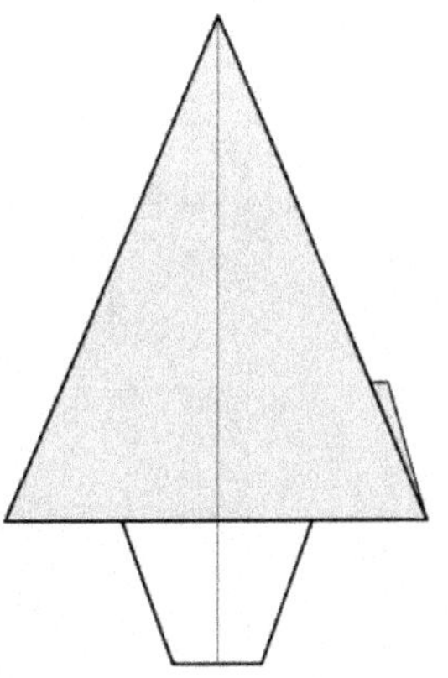

Sapin de Noël

Cloche

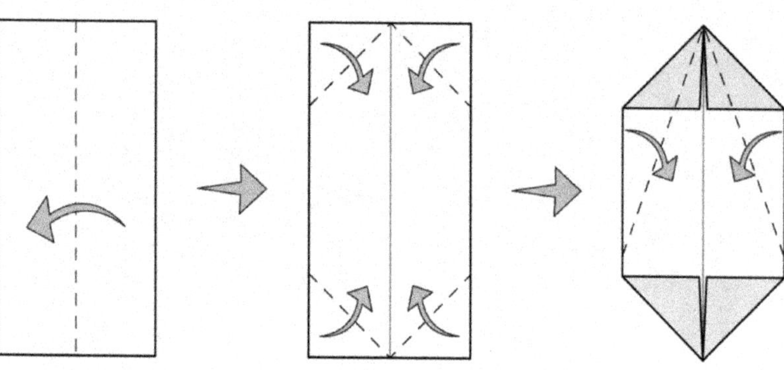

Étape 1

Prends une feuille rectangulaire (de la moitié de la taille d'une feuille A4) et plie-la en deux dans le sens de la longueur pour former un pli.

Étape 2

Plie tous les coins en diagonale jusqu'à la ligne médiane verticale.

Étape 3

Rabats le haut des deux côtés vers la ligne médiane verticale, comme indiqué sur le dessin.

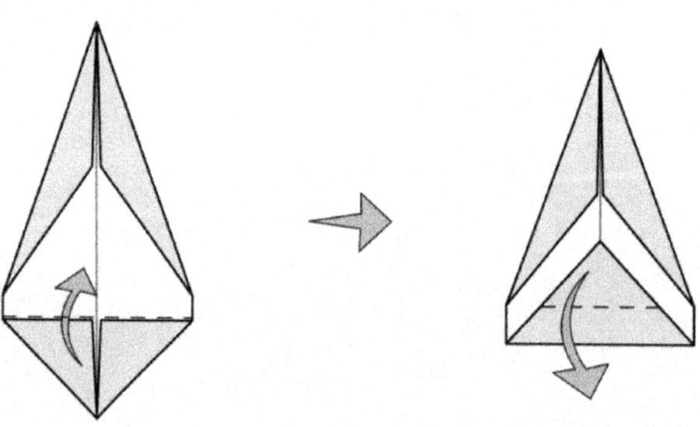

Étape 4

Plie le coin inférieur vers le haut, juste au-dessus des rabats de l'étape 2. Puis replie-le comme indiqué sur le dessin.

Cloche

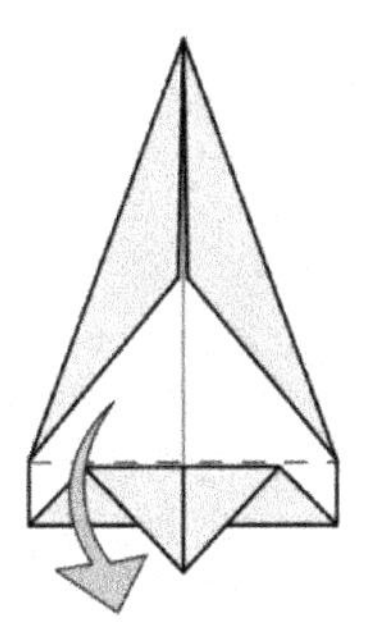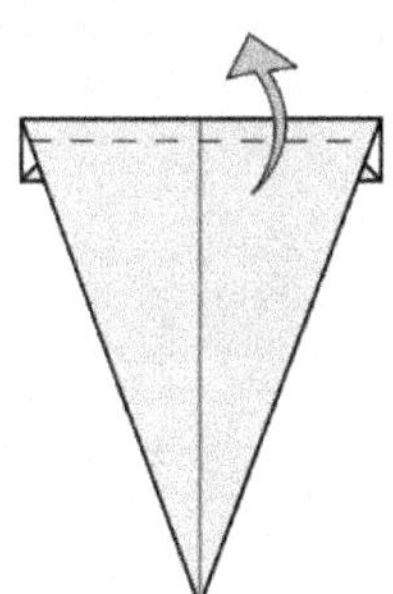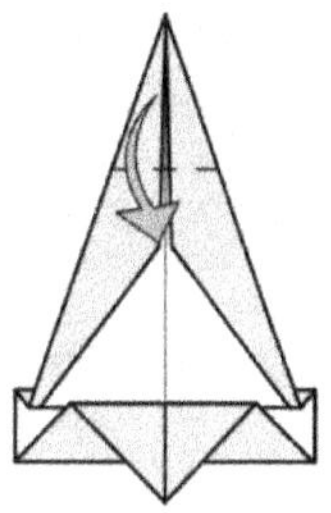

Étape 5

Maintenant, plie le haut de la figure vers le bas, juste au-dessus du rabat que tu viens de faire.

Étape 6

Plie-le à nouveau vers le haut en laissant un petit espace entre les deux plis.

Étape 7

Rabats le coin supérieur comme indiqué sur le dessin.

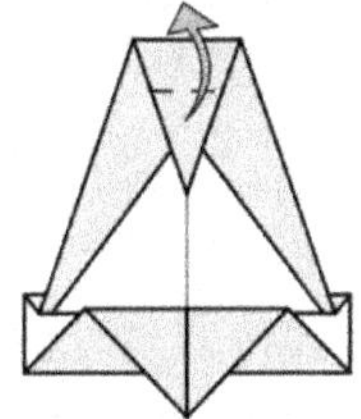

Étape 8

Ensuite, rabats-le dans l'autre sens comme indiqué sur le dessin.

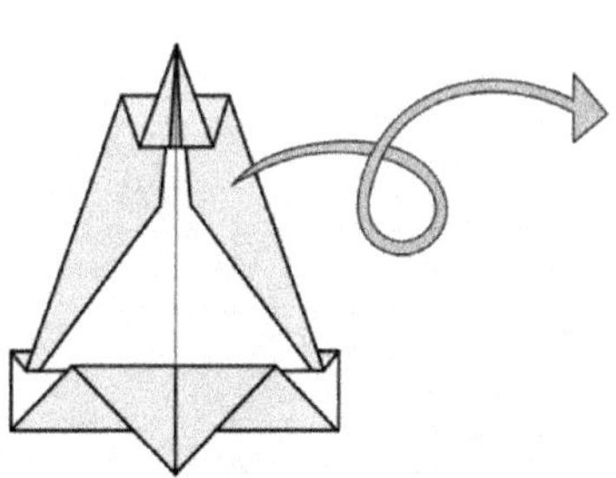

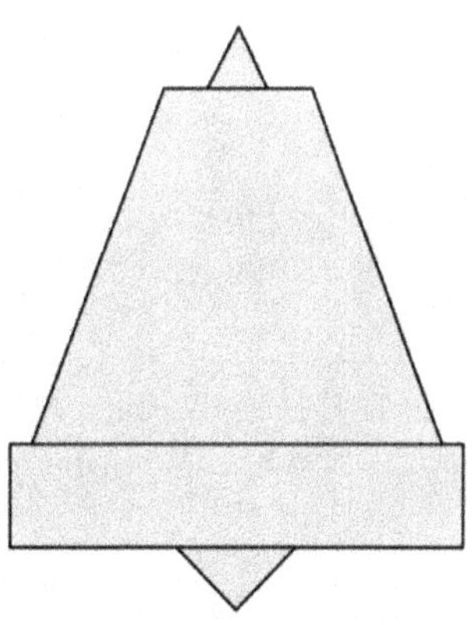

Étape 9

Retourne la figure.

Cloche

Couronne

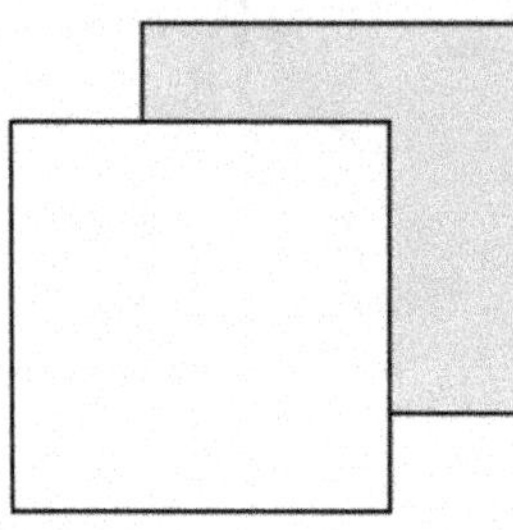

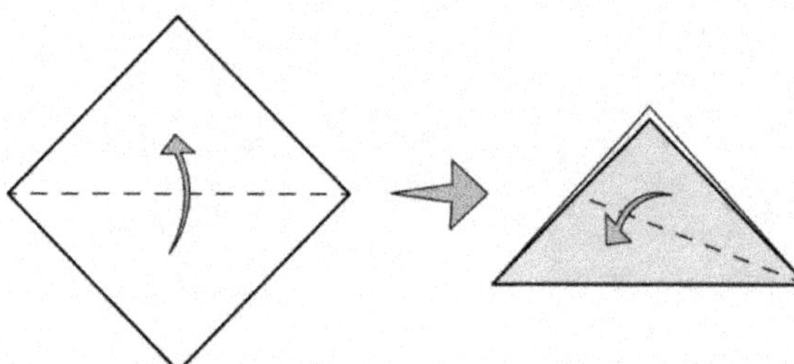

Astuce	Étape 1	Étape 2
Pour réaliser cette couronne, tu auras besoin de 8 feuilles carrées.	Plie l'une des feuilles en diagonale jusqu'à la moitié.	Plie la couche supérieure en deux comme indiqué sur le dessin.

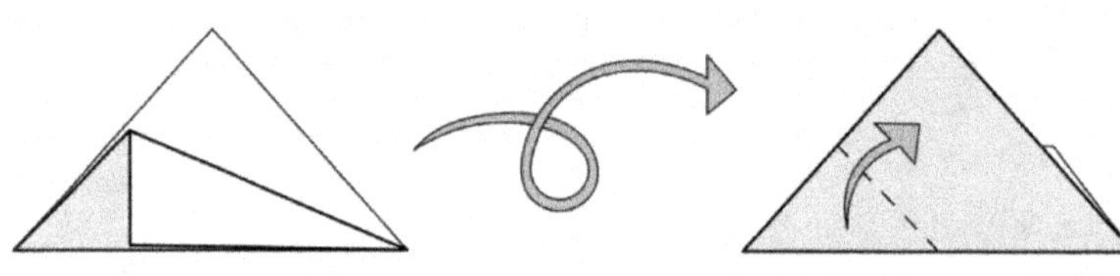

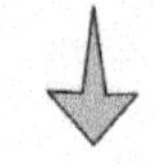

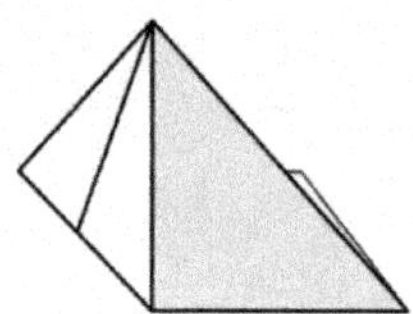

Étape 3

Retourne la figure, puis plie le coin inférieur gauche en diagonale de sorte qu'il rejoigne le coin supérieur.

Couronne

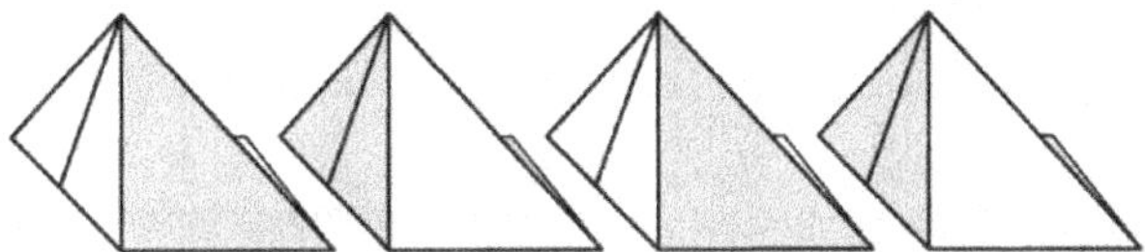

Tu as besoin de 8 pièces identiques pour ce modèle, alors répète ces étapes avec les 7 autres feuilles.

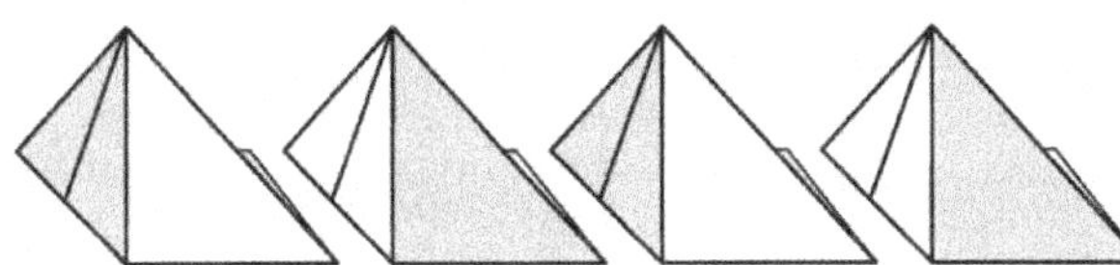

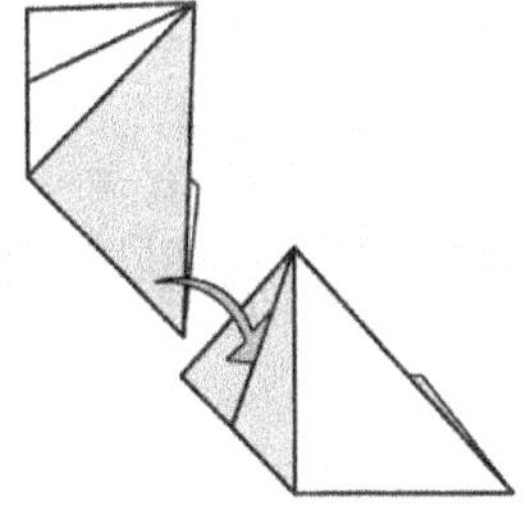

Prends 2 pièces et rentres-en une à l'intérieur de l'autre comme indiqué sur le dessin.

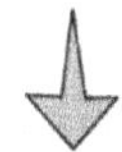

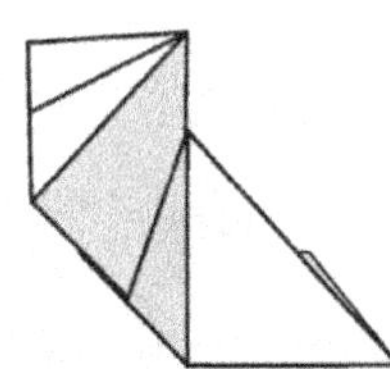

Continue d'emboîter les autres pièces les unes dans les autres jusqu'à former un cercle complet.

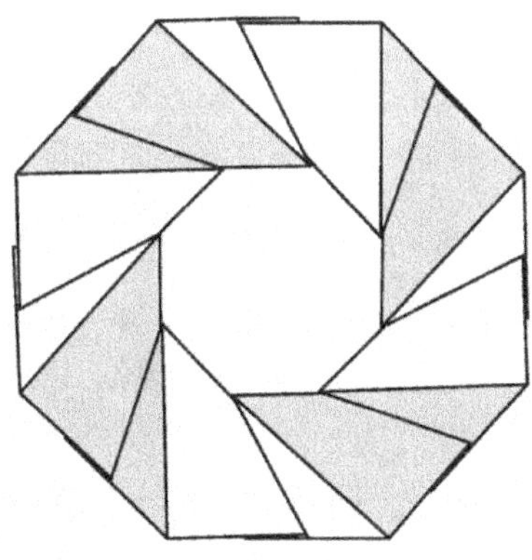

Visage de renne

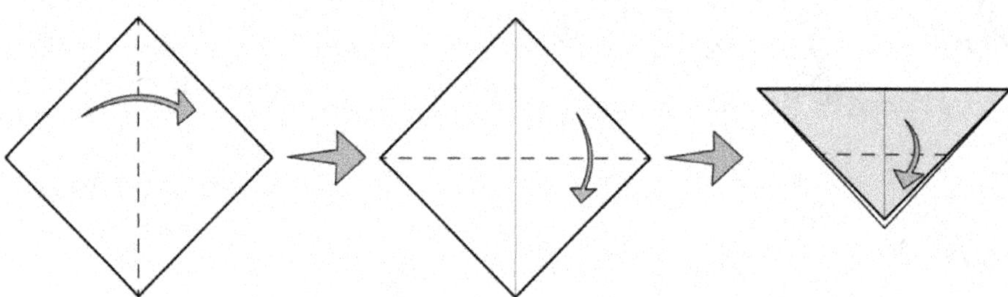

Étape 1

Plie la feuille de papier en diagonale, puis déplie-la pour former un pli vertical.

Étape 2

Plie la feuille en deux vers le bas.

Étape 3

Plie la totalité de la figure en deux comme indiqué sur le dessin, puis déplie-la pour former un pli.

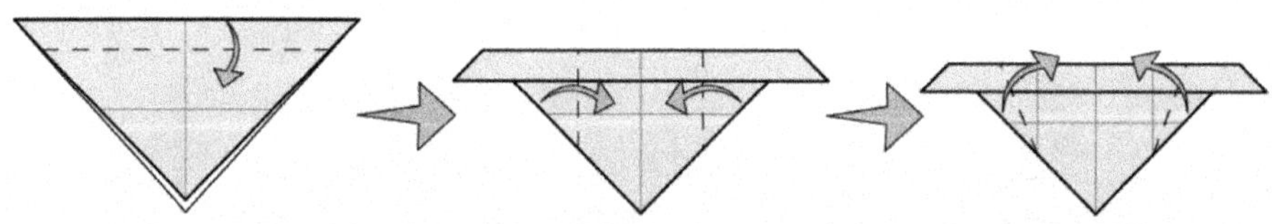

Étape 4

Plie le bord supérieur vers le bas comme indiqué. Puis plie les deux côtés en trois avant de les déplier.

Étape 5

Plie les deux côtés en diagonale vers le haut de sorte qu'ils rejoignent les plis que tu viens de faire.

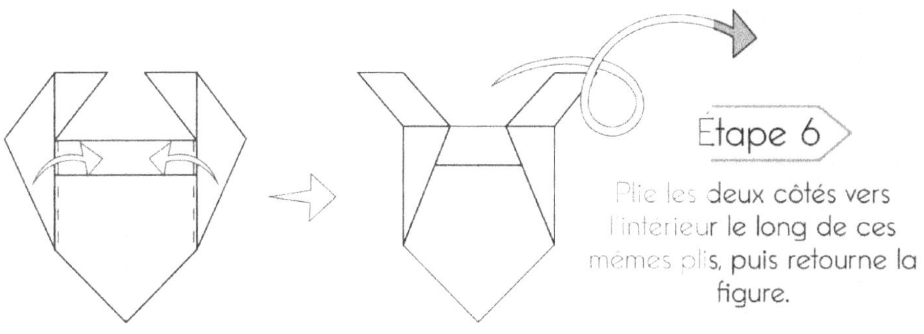

Plie les deux côtés vers l'intérieur le long de ces mêmes plis, puis retourne la figure.

Étape 7

Plie le coin inférieur de la couche superieure vers toi et le coin inferieur de la couche inferieure vers l'arriere.

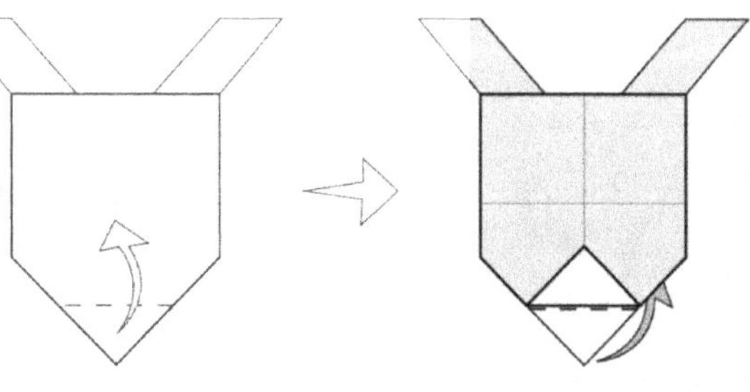

Étape 8

Rabats la pointe de la couche supérieure vers le bas pour former le nez du renne.

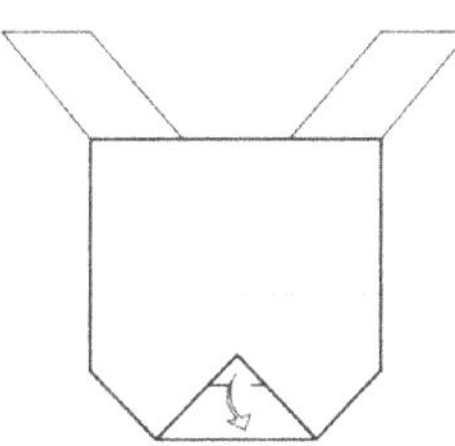

Botte du père Noël

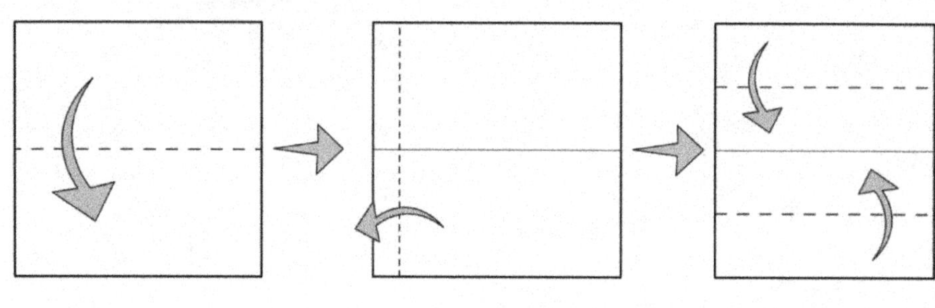

⟨ Étape 1 ⟩

Plie la feuille en deux vers le bas, puis déplie-la pour former un pli.

⟨ Étape 2 ⟩

Plie le côté gauche vers l'arrière, comme indiqué sur le dessin.

⟨ Étape 3 ⟩

Rabats les bords supérieur et inférieur sur la ligne médiane horizontale.

⟨ Étape 4 ⟩

Plie la figure en deux vers le bas.

⟨ Étape 5 ⟩

Plie le côté droit de la figure vers la gauche comme indiqué sur le dessin, puis déplie-le pour former un pli. Plie le côté droit en diagonale vers le bas pour qu'il rejoigne ce pli, puis déplie-le à nouveau.

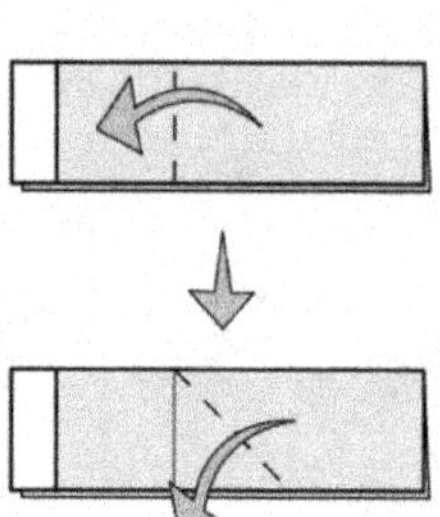

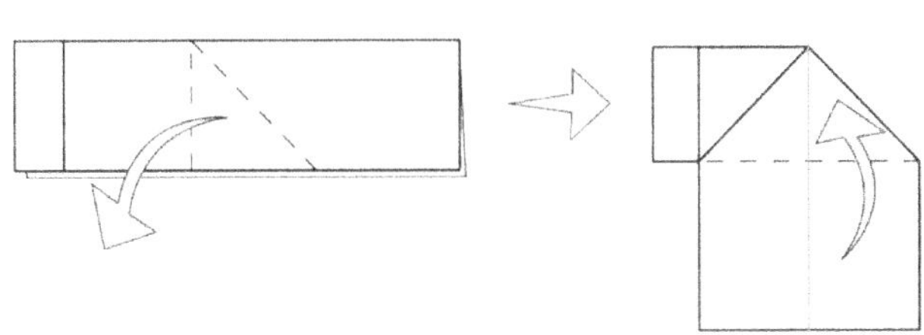

Étape 6

Suis les plis que tu as faits à l'étape précédente pour ramener la couche supérieure du côté droit vers la gauche. Plie ensuite le bas de la figure vers le haut, comme indiqué sur le dessin.

Étape 7

Plie la couche supérieure en deux vers la droite. Puis plie les extrémités des deux coins supérieurs en diagonale vers l'arrière.

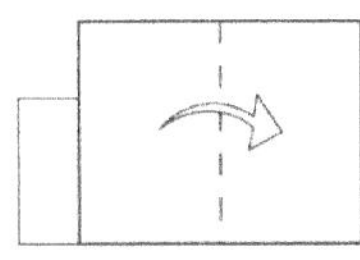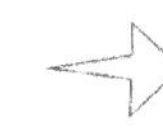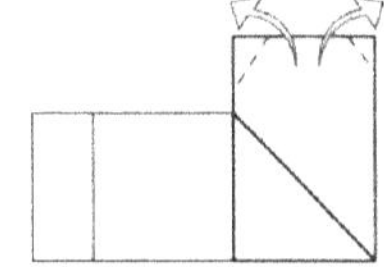

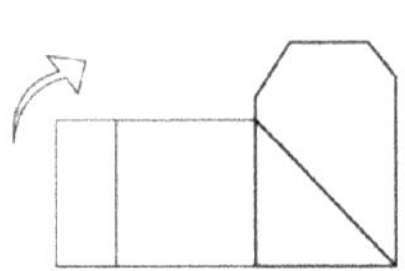

Étape 8

Fais tourner la figure.

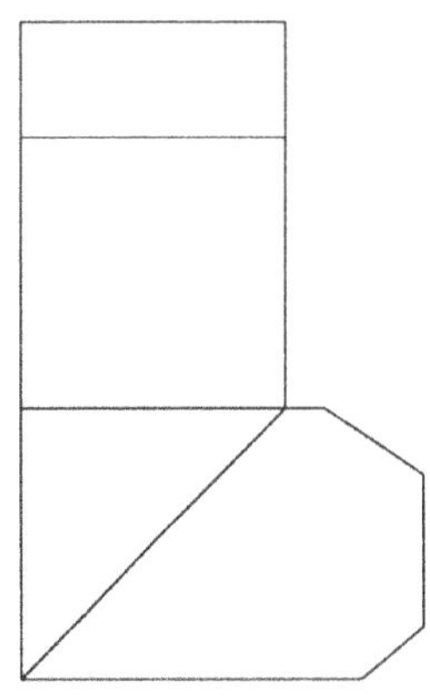

Botte du père Noël

Visage de lutin

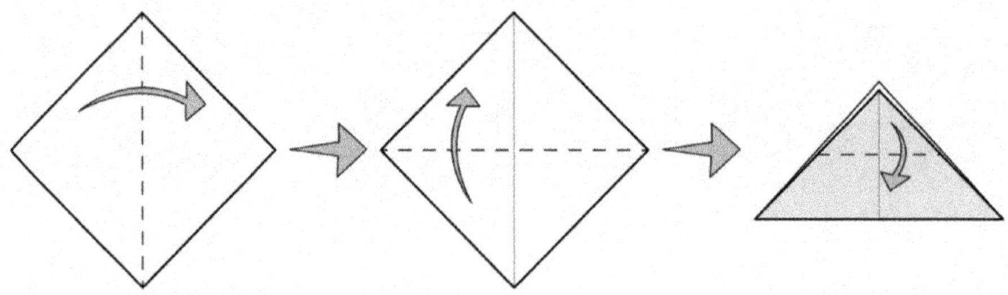

Étape 1

Plie la feuille de papier en diagonale, puis déplie-la pour former un pli. Ensuite, plie-la en deux vers le haut.

Étape 2

Rabats le coin supérieur de la couche supérieure vers le bas pour qu'il rejoigne le bord inférieur.

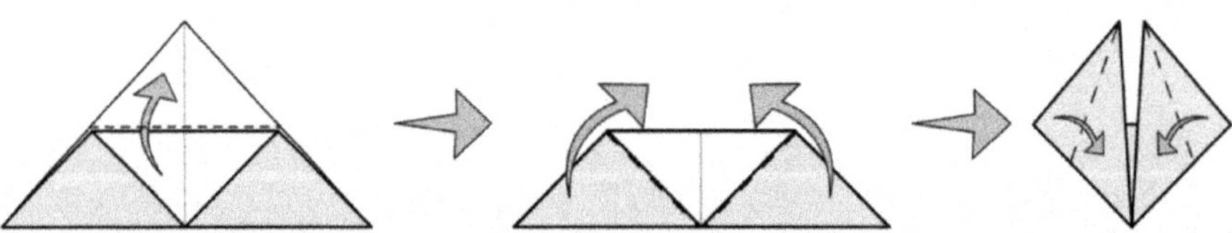

Étape 3

Plie le coin supérieur de la couche arrière vers l'arrière pour qu'il rejoigne le bord inférieur. Plie ensuite les deux coins latéraux vers le haut en direction de la ligne médiane verticale, en laissant un petit espace entre eux.

Étape 4

Plie les deux coins latéraux vers le bas comme indiqué sur le dessin.

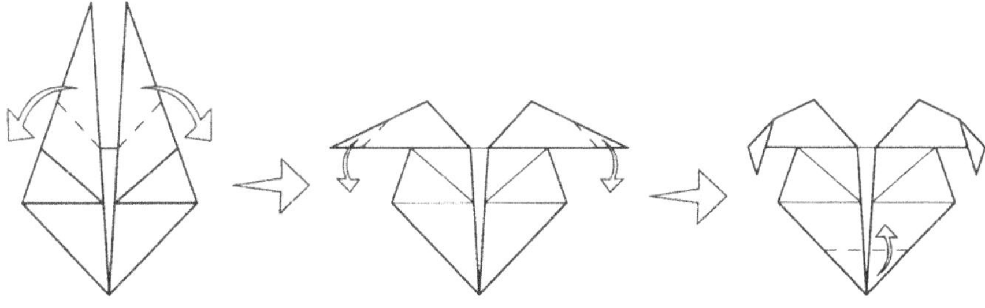

Étape 5

Plie le haut des deux coins vers le bas jusqu'à ce que leurs bords inférieurs se retrouvent à l'horizontale.

Étape 6

Rabats les bords de ces mêmes coins comme indiqué sur le dessin.

Étape 7

Rabats le coin inférieur comme indiqué sur le dessin.

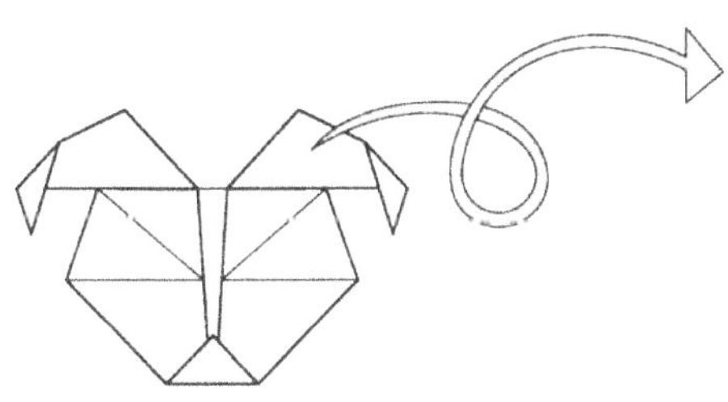

Étape 8

Retourne la figure.

Visage de lutin

Étoile

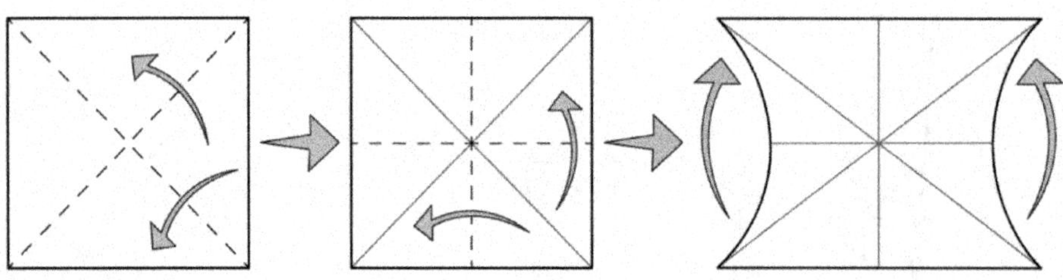

Étape 1

Plie la feuille le long des deux diagonales, puis déplie-la.

Étape 2

Plie la feuille dans le sens de la longueur et de la largeur, puis déplie-la à nouveau.

Étape 3

Rabats le bord supérieur pour qu'il rejoigne le bord inférieur tout en repliant les deux côtés pour former un triangle.

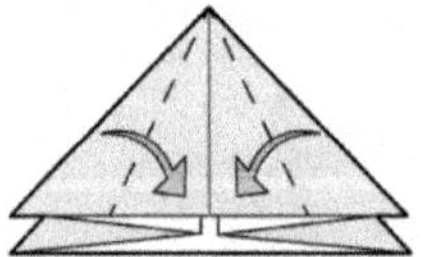  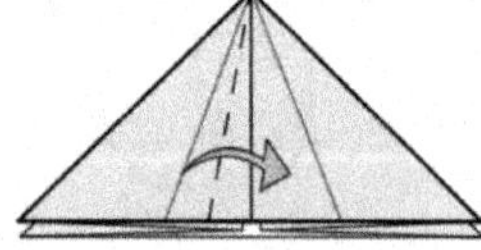

Étape 4

Rabats les coins latéraux de la couche supérieure jusqu'à la ligne médiane verticale, puis déplie-les.

Étape 5

Rabats le coin gauche vers l'intérieur, exactement au milieu de l'espace entre la ligne médiane verticale et le pli que tu viens de faire.

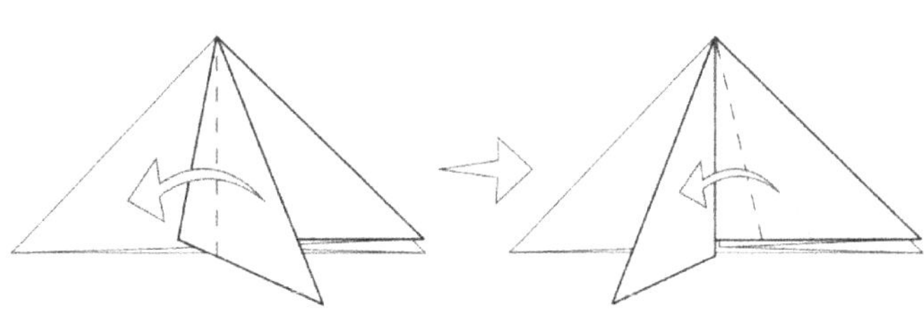

Étape 6

Replie-le vers l'extérieur le long de la ligne médiane verticale. Répète l'opération pour le coin droit.

Étape 7

Retourne la figure et répète l'opération en entier pour ce côté.

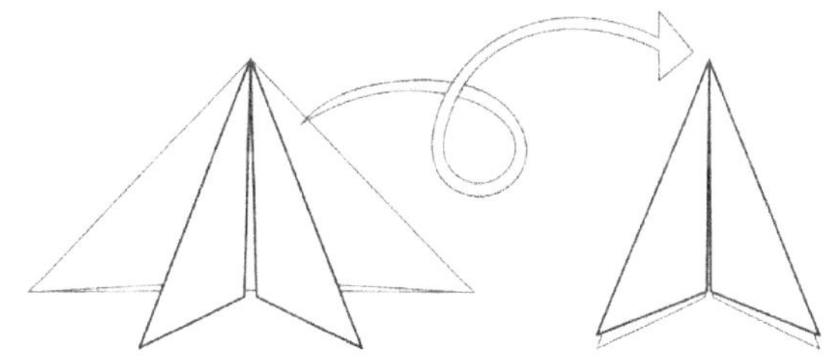

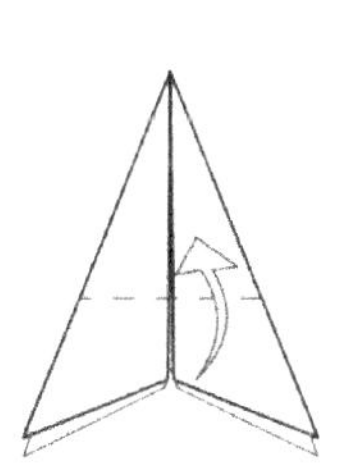

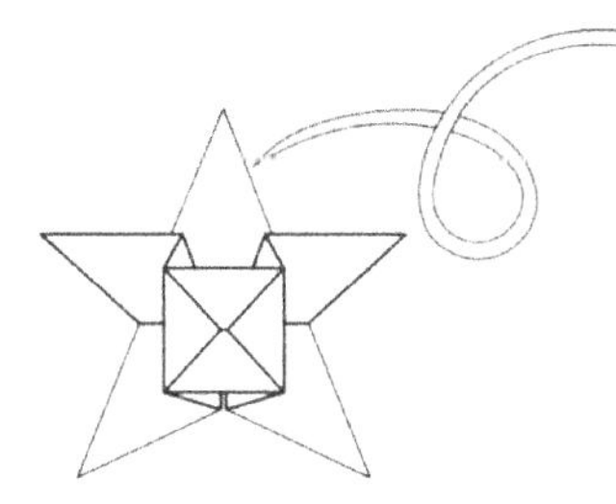

Étape 8

Ouvre la couche supérieure comme indiqué et aplatis la figure, puis retourne-la.

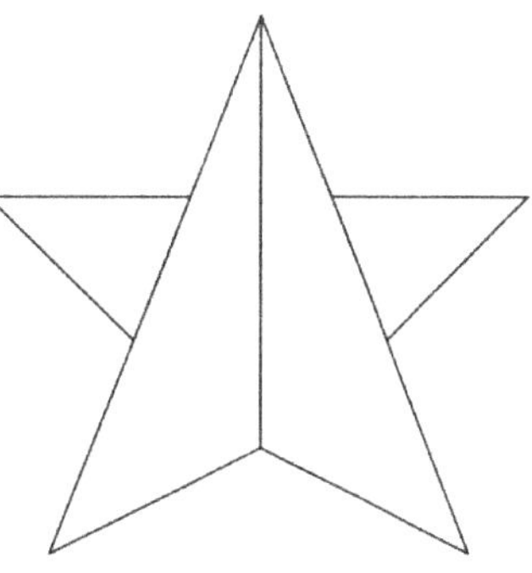

Étoile

Bonhomme de neige

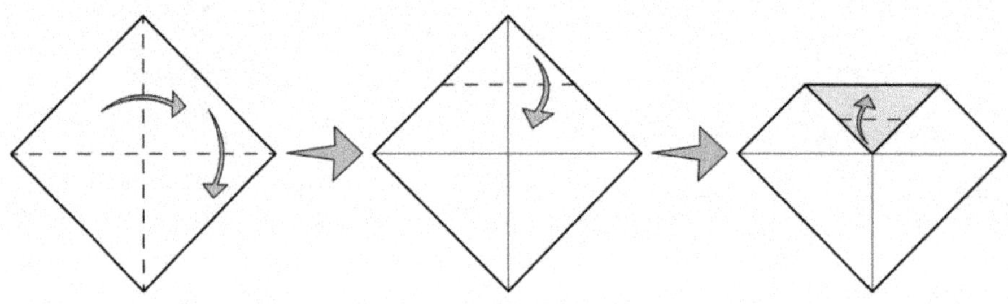

Étape 1

Plie la feuille le long des deux diagonales, puis déplie-la.

Étape 2

Rabats le coin supérieur jusqu'au centre de la feuille.

Étape 3

Replie le coin dans l'autre sens de sorte qu'il touche le bord supérieur, puis déplie-le.

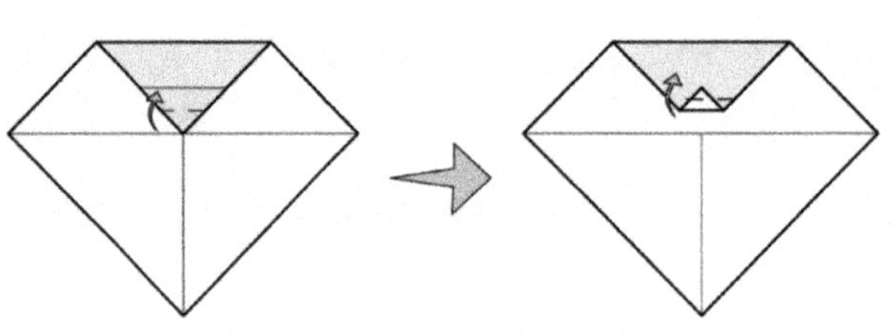

Étape 4

Plie la pointe vers le haut de sorte qu'elle rejoigne le pli que tu viens de faire, puis plie-la à nouveau vers le haut, comme indiqué sur le dessin.

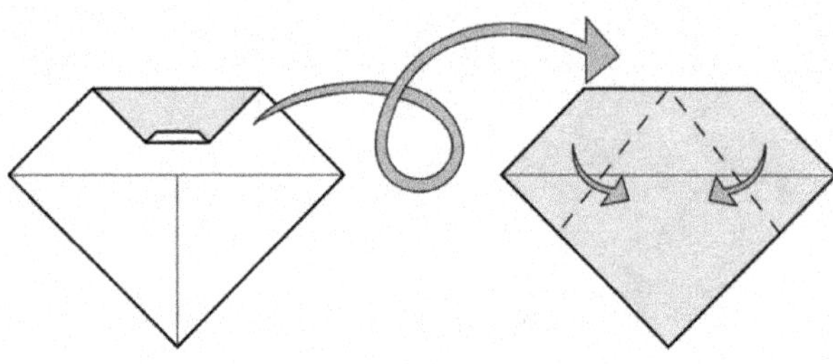

Étape 5

Retourne la figure et plie les deux coins latéraux comme indiqué sur le dessin.

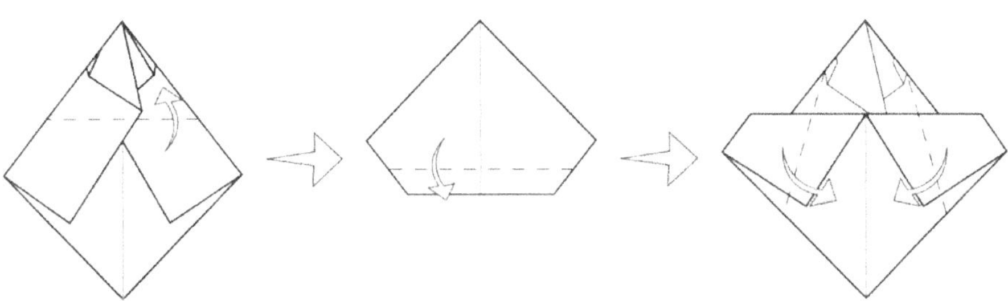

Étape 6

Rabats la partie inférieure de la figure comme indiqué sur le dessin.

Étape 7

Maintenant, rabats-la à nouveau vers le bas en laissant un petit espace entre les deux plis.

Étape 8

Plie les deux coins latéraux comme indiqué sur le dessin.

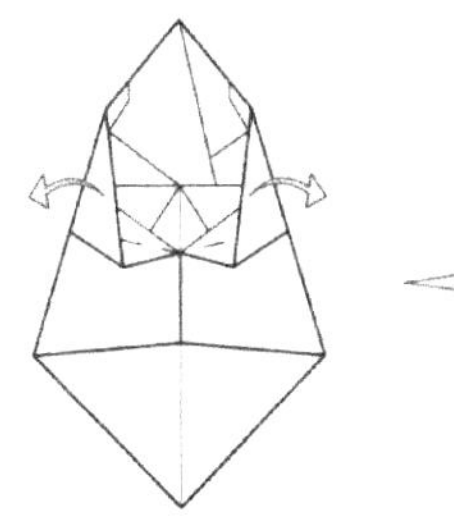

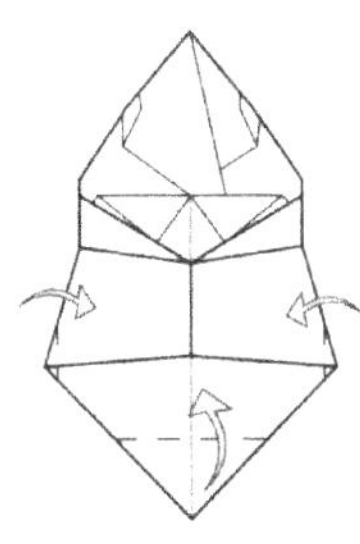

Étape 9

Ouvre les poches sur les côtés de la couche supérieure et aplatis le tout. Puis insère les pointes des coins latéraux et inférieurs comme indiqué sur le dessin.

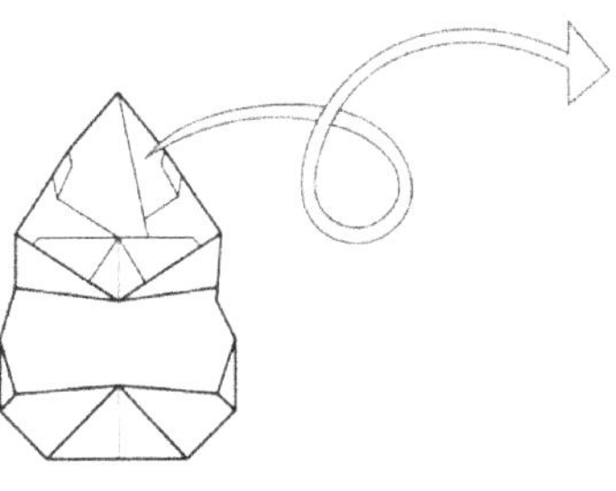

Étape 10

Retourne la figure.

Bonhomme de neige

Il s'agit du modèle avec la feuille pentagonale que tu as appris à réaliser au début de ce livre. Si tu as suivi ces étapes pour réaliser la feuille toi-même, tu peux ignorer l'étape 1, car tu as déjà tous les plis dont tu as besoin pour l'étape 2. S'il s'avère que tu disposais déjà d'une feuille pentagonale, tu devras alors suivre la première étape pour faire tous les plis que tu utiliseras plus tard.

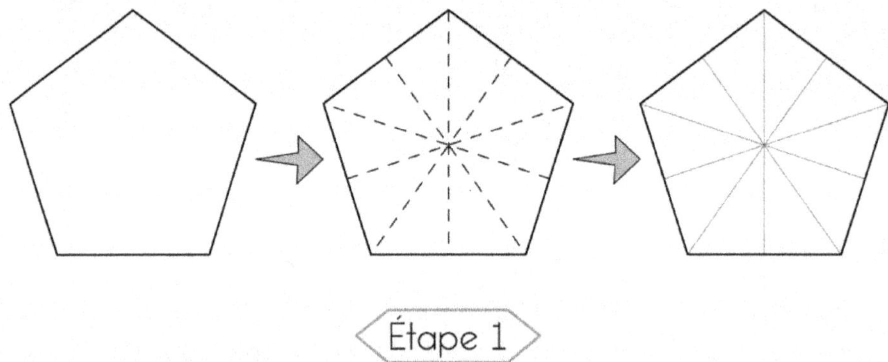

Étape 1

Si tu as déjà les plis sur ta feuille, tu peux passer à l'étape suivante. Sinon, plie la feuille le long de la ligne qui va de l'une des pointes au centre du côté opposé, puis déplie-la. Répète l'opération pour toutes les pointes de la feuille.

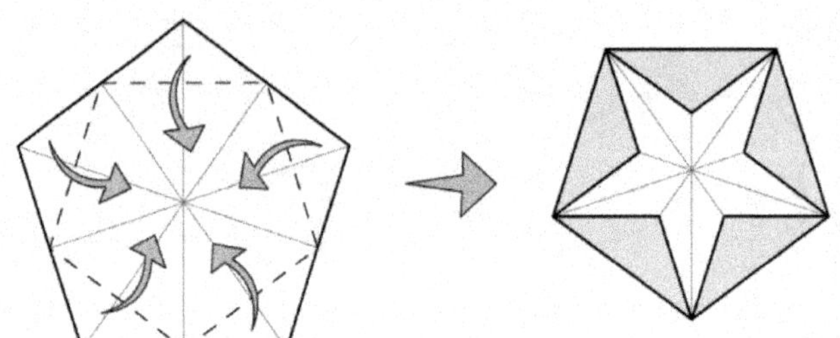

Étape 2

Rabats tous les coins vers le centre de la feuille, comme indiqué sur le dessin.

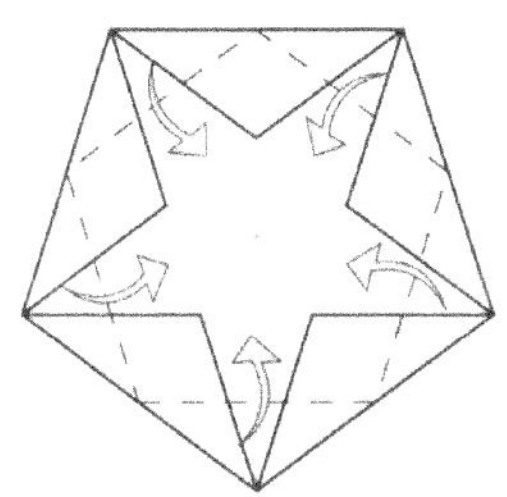  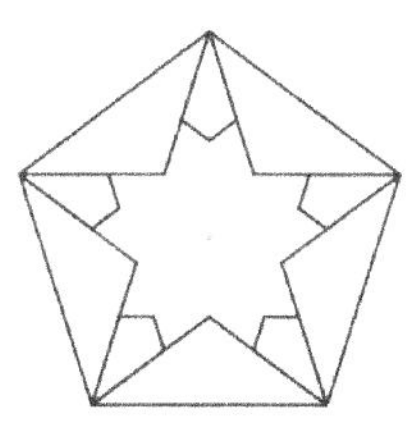

Étape 3

Rabats à nouveau
tous les coins vers le
centre de la feuille.

Étape 4

Retourne la figure

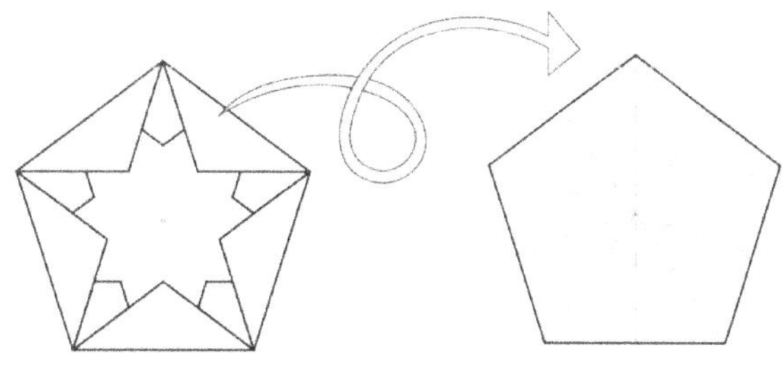

Étape 5

Plie le coin supérieur
vers le bas comme
indiqué, puis
deplie-le pour former
un pli.

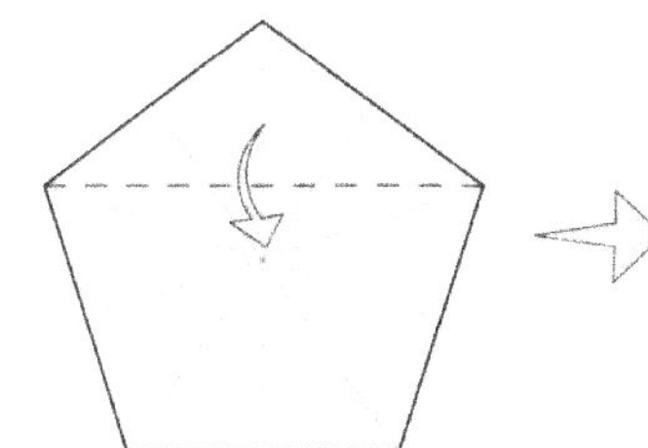 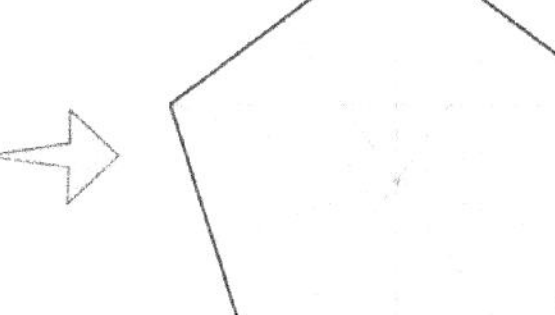

Coupelle en forme d'étoile

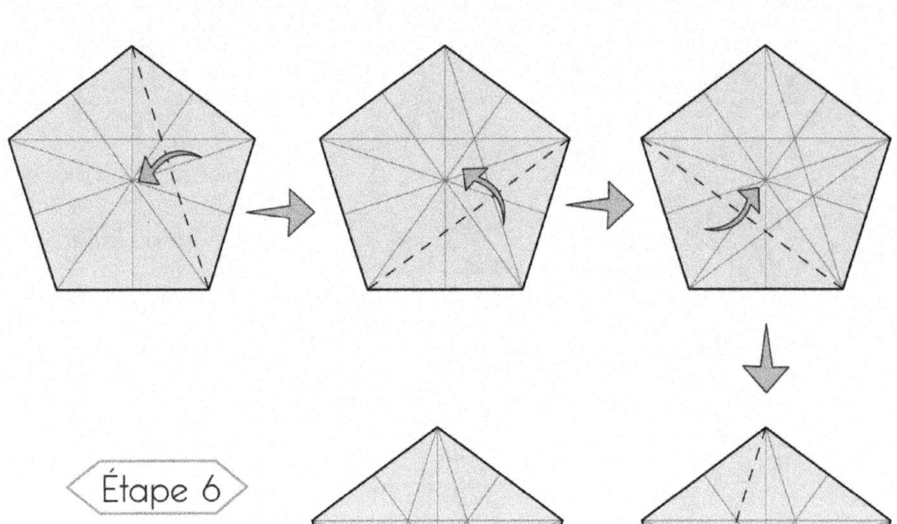

Étape 6

Répète l'opération pour tous les autres coins jusqu'à ce que ta figure ressemble au dessin.

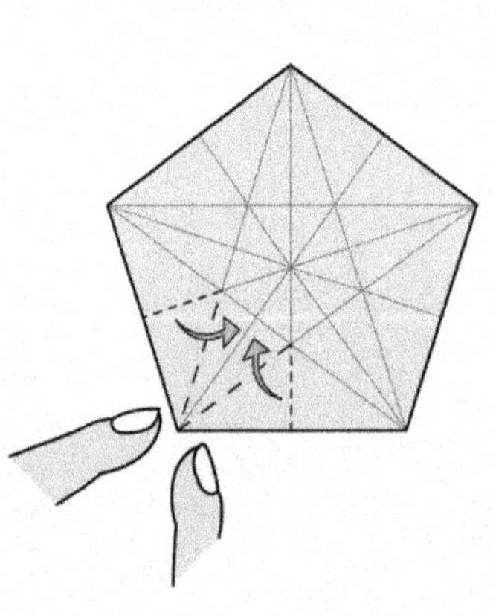

Étape 7

Pince chaque coin par en dessous de sorte que les plis intérieurs deviennent des plis vallée et que les plis extérieurs deviennent des plis montagne.

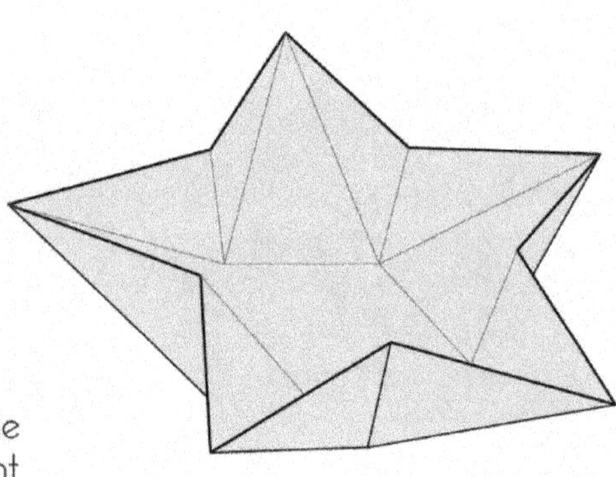

Coupelle en forme d'étoile

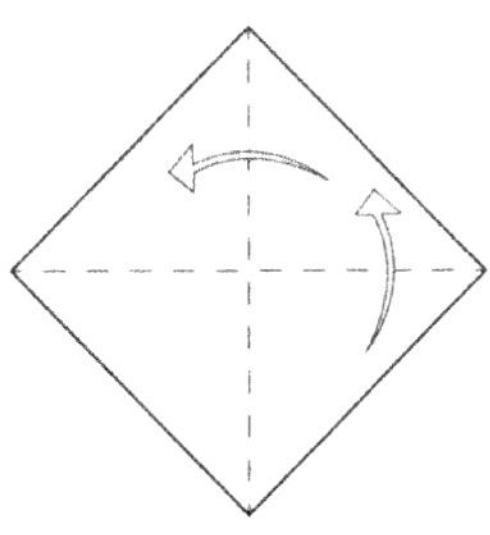

Étape 1

Plie la feuille le long des
deux diagonales, puis
déplie-la.

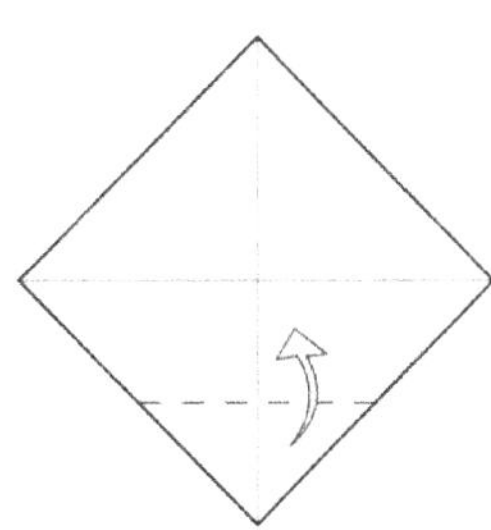

Étape 2

Rabats le coin inférieur
jusqu'au milieu de la feuille.

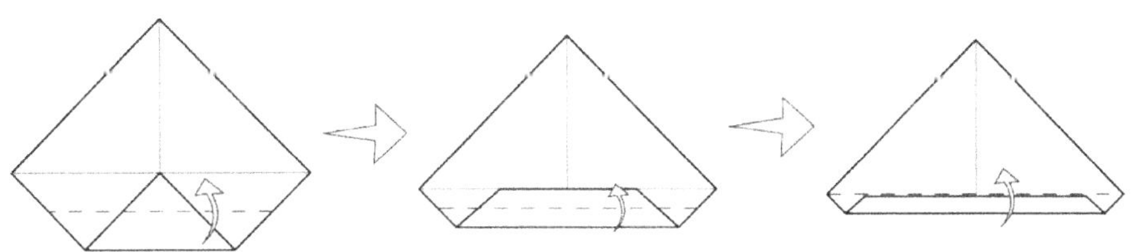

Étape 3

Rabats le bord inférieur jusqu'à la ligne
médiane horizontale trois fois de suite comme
indiqué sur le dessin.

Bonnet du père Noël

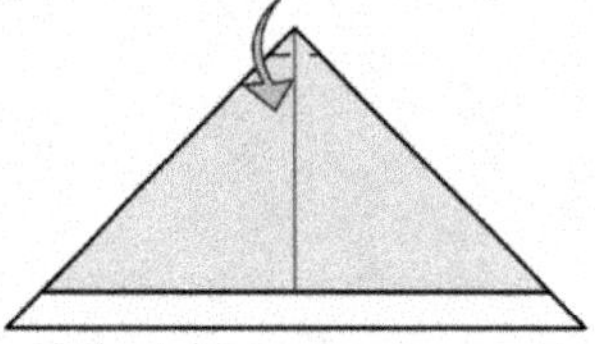  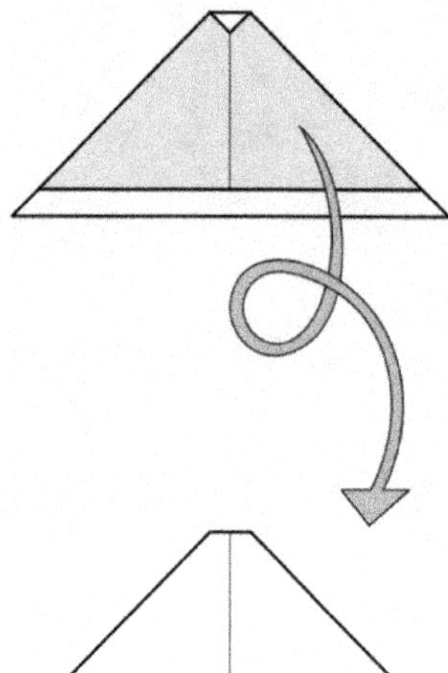

Plie le bord du coin supérieur vers le bas, puis retourne la figure.

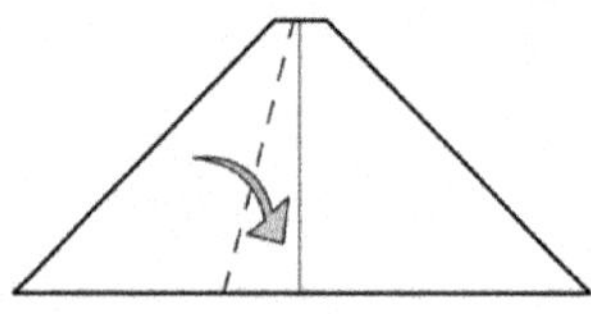

Plie le coin gauche comme indiqué sur le dessin, puis rabats-le vers le haut de sorte qu'il s'aligne avec le bord inférieur. Plie le coin droit vers la gauche comme indiqué sur le dessin.

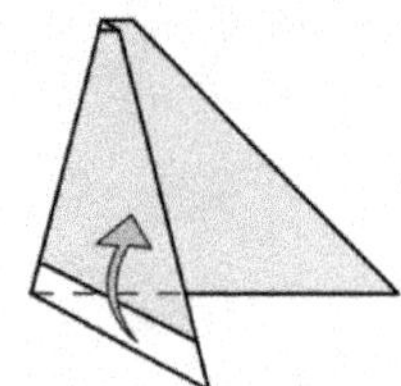   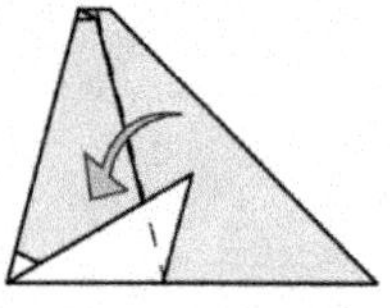

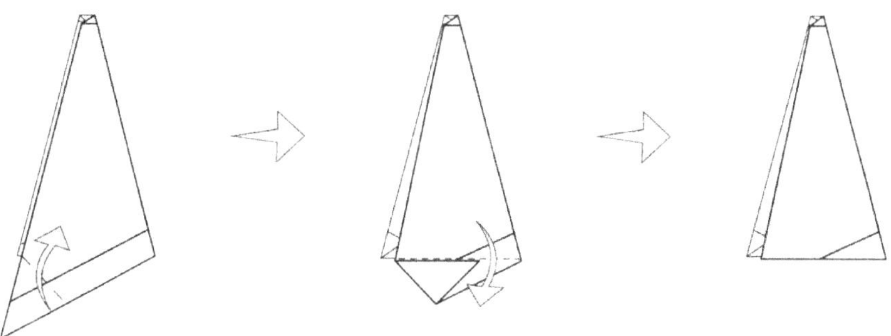

Étape 6

Plie le coin inférieur de la couche supérieure en diagonale vers le haut, puis plie-le vers l'arrière comme indiqué sur le dessin.

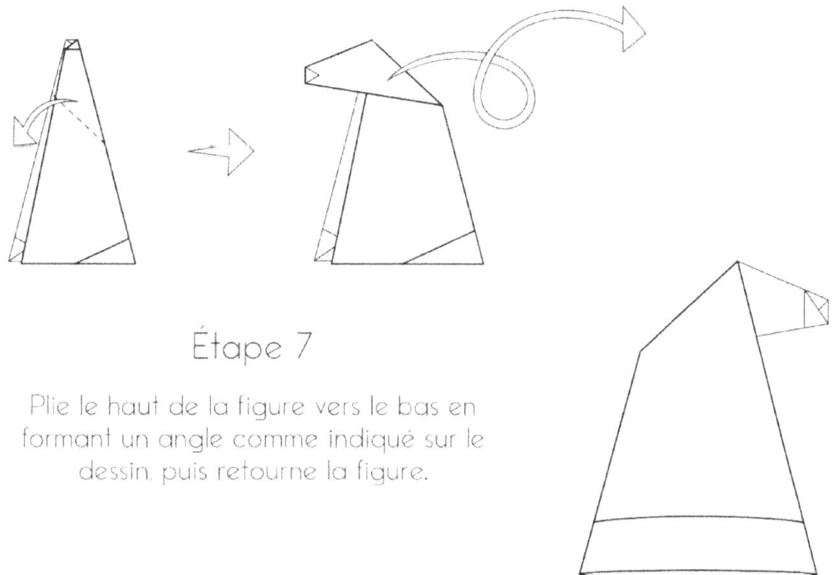

Étape 7

Plie le haut de la figure vers le bas en formant un angle comme indiqué sur le dessin, puis retourne la figure.

Bonnet du père Noël

Père Noël

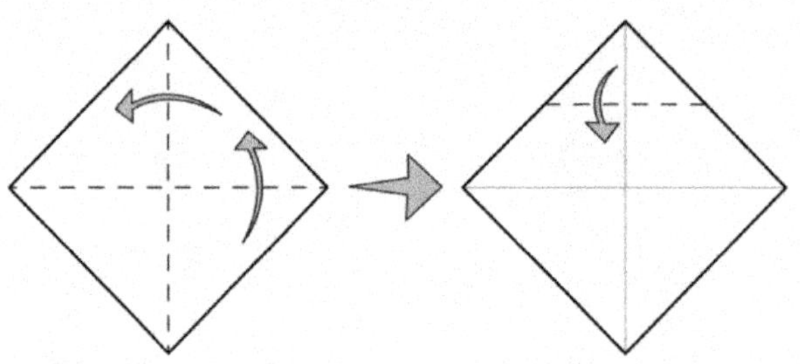

Plie la feuille le long des deux diagonales, puis déplie-la. Ensuite, rabats le coin supérieur jusqu'au milieu de la feuille.

Replie la pointe jusqu'à ce qu'elle rejoigne le bord supérieur, puis déplie-la. Enfin, plie-la à nouveau vers le haut de sorte qu'elle rejoigne le pli que tu viens de faire.

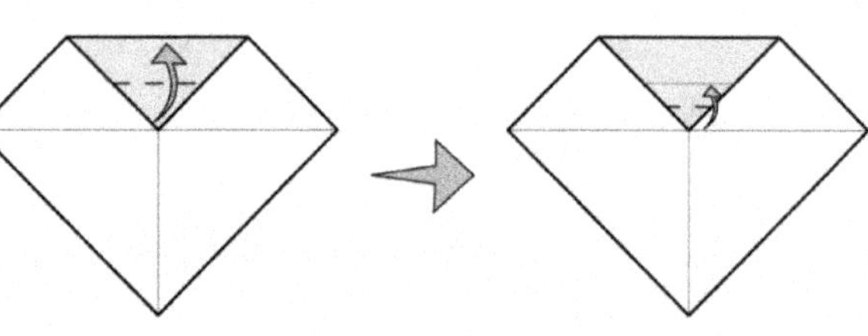

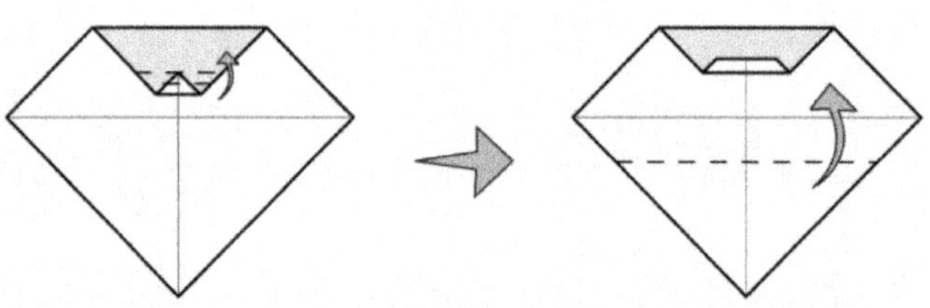

Plie à nouveau la pointe vers le haut deux fois de suite comme indiqué sur le dessin, puis ramène le coin inférieur vers le haut jusqu'à ce qu'il rejoigne le bord supérieur.

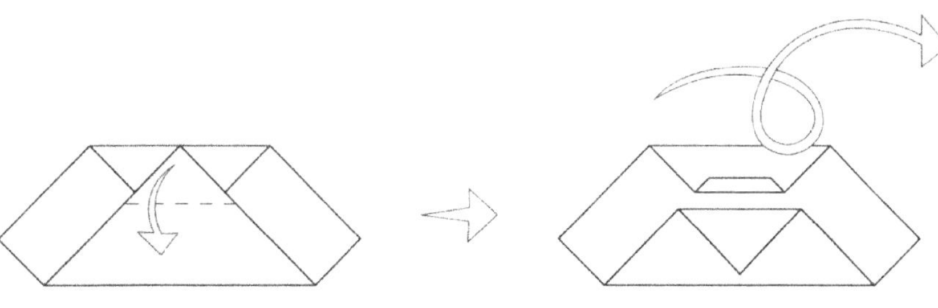

Étape 4

Plie ce coin vers le bas en laissant un petit espace entre ce rabat et celui que tu as fait avec le coin supérieur. Retourne ensuite la figure.

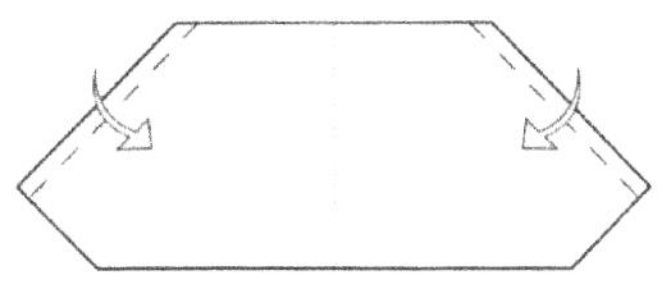

Étape 5

Plie les deux côtés latéraux vers l'intérieur, comme indiqué sur le dessin.

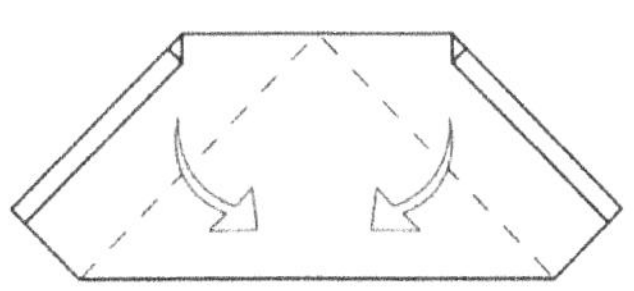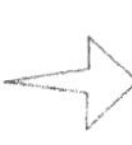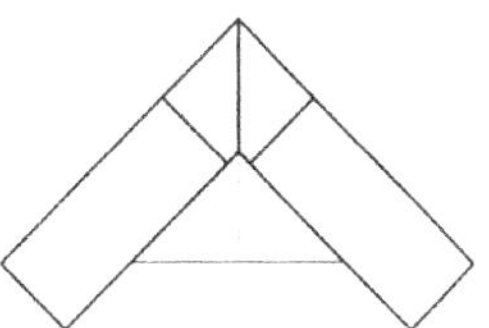

Étape 6

Plie les deux coins latéraux en diagonale vers le bas, comme indiqué sur le dessin.

Père Noël

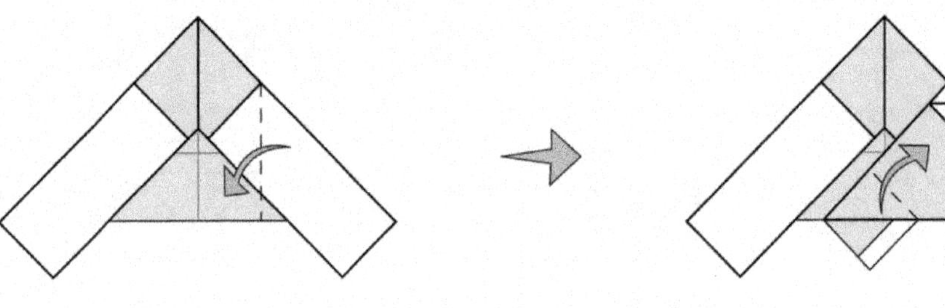

Divise la figure en trois et plie le côté droit vers l'intérieur. Ensuite, plie la pointe qui dépasse en bas en diagonale vers le haut, comme indiqué sur le dessin.

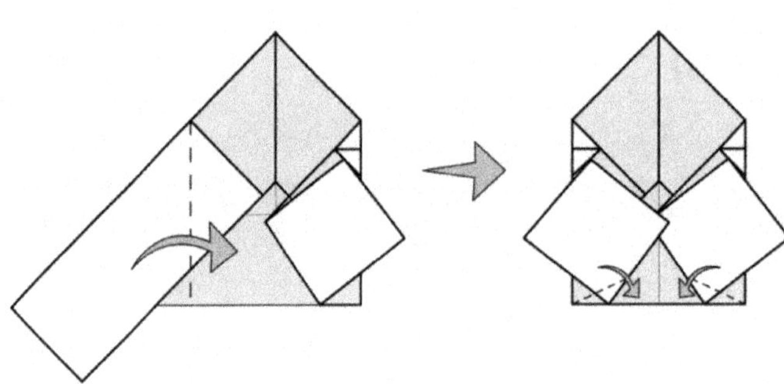

Répète l'étape précédente pour le côté gauche de la figure. Plie ensuite les coins inférieurs des deux rabats vers l'arrière, comme indiqué sur le dessin.

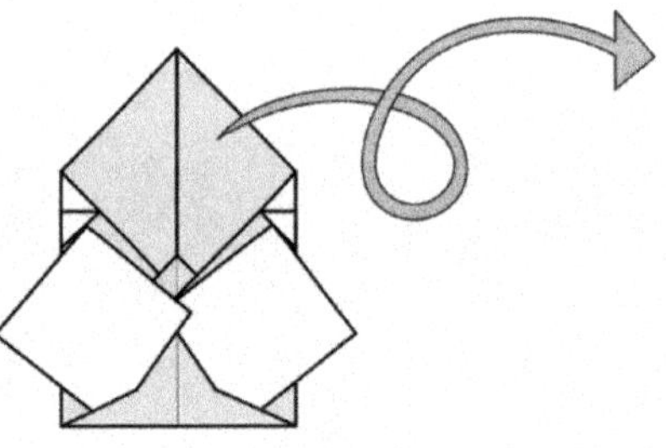

Retourne la figure.

Moufles

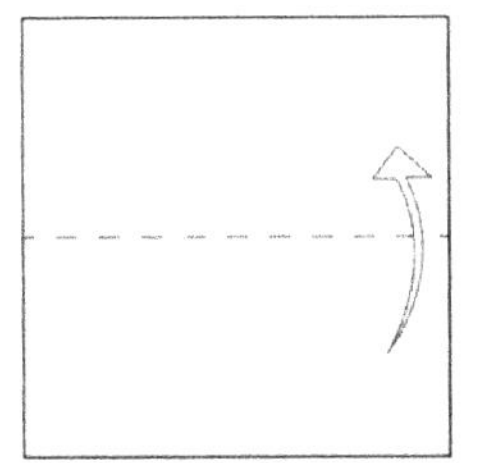  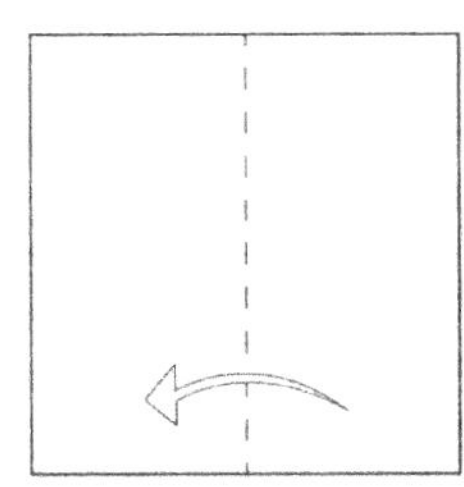 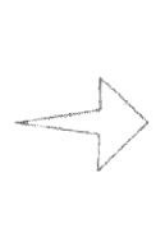 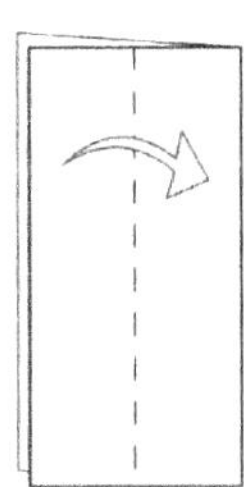

Étape 1

Plie la feuille en deux vers le haut, puis déplie-la pour former un pli.

Étape 2

Plie la feuille en deux vers la gauche.

Étape 3

Plie la couche supérieure en deux vers l'extérieur.

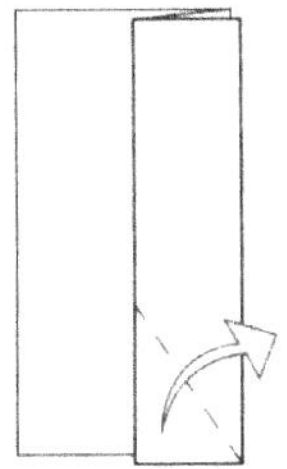  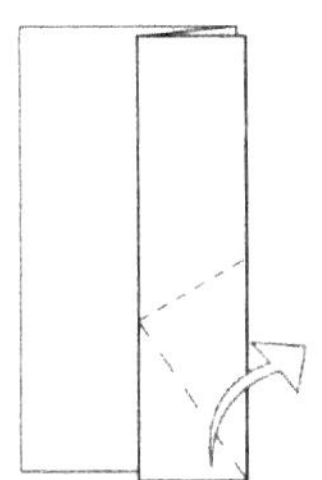 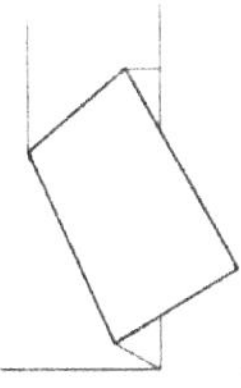

Étape 4

Plie le coin inférieur gauche de la couche supérieure vers le haut en diagonale, comme indiqué sur le dessin, puis déplie-la.

Étape 5

En suivant le pli que tu viens de faire, ouvre la couche supérieure comme indiqué sur le dessin, puis aplatis-la.

Moufles

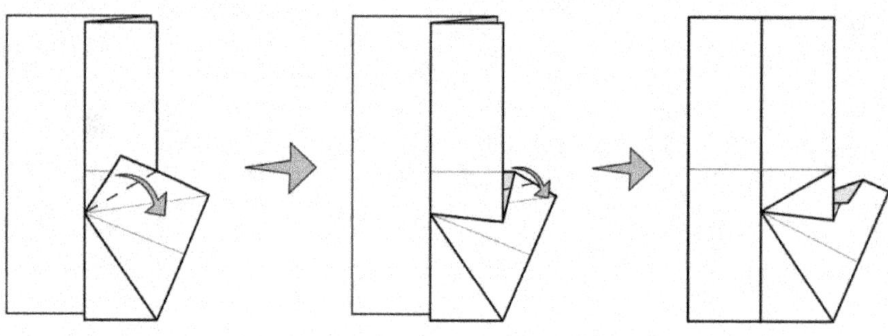

Étape 6

Replie le coin supérieur
du rabat que tu viens
de faire.

Étape 7

Après l'étape précédente, tu verras qu'il y
a un rabat entre les couches supérieure et
inférieure de la figure. Plie-le comme indiqué
sur le dessin.

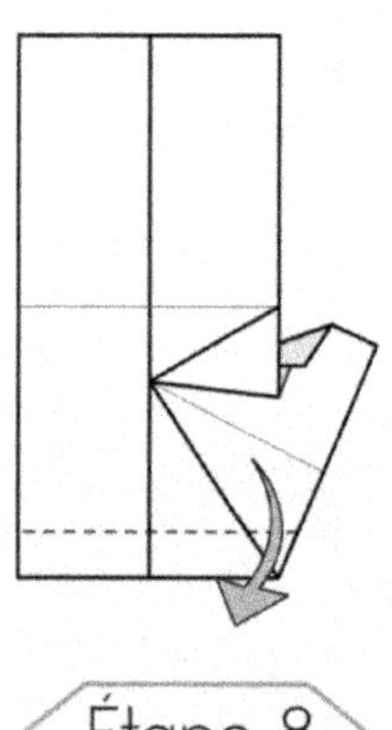
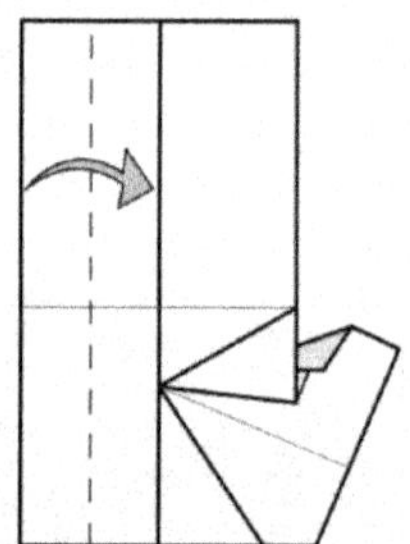

Étape 8

Plie le bord inférieur de la
figure vers l'arrière.

Étape 9

Plie le bord gauche vers
l'intérieur jusqu'à ce qu'il
rejoigne la ligne médiane
verticale.

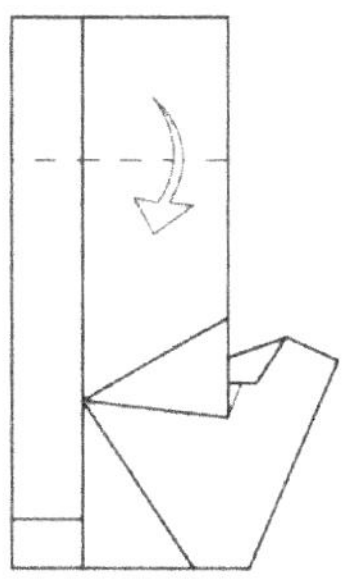  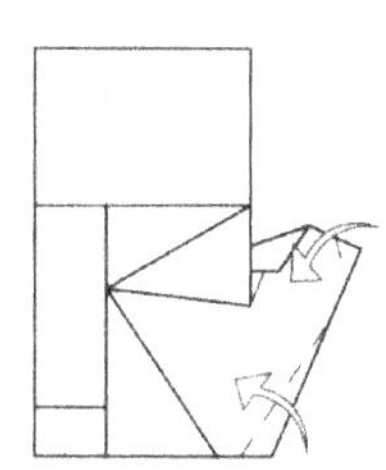

Étape 10

Plie le bord supérieur vers le bas jusqu'à ce qu'il rejoigne la ligne médiane horizontale, puis replie les coins du rabat sur la droite comme indiqué.

Étape 11

Rabats les pointes des deux coins supérieurs en diagonale.

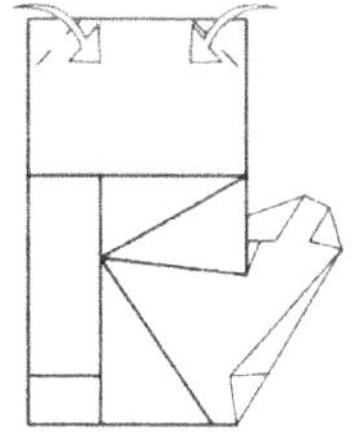

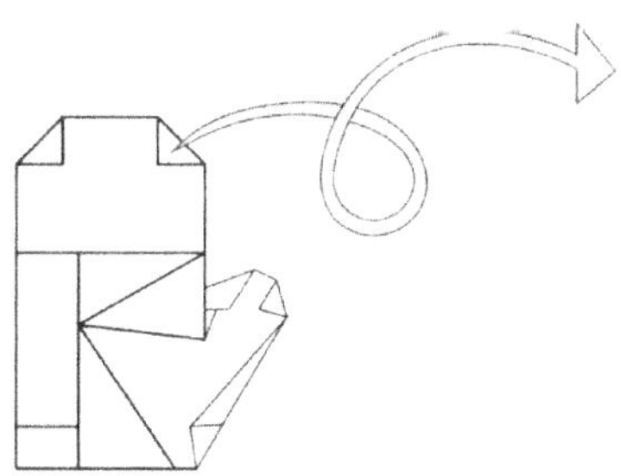

Étape 12

Retourne la figure.

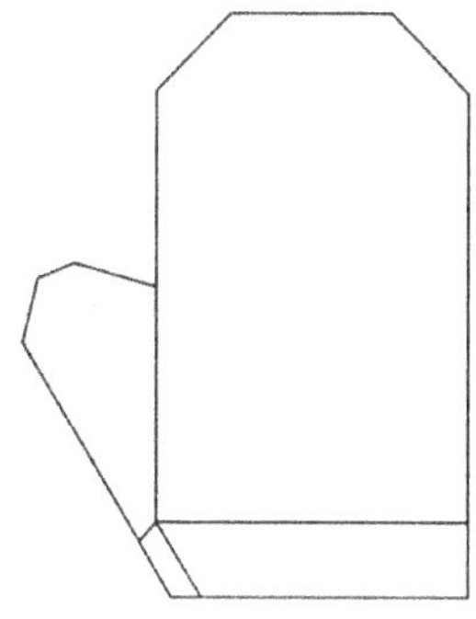

Moufles

Paquet-cadeau

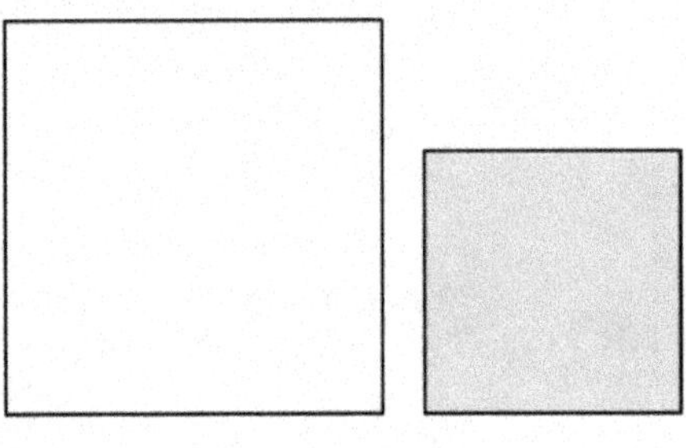

Tu auras besoin de 2 feuilles carrées pour réaliser ce paquet cadeau. L'une des feuilles doit faire les 2/3 de la taille de l'autre.

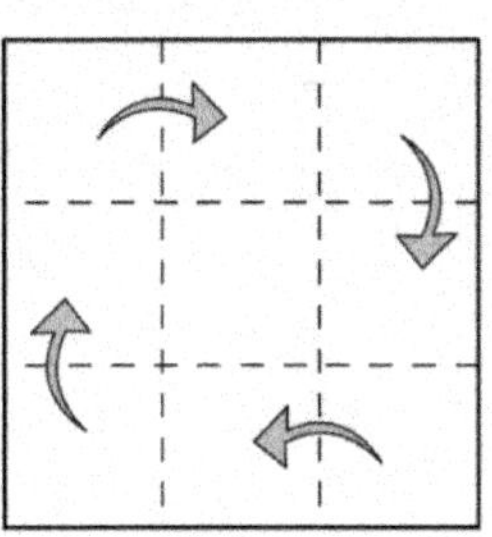

Commence par la plus grande feuille. Plie-la en trois dans le sens de la longueur et dans le sens de la largeur, puis déplie-la.

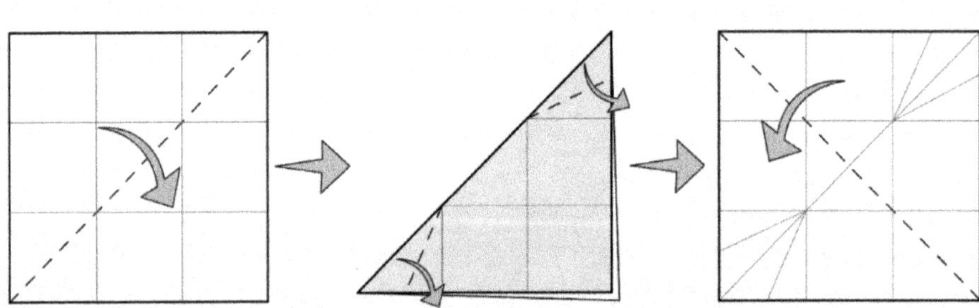

Étape 2
Rabats la feuille en diagonale vers la droite.

Étape 3
Plie les coins en haut à droite et en bas à gauche jusqu'au pli le plus proche que tu as réalisé à l'étape 1. Ensuite, déplie le tout.

Étape 4
Rabats la feuille en diagonale vers la gauche, puis répète les étapes précédentes.

 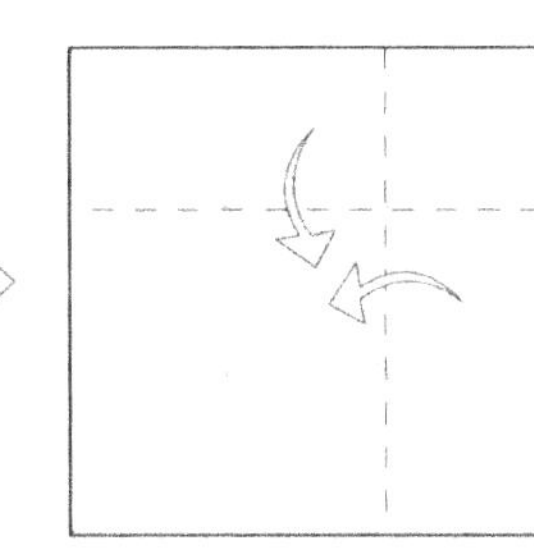

Étape 5

Plie les bords supérieur et droit à mi-hauteur en suivant tous les plis que tu as faits jusqu'à présent de sorte qu'ils soient perpendiculaires au reste de la feuille. Tu verras que le coin entre les deux côtes dépasse.

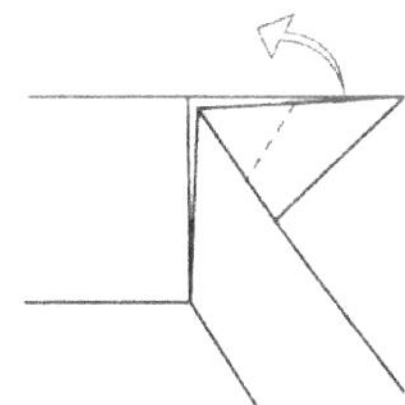 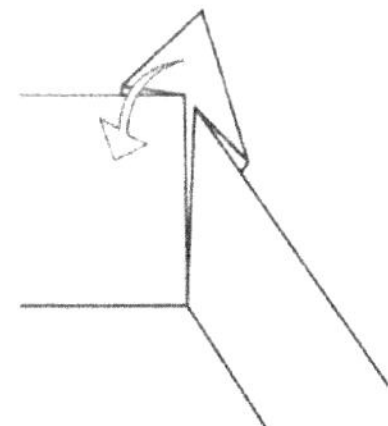 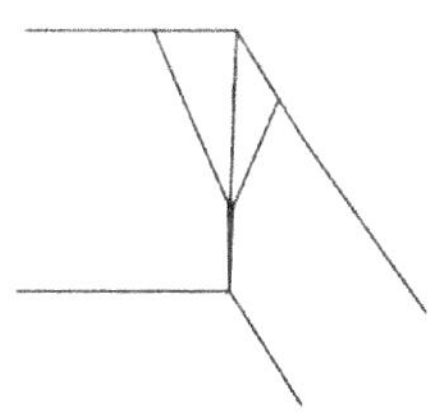

Étape 6

Maintiens les deux côtes en place en pliant ce coin comme indiqué sur les dessins.

Étape 7

Répète les étapes précédentes pour tous les bords et tous les coins. Ta boîte est prête !

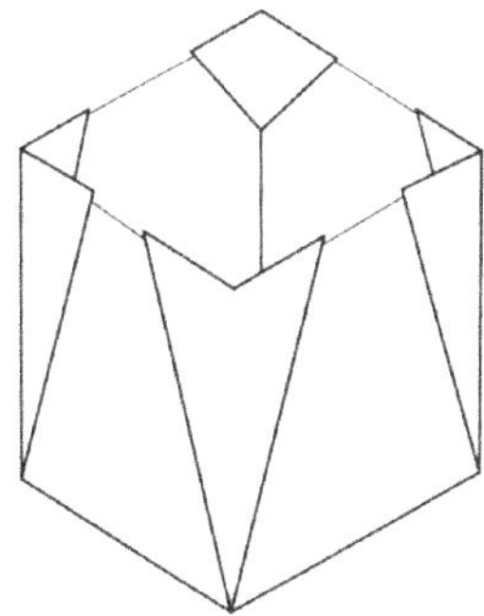

Paquet-cadeau

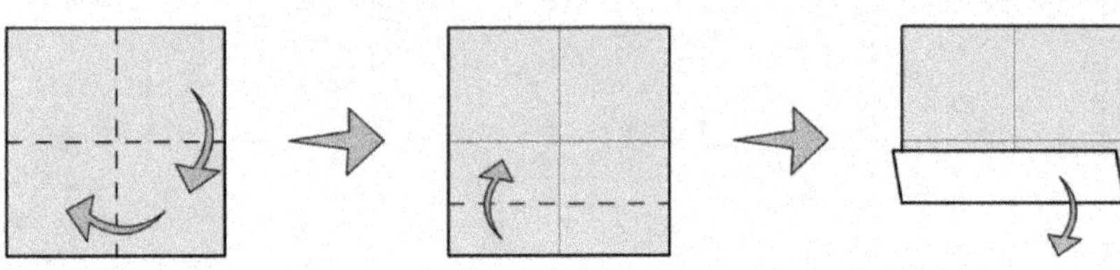

Étape 8

Utilise maintenant la plus petite feuille pour fabriquer le couvercle. Plie-la dans le sens de la longueur et de la largeur, puis déplie-la.

Étape 9

Rabats le bord inférieur un peu en dessous de la ligne médiane horizontale.

Étape 10

Répète l'étape précédente pour tous les autres côtés de la feuille, puis répète les étapes 2 à 7 pour former le couvercle.

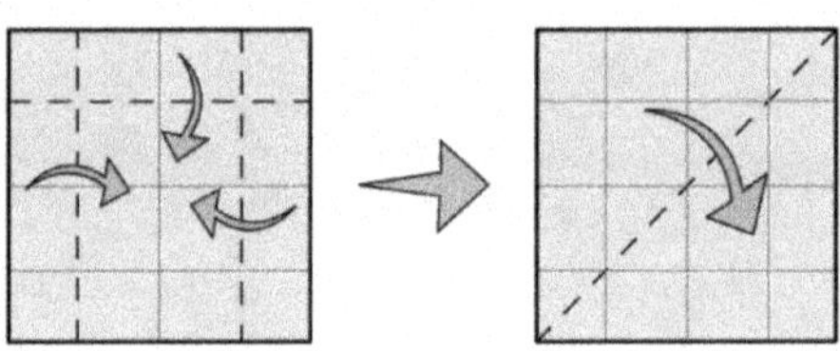

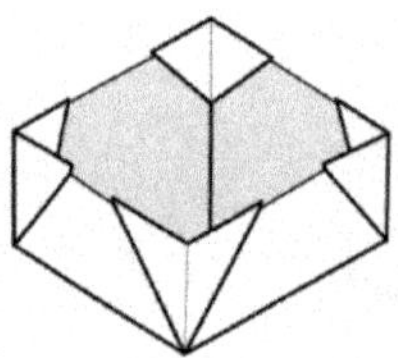

Étape 11

Pose le couvercle sur la boîte. Ton paquet-cadeau est prêt !

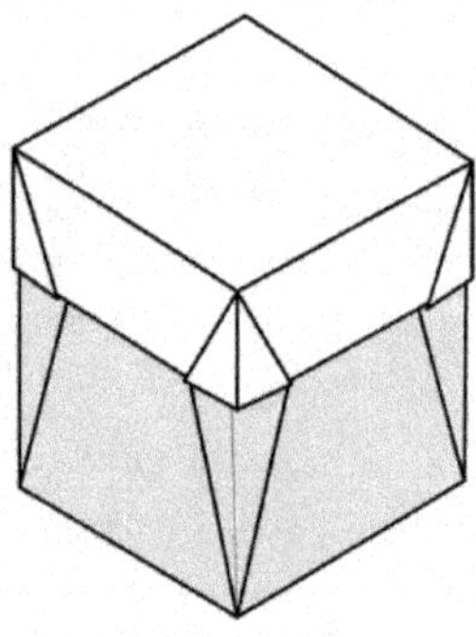

Lutin

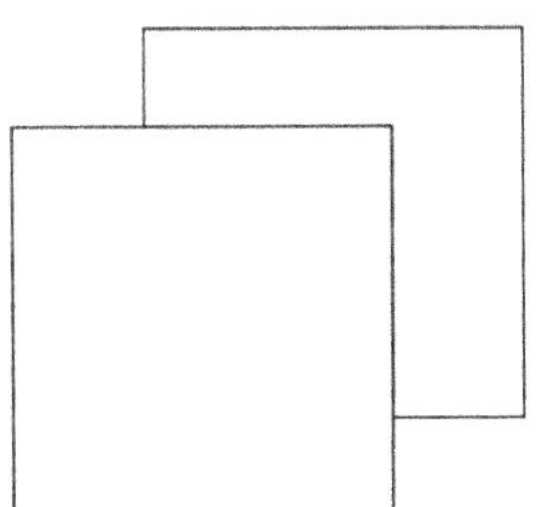

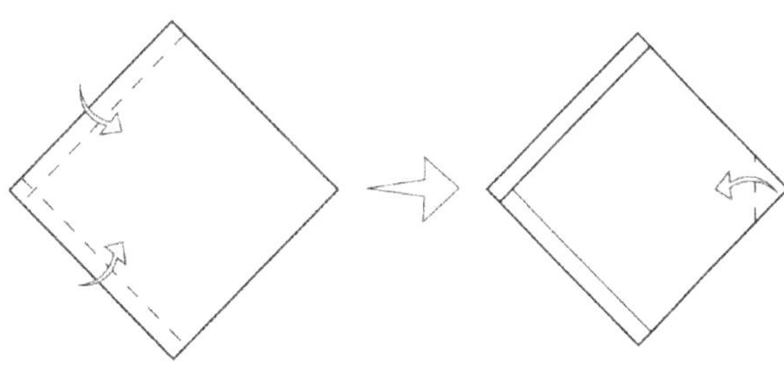

Astuce

Tu auras besoin de 2 feuilles carrées pour réaliser ce lutin.

Étape 1

Rabats legerement les coins de l'un des côtés de la première feuille.

Étape 2

Rabats le coin du coté opposé.

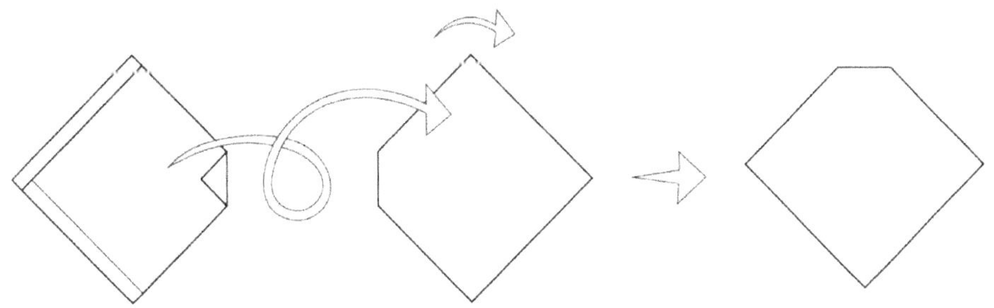

Étape 3

Retourne la figure, puis fais-la tourner de sorte que le côté droit soit orienté vers le haut.

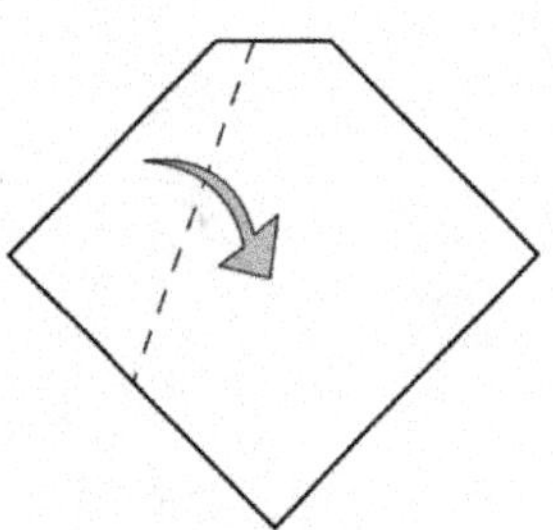  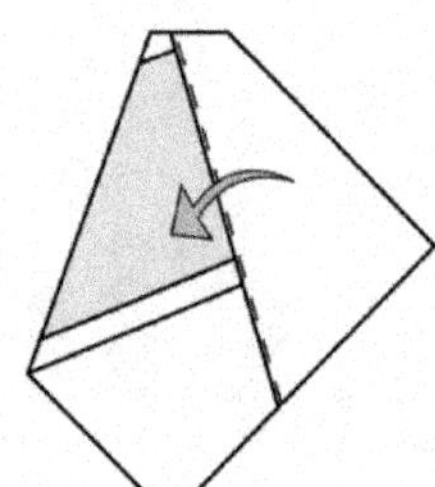

Étape 4

Plie le côté gauche vers
le bas en biais, comme
indiqué sur le dessin.

Étape 5

Plie également le côté droit vers
le bas, par-dessus le rabat que tu
viens de faire.

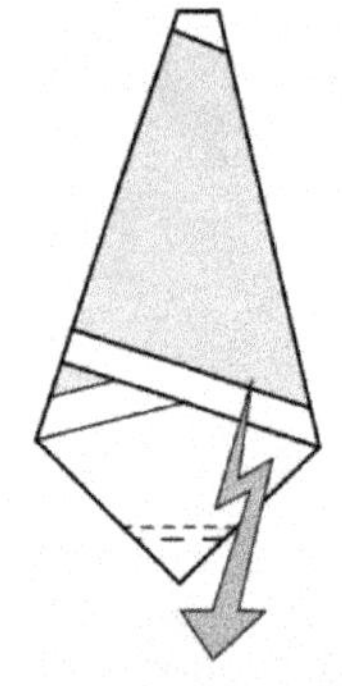 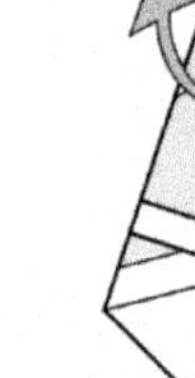

Étape 6

Plie le coin inférieur en
zigzag comme indiqué
sur le dessin.

Étape 7

Plie le haut de la
figure en biais comme
indiqué sur le dessin.

Étape 8

Rabats le bord de
cette section comme
indiqué sur le dessin.

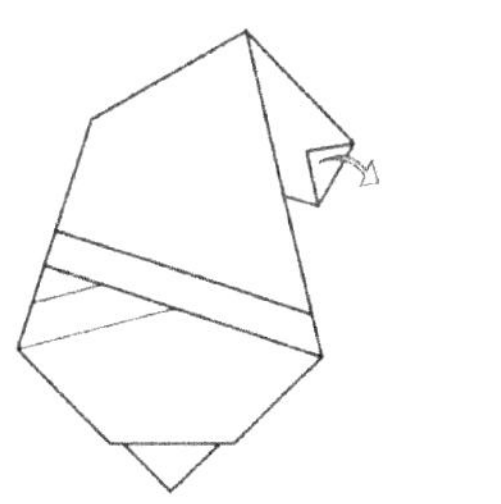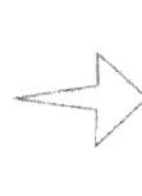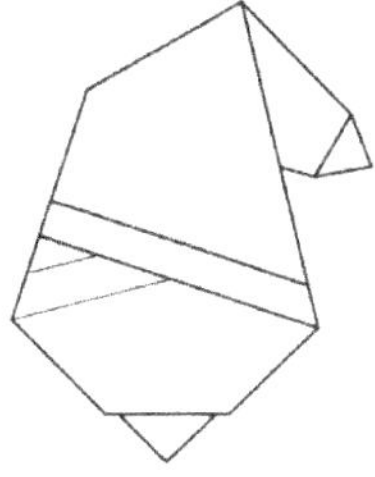

Étape 9

Déplie la couche supérieure à l'extrémité de cette section. Le visage
du lutin est prêt !

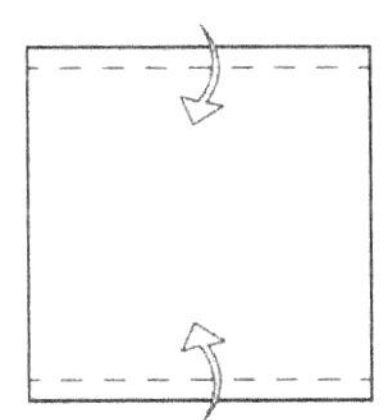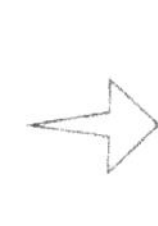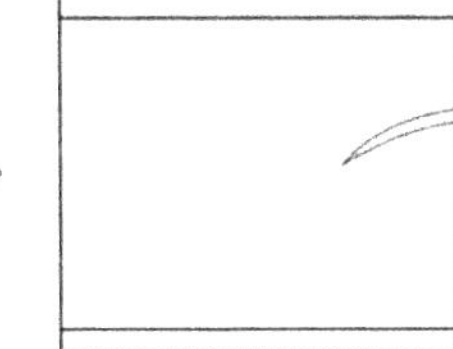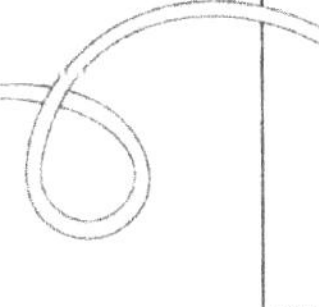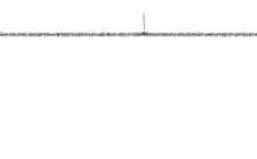

Étape 10

Prends la deuxième
feuille et rabats
légèrement les bords de
deux côtés opposés.

Étape 11

Retourne la figure.

Étape 12

Plie la feuille en
deux verticalement.
puis déplie-la.

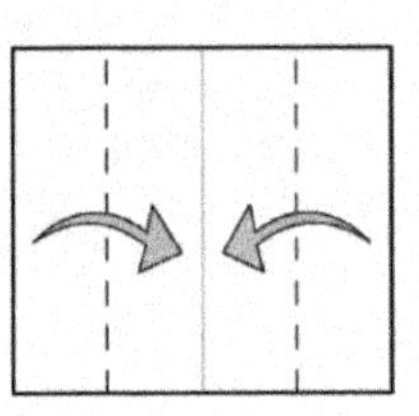  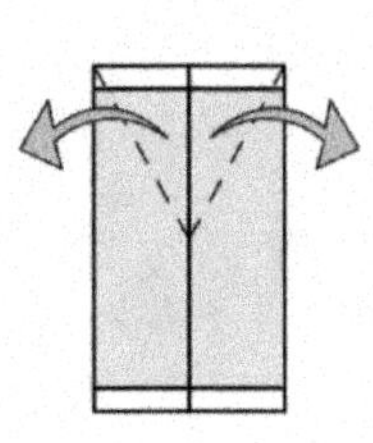

Étape 13

Rabats les deux bords latéraux jusqu'à la ligne médiane verticale, puis plie leurs coins supérieurs vers l'extérieur, comme indiqué sur le dessin.

Étape 14

Rabats le haut de la figure comme indiqué sur le dessin pour former le corps du lutin.

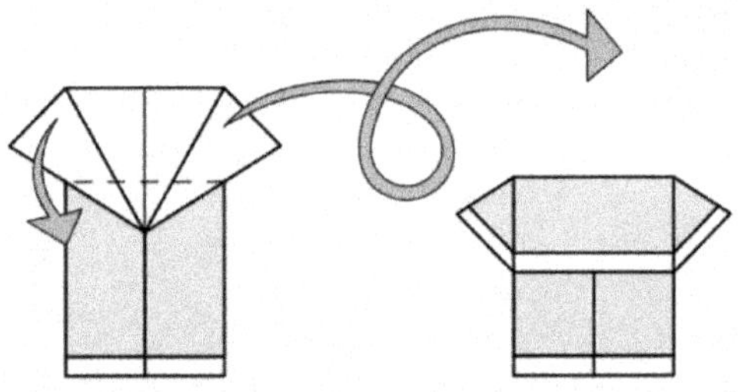

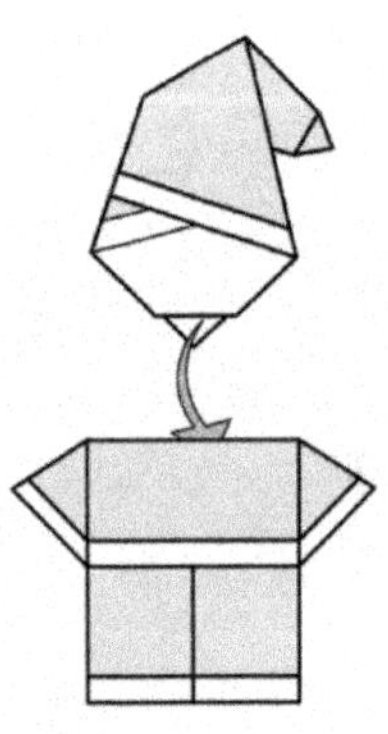

Étape 15

Sers-toi du coin inférieur du visage du lutin avec le motif en zigzag pour l'attacher à son corps.

Lutin

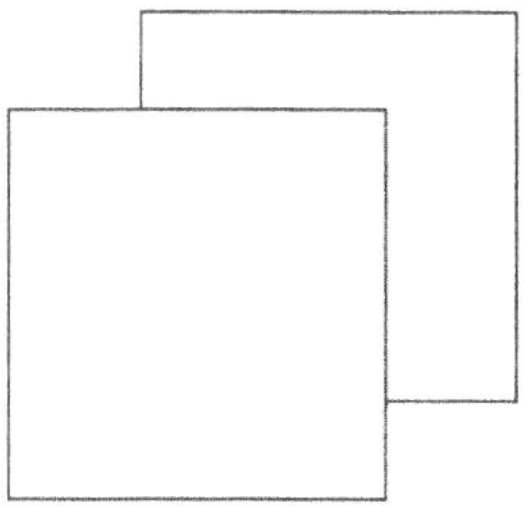

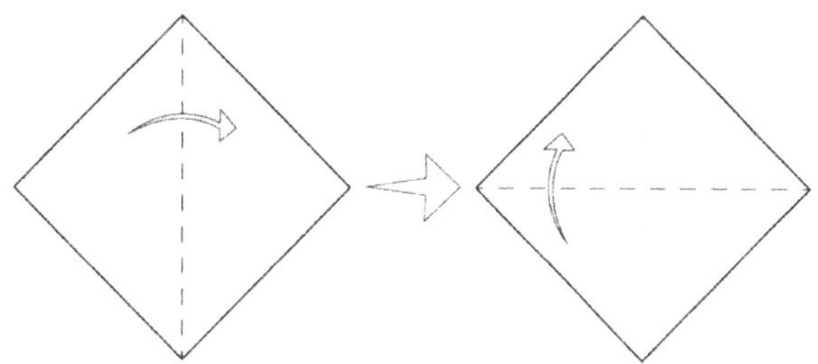

Astuce

Tu auras besoin de 2 feuilles carrées pour réaliser ce renne.

Étape 1

Plie la première feuille en diagonale, puis déplie-la pour former un pli vertical.

Étape 2

Plie la feuille en deux vers le haut.

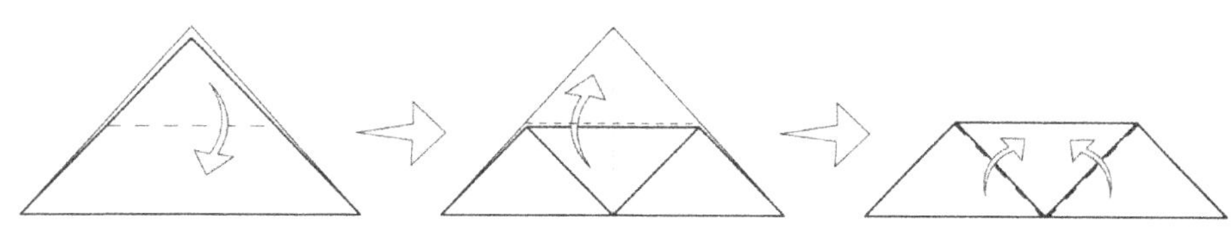

Étape 3

Rabats le coin de la couche supérieure jusqu'à ce qu'il rencontre le bord inférieur.

Étape 4

Rabats le coin de la couche de derrière jusqu'à ce qu'il rencontre le bord inférieur.

Étape 5

Plie les deux coins latéraux vers la ligne médiane verticale, en laissant un petit espace entre eux.

Renne

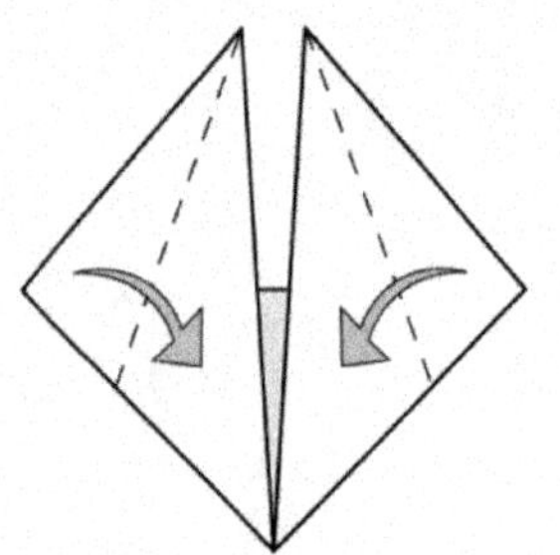

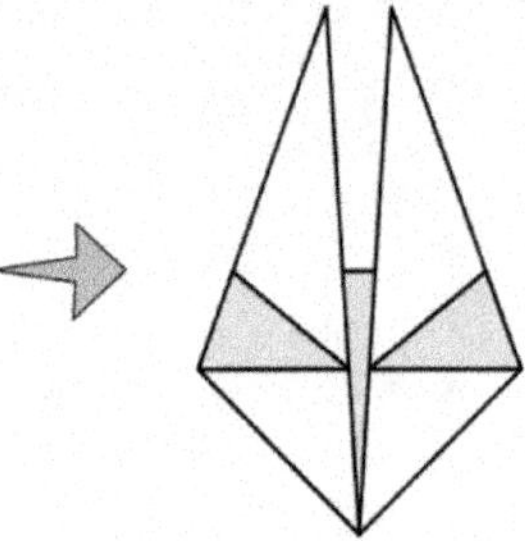

Étape 6

Plie les deux coins latéraux en deux comme indiqué sur le dessin.

Étape 7

Rabats le haut des deux coins en biais comme indiqué sur le dessin

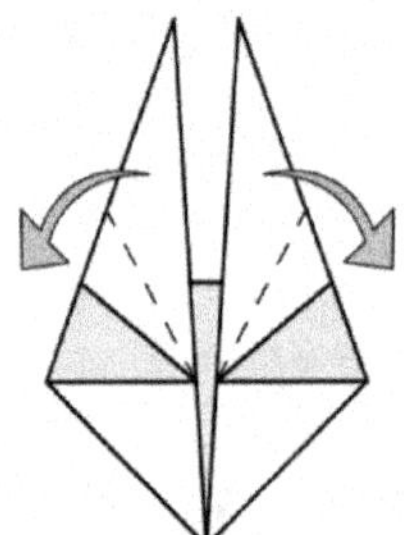

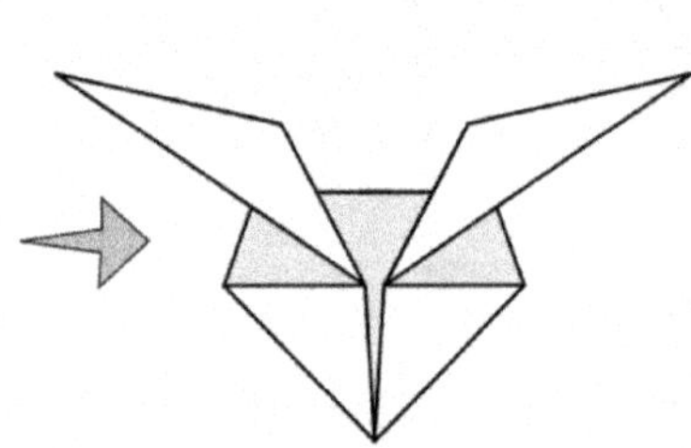

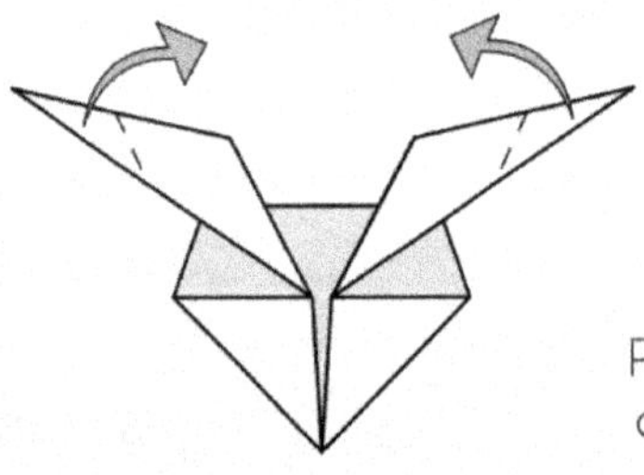

Étape 8

Plie les pointes de ces mêmes coins vers le haut, comme indiqué sur le dessin. Retourne la figure et le visage du renne est prêt !

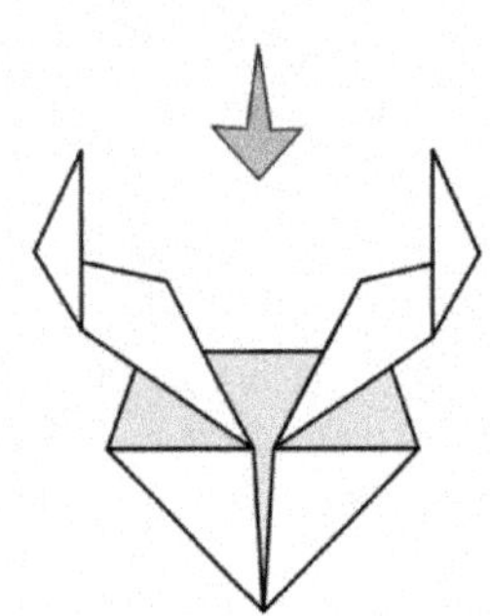

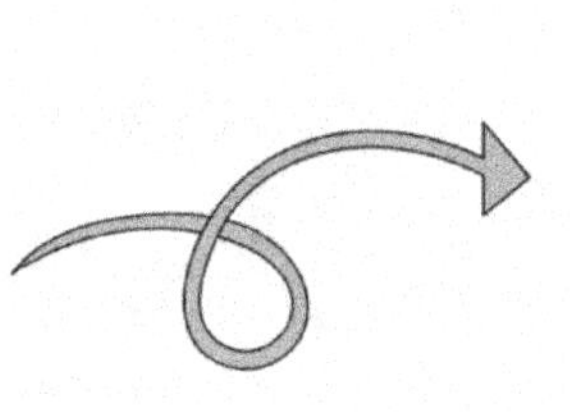

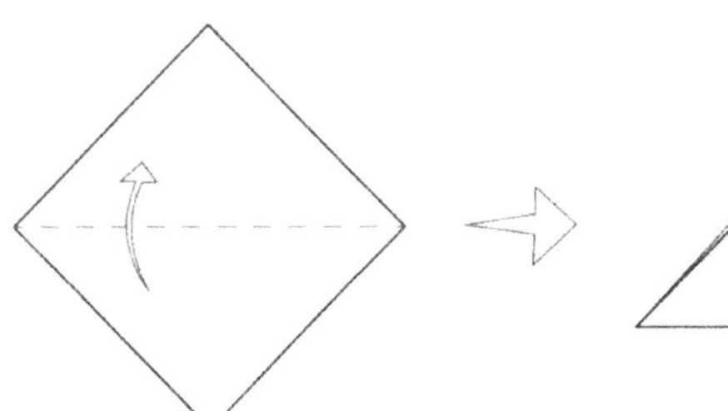

Étape 9

Prends la deuxieme feuille
et plie-la en diagonale
vers le haut. Ensuite, plie-la
en deux et deplie-la pour
former un pli.

Étape 10

Plie le coin supérieur de la
couche supérieure vers le bas
en veillant à ce qu'il dépasse
du bord inférieur, comme
indiqué sur le dessin. Rabats
ensuite les deux coins
latéraux vers la ligne
médiane.

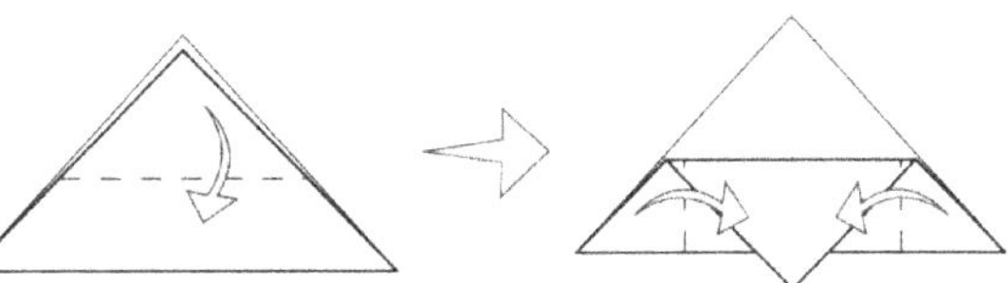

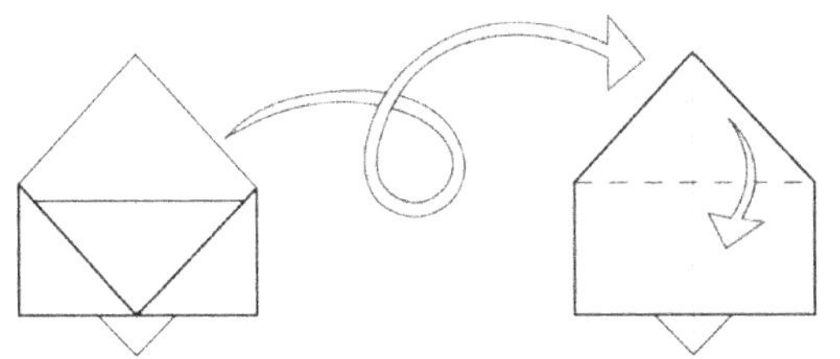

Étape 11

Retourne la figure, puis plie
le coin superieur vers le bas
comme indiqué et déplie-le
pour former un pli.

Renne

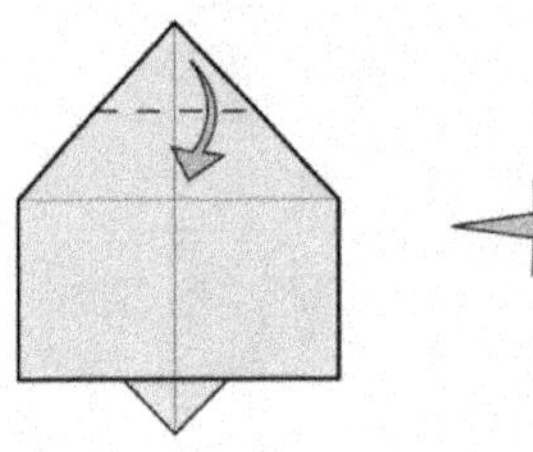 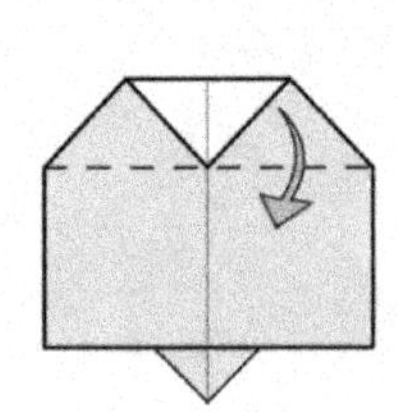

Étape 12

Rabats le coin supérieur pour qu'il rejoigne le pli que tu viens de faire, puis plie-le à nouveau en suivant ce même pli.

Étape 13

Plie la figure en deux vers l'arrière et fais-la pivoter sur le côté. Le corps du renne est prêt !

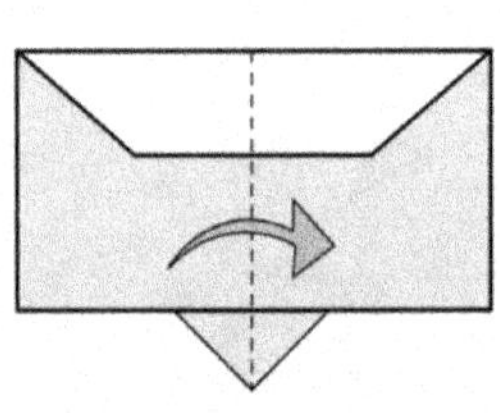 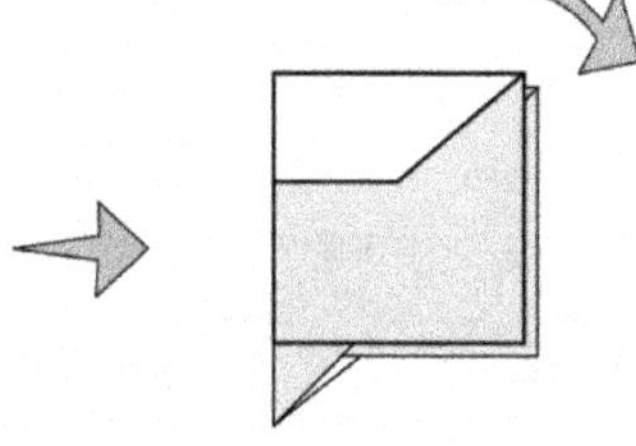

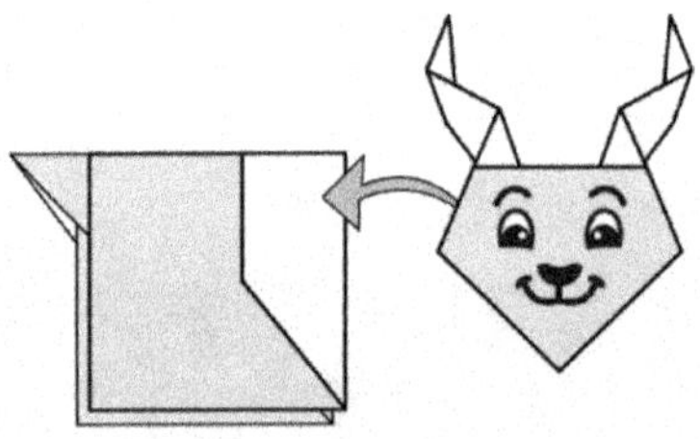

Étape 14

Pose le visage du renne sur son corps. Et voilà, tu as terminé !

Renne

Astuce

Tu auras besoin de 2 feuilles carrées pour réaliser cette décoration en diamant.

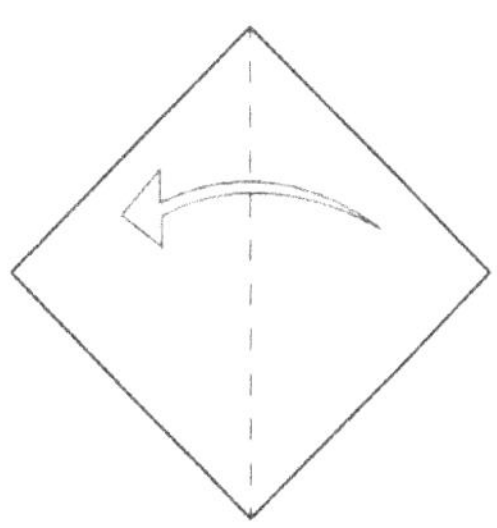

Étape 1

Plie la première feuille en diagonale, puis deplie-la pour former un pli vertical.

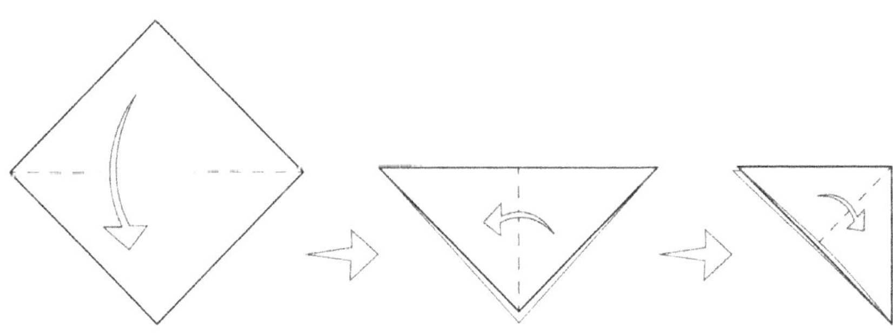

Étape 2

Plie la feuille en deux vers le bas.

Étape 3

Plie la feuille en deux vers la gauche.

Étape 4

Rabats la couche superieure en diagonale, puis deplie-la pour former un pli.

Décoration en diamant

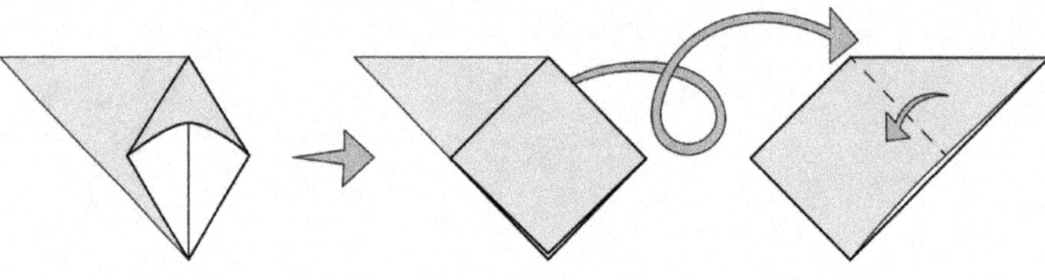

Tire la couche supérieure uniquement vers la droite le long du pli que tu viens de faire et aplatis comme indiqué sur le dessin. Retourne ensuite la figure et répète l'opération de l'autre côté.

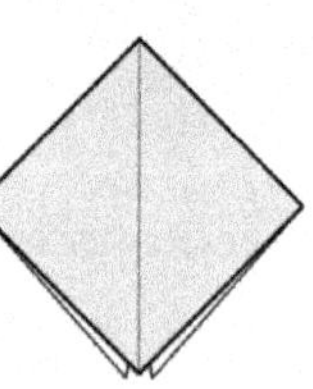

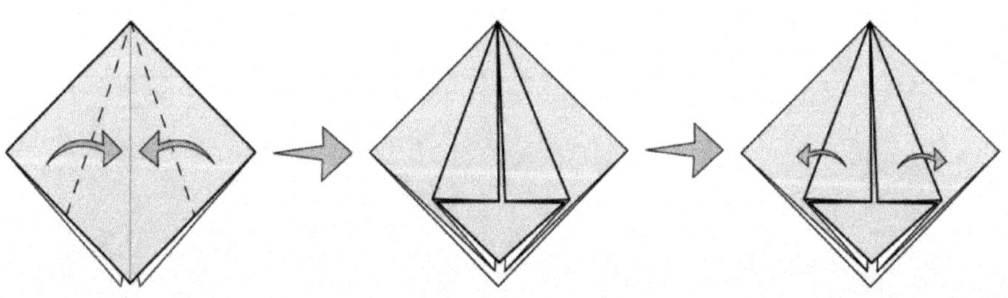

Rabats les deux côtés jusqu'à la ligne médiane verticale.

Déplie-les pour former des plis.

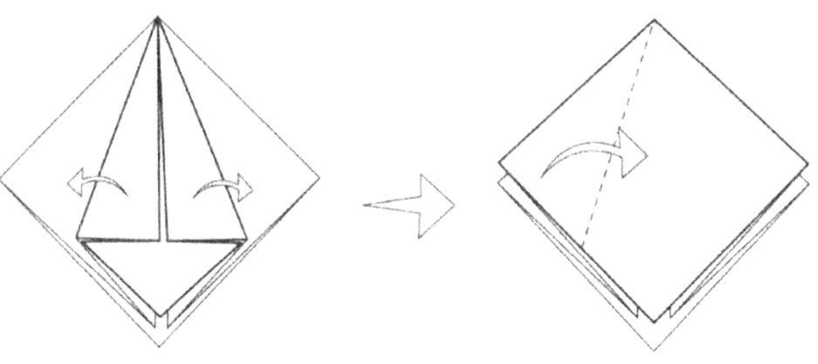

Étape 8

Tire la couche supérieure uniquement vers la gauche le long du pli que tu viens de faire pour l'ouvrir.

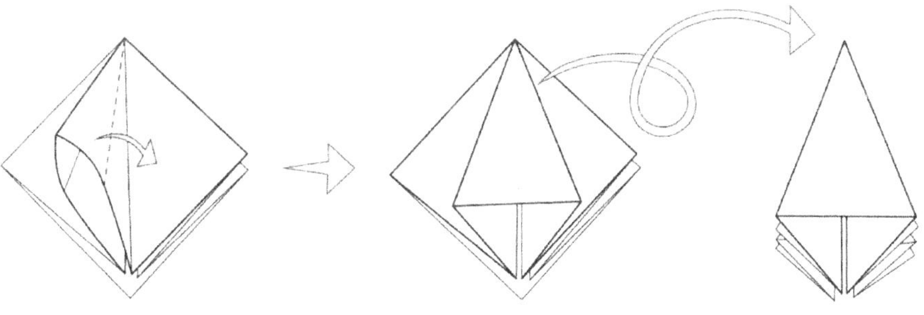

Étape 9

Aplatis la figure comme indiqué sur le dessin, puis retourne-la.

Étape 10

Répète l'étape précédente de l'autre côté.

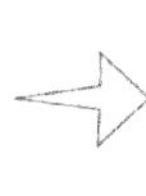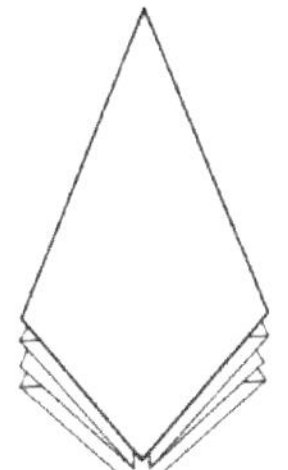

Étape 11

Prends la deuxième feuille et repète toutes les étapes précédentes de sorte que tu te retrouves avec 2 pièces identiques.

Décoration en diamant

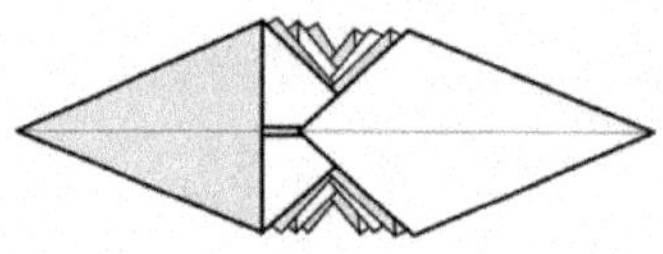

Assemble les deux figures comme indiqué pour faire tenir les rabats en place.

Insère le rabat de la figure de droite dans la poche de la figure de gauche, puis plie-les en deux. Maintenant, rentre le rabat de la figure de gauche dans la poche de la figure de droite, puis plie-les en deux, et ainsi de suite jusqu'à ce que tous les rabats soient en place.

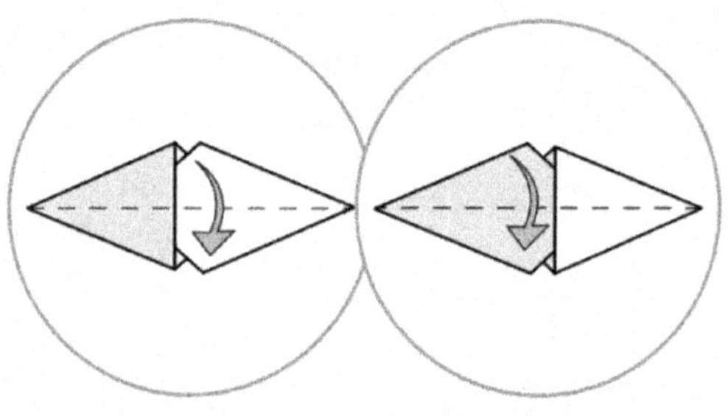

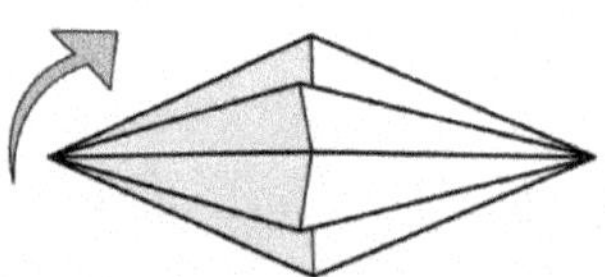

Fais tourner la figure et ta décoration en diamant est prête !

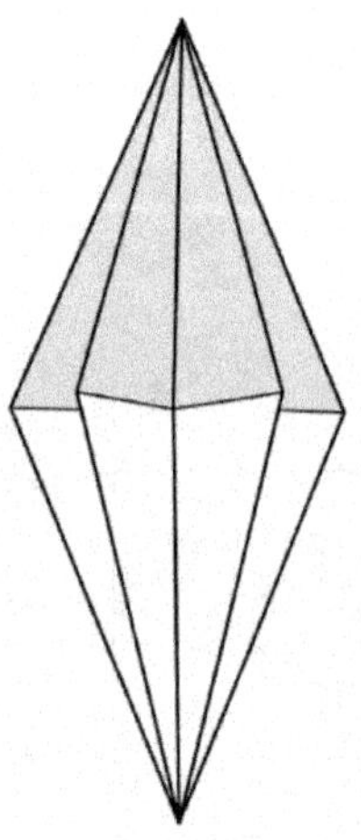

Décoration en diamant

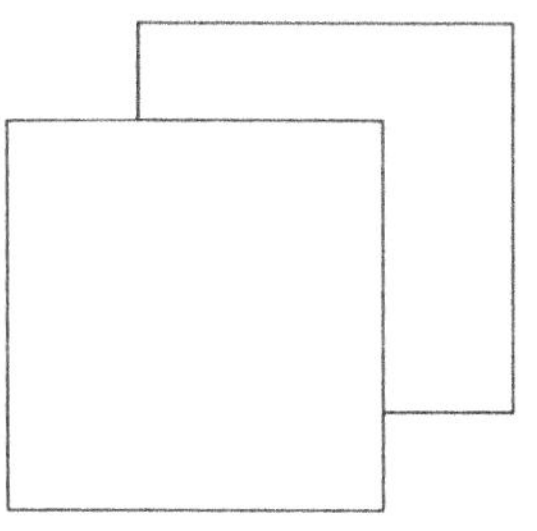

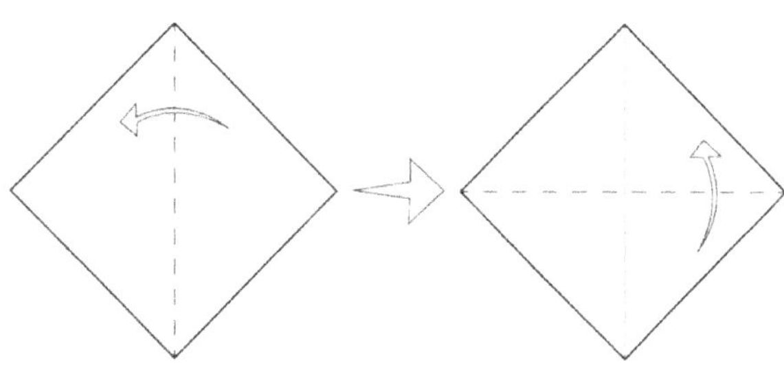

Astuce

Tu auras besoin de 2 feuilles carrées pour réaliser cet ange.

Étape 1

Plie la première feuille en diagonale, puis déplie-la pour former un pli vertical.

Étape 2

Plie la feuille en deux vers le haut.

Étape 3

Rabats les deux côtés sur la ligne médiane verticale et déplie-les pour former des plis. En partant du point où ces plis rejoignent le bord inférieur, plie les deux coins vers le haut et vers l'intérieur afin qu'ils se retrouvent entre les deux couches de la feuille.

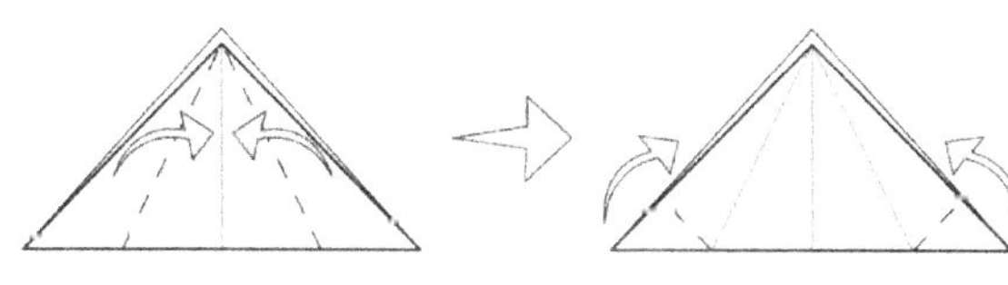

Étape 4

Rabats à nouveau les deux coins latéraux jusqu'à la ligne médiane verticale.

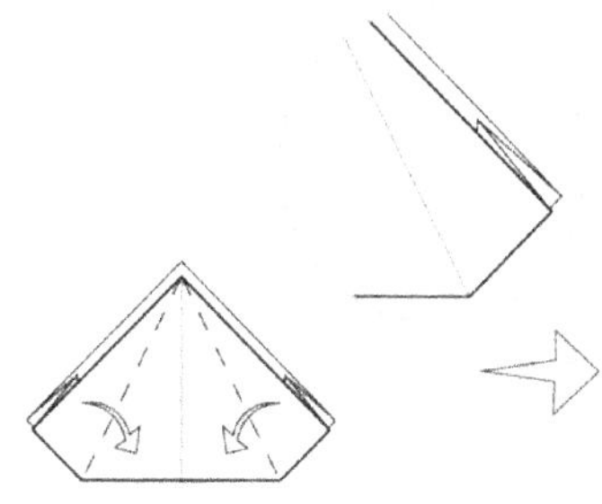

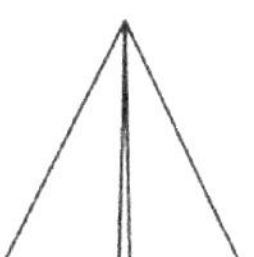

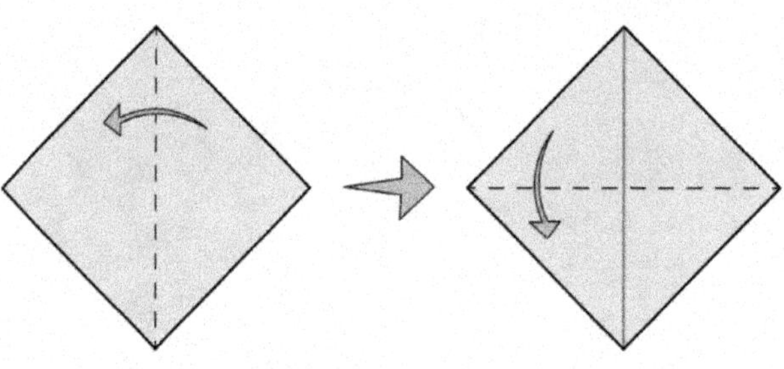

Étape 5

Prends la deuxième feuille et plie-la en diagonale, puis déplie-la pour former un pli vertical. Plie-la ensuite en deux vers le bas.

Étape 6

Rabats le côté droit de la couche supérieure jusqu'à ce qu'il rejoigne le bord supérieur, puis déplie-le. Répète l'opération de l'autre côté, comme indiqué sur le dessin.

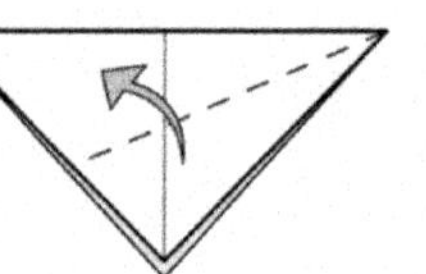  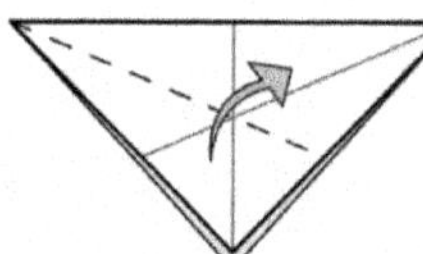

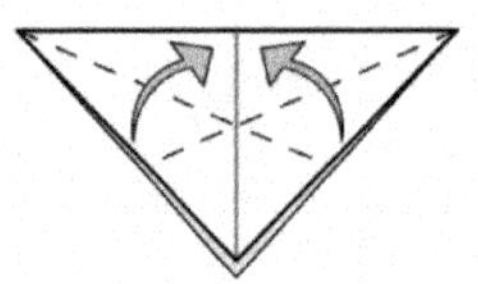  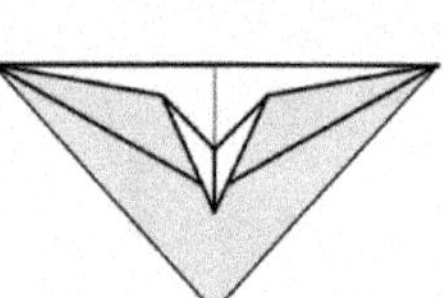

Étape 7

Sers-toi des plis que tu viens de faire pour plier la couche supérieure de la figure. Tu verras un petit rabat se former au centre du pli.

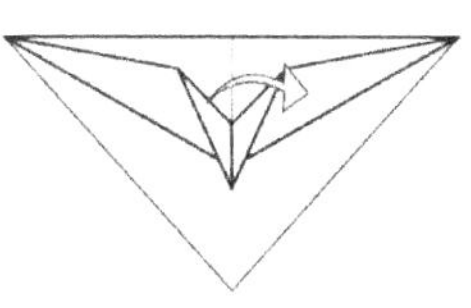  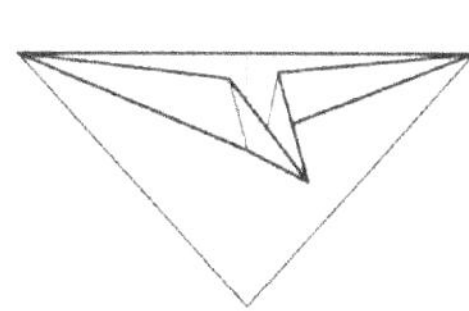

Étape 8

Plie ce petit rabat vers la droite, puis aplatis-le comme indiqué sur le dessin.

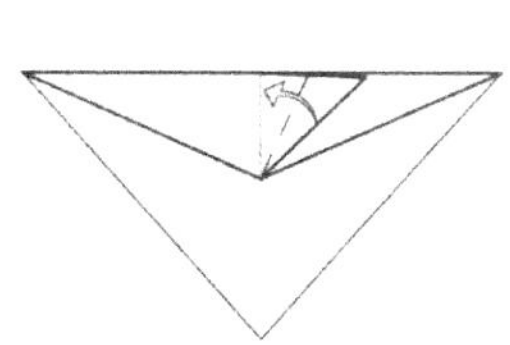 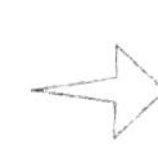 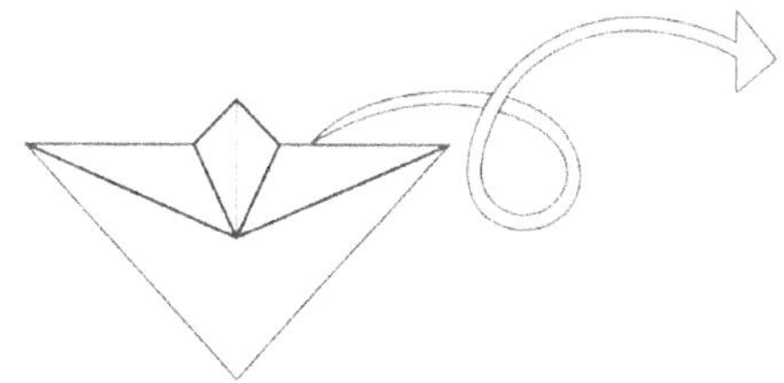

Étape 9

Maintenant, rabats-le jusqu'à la ligne médiane verticale et déplie-le pour former un petit pli. Utilise ensuite ce pli pour l'ouvrir et l'aplatir comme indiqué sur le dessin.

Étape 10

Retourne la figure.

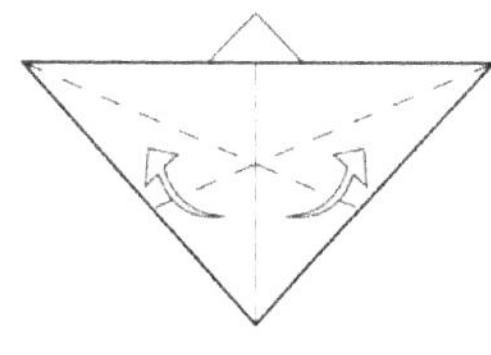 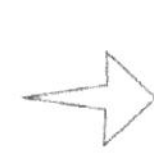 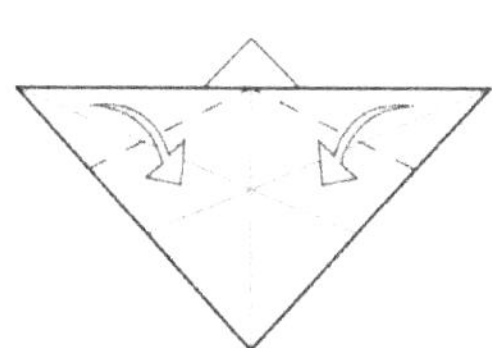

Étape 11

Rabats le côté droit de la couche supérieure jusqu'à ce qu'il rejoigne le bord supérieur et déplie-le. Répète l'opération de l'autre côté, comme indiqué sur le dessin.

Étape 12

Ensuite, rabats les coins latéraux en biais comme indiqué sur le dessin.

Ange

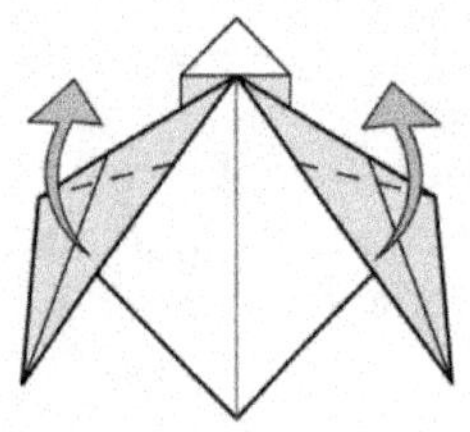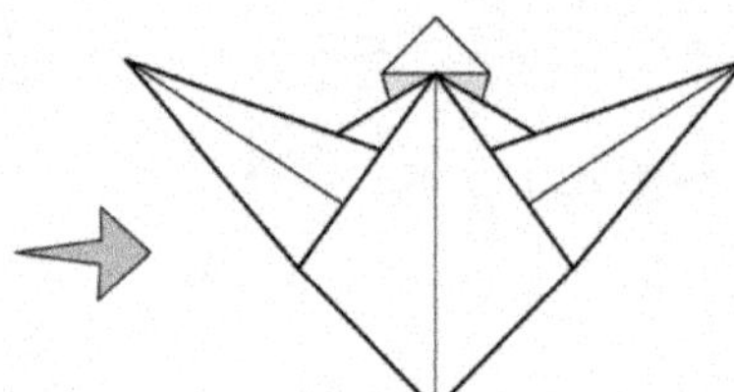

Replie les deux côtés vers le haut, à nouveau en biais mais à un angle différent, comme indiqué sur le dessin.

Plie les coins supérieurs et latéraux de la couche inférieure comme indiqué sur le dessin, puis retourne la figure.

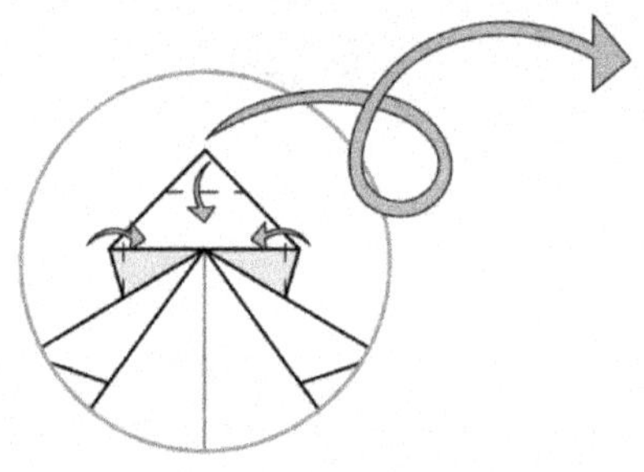

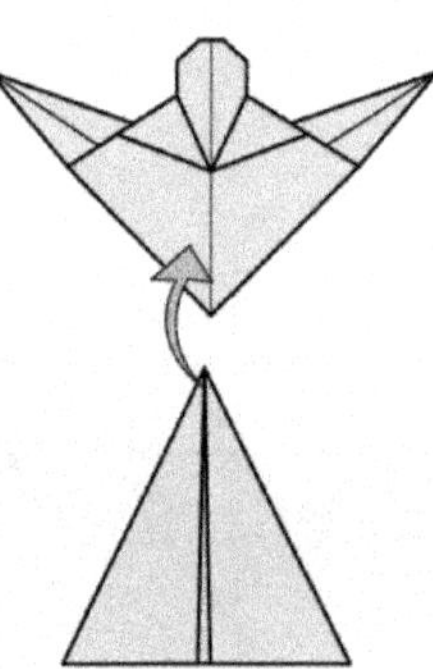

Insère la première figure entre les couches de celle-ci. Ton ange est prêt !

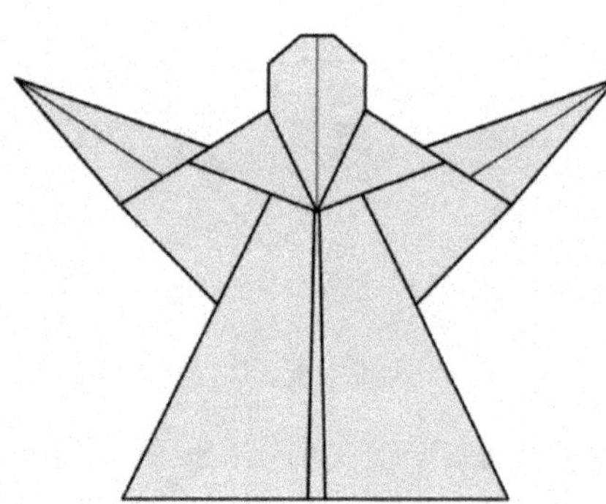

Conclusion

Félicitations pour être arrivé(e) à la fin de ce livre sur les origamis ! J'ai la certitude que tu es maintenant un(e) expert(e) dans l'art de fabriquer des figures en te servant de simples feuilles de papier !

J'espère que ce périple a été amusant et que tu as découvert un nouveau passe-temps avec les origamis. Si c'est le cas et que tu souhaites continuer à apprendre et à t'amuser, jette un coup d'œil à nos autres livres sur les origamis. Il y en a pour tous les goûts !

Enfin, si tu as apprécié ce livre, nous te serions très reconnaissants de nous faire part de ton avis sur Amazon. C'est notre façon d'apprendre et de grandir avec toi pour continuer à proposer des livres amusants et de qualité !